DEATH
OF A
NAZI ARMY

Also by William B. Breuer:

DEATH
OF A
NAZI ARMY
The Falaise Pocket

William B. Breuer

STEIN AND DAY/*Publishers*/New York

First published in 1985
Copyright © 1985 by William B. Breuer
All rights reserved, Stein and Day, Incorporated
Designed by Louis A. Ditizio
Printed in the United States of America
STEIN AND DAY/*Publishers*
Scarborough House
Briarcliff Manor, N.Y. 10510

Library of Congress Cataloging in Publication Data
Breuer, William B., 1923-
   Death of a Nazi army.

   Bibliography: p.
   Includes index.
   1. Falaise Gap, Battle of, 1944.   I. Title.
D756.5.F34B73   1985   940.54′21   84-40736
ISBN 0-8128-3024-5

Dedicated to the memory of
Colonel Harry A. "Paddy" Flint,
killed in action while ahead of
his front lines during the Normandy breakout.

Indomitable, courageous, beloved
by his men, a symbol of the
American soldier's fighting spirit

CONTENTS

PHOTOGRAPHS

MAPS

PROLOGUE

The bold, blaring headline in the July 21, 1944, edition of the *New York Herald-Tribune* told it all:

ALLIES IN FRANCE BOGGED
DOWN ON ENTIRE FRONT

Seven weeks after Anglo-American assault troops had stormed ashore on D-Day in Normandy in the mightiest airborne-amphibious operation in history, a choking pall bordering on panic hovered over the highest councils of the military and government in the United States and Great Britain. So deep was the concern that Allied solidarity, at its zenith on the eve of D-Day, was shaken to its foundations and nearly split wide open.

Instead of breaking out of Normandy and racing for Paris and then on into Germany as planned, the powerful Anglo-American armies had stalled not far from the D-Day landing beaches. Nearly one and a half million American, British, and French troops and their equipment were bottled up in the narrow confines of the Cotentin Peninsula, which thrust out into the English Channel like a sore thumb, and along a thin strip of the Calvados coast in front of the ancient Norman cathedral city of Caen.

During the first two weeks of July the savage fighting in the swamps and hedgerows (known as the bocage) north of the strategically crucial medieval town of St.-Lô raged relentlessly. "The most

11

monstrous bloodbath, the like of which I have not seen in eleven years of war," exclaimed the German commander in the sector Lieutenant General Dietrich von Choltitz.

Young foot soldiers and tankers of Lieutenant General Oma Bradley's First Army, many not long removed from high schoo proms and jukebox emporiums back in the States, had been hacking through the treacherous bocage against tenacious Germans who'c been ordered not to give up "a single foot of ground." America gains, if any, were measured in yards; a half-mile advance was haileс as a major tactical achievement.

The hedgerows provided a natural defense for the Germans, infi nitely more formidable than any conceivable man-made barriers For centuries the flatlands of the lower Cotentin Peninsula had been divided and subdivided into small pastures by means of thick earth en walls. Many of these walls were eight to ten feet high, and long snakelike roots packed the dirt together much as reinforcing stee would strengthen concrete.

A thick, thorny growth of trees, bushes, and brambles crowned each wall. The earthen mounds furnished ideal protection for defenders and the tangled vegetation provided natural concealment. An American infantryman, with sudden death lurking at all times, could see ahead for only fifty to one hundred yards—to the next hedgerow. Tough, tenacious, and motivated, the outnumbered and outgunned Feldgrau (field gray; the typical German soldier was called after the color of his uniform) burrowed into the thick hedgerow walls, and armed with a formidable array of machine guns, automatic rifles, and Panzerfauste (rocket launchers) took a frightful toll among American attackers.

At cemeteries behind the lines, the bodies of young Americans, each shrouded in a mattress cover, were stacked up in long rows awaiting interment by grim-faced burial details. The U.S. First Army had suffered more than 61,000 casualties since D-Day, including 11,268 killed by July 20.

The gods of war appeared to favor the German defenders; rains persisted a.id turned much of the terrain into quagmire. Allied fighter-bomber attacks were curtailed when the planes weren't grounded. The chopped-up fields made it difficult and sometimes impossible to utilize one of First Army's most potent assets—swarms of fast, highly maneuverable tanks. The mighty American army was virtually trapped in the bocage.

As the dogfaces (as American foot soldiers called themselves) and the Feldgrau were slaughtering each other in the swamps and hedgerows, massive bloodletting was also taking place along the eastern sector of the front where the British, under General Bernard Law Montgomery, had been stalled since D-Day. Hoping to break the stalemate and send his tanks racing for Paris, Montgomery on July 18 launched Operation Goodwood (named after a popular English horse-racing track). The all-out assault was an awesome display of Allied power, a deluge of explosives the like of which had never been known.

A mighty armada of the Royal Air Force and the U.S. Eighth Air Force of 1,728 heavies and 412 medium bombers saturated with seven hundred tons of explosives a tiny patch of Norman countryside of only twenty-five square miles, after which guns of the British Second Army sent 45,000 shells screaming into this same pulverized locale. On the heels of this thunderous bombardment, 1,500 tanks and 250,000 foot soldiers jumped off and headed across rolling pasture land toward the smoke-shrouded German lines around Caen. Ahead of this massive attacking force 796 Allied fighter-bombers circled the tortured battleground and swooped down on any German, gun, tank, or vehicle that tried to move, much like hawks would pounce on hapless prairie chickens.

German grenadiers (infantrymen) and panzers rallied quickly from the furious rain of explosives and by noon of the first day were resisting with customary ferocity. For three days the British and Canadians slugged ahead for a total of six or seven miles where they ran into a screen of German 88-millimeter guns and took a fearful beating. Goodwood was stopped cold. It had been a disaster. Empire forces had lost 5,000 men killed, wounded, or missing in the three-day carnage, and 500 knocked-out tanks, burned and twisted, dotted the pastures and woods. The gate to Paris had been slammed shut by the stubborn Germans.

At SHAEF (Supreme Headquarters, Allied Expeditionary Force) at Southwick House outside Portsmouth, England, General Montgomery had been the target of bitter verbal abuse for weeks while his 21st Army Group was stalled nine miles inland from the Calvados coast outside Caen, Montgomery's D-Day objective. The most vocal critics were not American but British. As the diminutive, nonsmoking, teetotaling hero of El Alamein was in command of all Anglo-American ground forces, he was held at fault for the stalemate bloodbath in Normandy. It had been openly discussed at SHAEF who would replace Montgomery, the methodical battle commander whose arrogance, braggadocio, and unorthodox mannerisms had long grated on the nerves of fellow generals, British and American alike. With the failure of Goodwood and its expenditure of enormous amounts of explosives, lives and equipment, a new round of invective was poured onto Montgomery's head.

Suave, pipe-smoking British Air Marshal Arthur Tedder, deputy to Supreme Commander Dwight D. Eisenhower, exploded: "We've been taken for suckers by Montgomery!" Another British general at SHAEF howled: "Monty does a lot of [personal] publicity stuff. I don't believe he's a general at all, just a film star!" Eisenhower's American naval aide, Commander Harry C. Butcher, referred to Montgomery as Chief Big Wind, a monicker that caught on around SHAEF.

The German strategy of fighting savagely for every foot of ground to seal the invaders into the Normandy bridgehead stunned Allied planners who had taken it for granted that once the Anglo-Americans were ashore in great strength the Wehrmacht generals would follow accepted tactical doctrine and conduct a withdrawal to the first natural defensive barrier, the Seine River. But the German army in France was not going by the military textbook—Adolf Hitler, supreme warlord of the Third Reich, had taken over strategy from his professionals.

In World War I, Hitler had been an infantry corporal and for four years fought in the muddy trenches on the Western Front. He had received the Iron Cross for gallantry, a high decoration for one of his lowly rank. He was a man of enormous energies with a lifestyle few others could have endured. Long before he had assumed an incredibly heavy workload.

The Fuehrer, from the perspective of his battle headquarters at Wolfsschanze (Wolf's Lair), hundreds of miles to the east near Rastenburg in East Prussia behind the flaming Russian front, was optimistic about the situation in far-off Normandy. Part of this rose-colored viewpoint was the result of the high-level toadies who surrounded him keeping from the Fuehrer depressing reports of the looming German disaster in France.

Hitler had made up his mind: the Battle of France would not be fought along the barrier of the Seine River but in the tangled hedgerows and rolling green pastures of Normandy.

Few German generals dared to disagree with Hitler. One of those who did was Field Marshal Erwin Rommel, the dynamic leader of Army Group B whose dubious task was to keep the Allies bottled up in Normandy. Rommel had repeatedly warned Hitler and the German high command that "the dam is bound to burst at any minute." His warnings fell on deaf ears at far-off Wolfsschanze.

Rommel had taken a sacred oath of allegiance to the Fuehrer and received his field marshal's baton personally from the Nazi leader in 1941, becoming at age fifty the youngest of that exalted rank in German history. Since that zenith of the Wehrmacht's fortunes three years before, Erwin Rommel, devout Catholic, devoted husband and doting father, had grown increasingly disillusioned with his patron. He was convinced that Hitler was taking the Fatherland hell bent down the road to ruin and destruction and was mindlessly butchering the flower of German youth. "The man is mad!" Rommel had exploded to his staff many times.

Since February 1944, Rommel, a household hero whose popularity rivaled that of Hitler himself, had been playing a dangerous game. At that time he had been approached by Dr. Karl Stroelin, Oberburgermeister of Stuttgart, who informed Rommel for the first time of the existence of an ultra-secret conspiratorial group of high ranking German generals, active and retired, and prominent civilian officials known as the Schwarze Kapelle (Black Orchestra). The group's goal: to arrest or execute Hitler.

Eliminating the Fuehrer from the scene could result in a bloody fight between the German Army and Hitler's elite SS troops unless a widely respected, dominating figure surfaced immediately to lend his name to the conspiracy, Dr. Stroelin told his solemn-faced listener. "That figure is you, Herr Rommel," the Stuttgart mayor intoned. "Only you can save Germany."

Pondering the matter for long, silent minutes, Rommel replied: "I believe it is my duty to come to the rescue of Germany."

Since that time, Field Marshal Rommel had hatched a plan to present to the Anglo-Americans in which the Wehrmacht in Normandy would be surrendered at the same time Hitler was arrested or assassinated. Several high-ranking German officers in the West, including Rommel's trusted chief of staff, the astute, bespectacled Lieutenant General Hans Spiedel would cross the battle lines in Normandy and negotiate a truce under which Rommel would pull back the Wehrmacht to the Siegfried Line at the border of the Reich. In return the Allies would immediately cease bombing German cities and installations. Then a permanent peace would be worked out short of the unconditional surrender demand of President Franklin D. Roosevelt and Prime Minister Winston Churchill. The Wehrmacht would continue to battle the Russians to "keep the Bolshevik barbarians from overrunning Europe."

These were hectic and draining days for Erwin Rommel. On the one hand he exerted his enormous energies and brilliant generalship to hold the Anglo-Americans at bay in order to have bargaining leverage at the peace negotiations. On the other hand a great many of his waking hours were devoted to the delicate and perilous task of wooing SS generals in Normandy in supporting him in the revolt. By mid-July Rommel had secured pledges of cooperation from top army and SS generals in France. It was time to actively seek contact with Anglo-American leaders. The "Revolt of the Generals" would not take place in Berlin, as Schwarze Kapelle conspirators had long planned, but in Normandy.

Now fate intervened. Shortly after 6 P.M. on July 17, Rommel and several aides were speeding along a French road on the way back to Army Group B headquarters after visiting the front. Suddenly two Royal Air Force fighter-bombers zoomed in at tree-top level and riddled the Mercedes with 20-millimeter shells. The driver was killed, the car went out of control and smashed into a ditch, tossing an unconscious Rommel onto the road.

The field marshal was rushed to a civilian hospital in nearby Livarot, then on to a Luftwaffe medical center at an airfield outside Bernay. German doctors found that Rommel had a fracture at the base of the skull, two fractures of the left temple, and his left cheekbone had been crushed. He had a severe concussion, his left eye was badly damaged and his scalp had been ripped open. The Luftwaffe doctors gave him little chance to live.

The Revolt of the Generals in Normandy had been brought to a screeching halt by the machine guns of two RAF pilots.

All the while Anglo-American leaders had been grappling for a

16

solution to the bloody stalemate in Normandy, they were beset by another crisis of equal portent. For six weeks London had been under murderous attack by German missiles. The capital was defenseless against the round-the-clock assault from the sky; the attacks threatened to bring Great Britain to its knees, and possibly the entire Allied cause in the West. Swarms of the Führer's "vengeance weapons"—pilotless aircraft packed with explosives and named the V-1—were being launched from ramps along the Pas de Calais in France. With an air speed of 440 miles per hour (far faster than any Allied airplane), the flying-bomb's motor was timed to cut off over London, after which the V-1 would plummet soundlessly to earth and explode with the force of a blockbuster bomb.

Codenamed Target 42 by the Germans, the city of London lived in constant fear and chaos since the first V-1 exploded on June 12, only six days after D-Day in Normandy. Since then, hundreds of flying-bombs had rained down on the British capital. Thousands of Londoners were homeless, and the threat of an epidemic due to smashed water lines and sewers increased official worries. An evacuation program for children, women, the elderly, and the sick was hurriedly launched, and more than one million Londoners were whisked to the countryside. This mass exodus from Target 42 resulted in a severe strain on British railways and slowed the vital flow of ammunition and supplies to the Normandy front.

In dark corners of British government buildings, there was hushed talk that unless something was done about the flying bombs England might have to sue for peace. Allied Supreme Commander Eisenhower, an American, already deeply worried over the Normandy stalemate, now was forced into an anguishing decision: a large portion of the powerful Anglo-American heavy-bomber force would be diverted from support of the Normandy fighting and begin pounding V-1 launching sites along the Pas de Calais. This crisis-bombing operation was codenamed Crossbow.

More than two thousand antiaircraft guns were rushed to the south coast of England. Home Secretary Herbert Morrison "demanded" that the Allies invade the strongly held Pas de Calais to capture the launching sites. In fair weather and foul, Hitler's "vengeance weapons" rained onto London, often one hundred fifty to two hundred each day. By early July, three hundred thousand London houses and thousands of other buildings had been destroyed.

In desperation—as national survival hung in the balance—on

July 13 Prime Minister Churchill proposed to the British Chiefs of Staff that they consider the all-out use of poison gas against Germany to "shorten the war" or to conclude a situation where there was "danger of a stalemate."

Churchill then began vigorously promoting another innovative scheme to halt the deluge of V-1 bombs on London: He would select one hundred small, undefended German towns and Royal Air Force bombers would wipe them out, one at a time, "until Herr Hitler calls off his dogs."

Launching bacteriological warfare against the German homeland, with all its hideous consequences, was seriously considered. Great Britain had developed a top-secret bacteriological agent against which there was no known remedy. Using the agent as a retaliatory weapon against Nazi Germany was ruled out—large quantities would not be ready for at least a year.

Great pressures were brought on General Eisenhower to scrap previous plans for prosecuting the war by driving directly against Germany and to cancel a proposed Allied landing in southern France set for August 15 and instead to invade the Pas de Calais.

Faced with the monumental twin crises of having 1,500,000 Allied soldiers bottled up in Normandy not far from the D-Day landing beaches and an English civilian population daily suffering an ordeal of death and destruction by robot bombs, a fateful decision was made at the highest levels of the British and American governments and military. Frightful as was the carnage being heaped on London's civilians, Hitler's vengeance weapons were not greatly affecting the prosecution of the war. So London would have to endure the robot bombs, and an all-out effort would be made to break out of Normandy and overrun the V-1 launching sites along the Pas de Calais. This would be accomplished while American and British forces followed the general plan for destroying Nazi Germany by driving into the heart of the Reich.

DEATH
OF A
NAZI ARMY

Thunder Over Normandy

A Murder Plot
Misfires

EARLY ON THE morning of July 20, 1944, a black trimotor Junkers transport plane lifted off from Rangsdorf Airfield outside rubble-strewn Berlin and set a course for Adolf Hitler's battle headquarters, *Wolfsschanze*. The "wolf's lair" was a sprawling complex of buildings and underground bunkers set among thick woods outside Rastenburg, East Prussia. On board the aircraft were a decorated young German count, Colonel Klaus von Stauffenberg, and his aide and longtime close friend, Lieutenant Colonel Werner von Haeften.

There was nothing unique about the appearance or demeanor of the two Wehrmacht officers to betray to the casual eye that they were embarked upon a desperate and perilous mission. If all went well, within the next six hours von Stauffenberg would violate his devout principles and murder a human being in cold blood. His target: Adolf Hitler, supreme warlord of the Third Reich.

Count von Stauffenberg was tall, lean, and exceedingly handsome, although the previous year he had lost an arm, part of the other hand, an eye, and a piece of his scalp when strafed by American fighter-bombers while fighting in Tunisia with the 10th Panzer Division. He would be the "hit man" for *Schwarze Kapelle* (Black Orchestra). Only days before, having grown weary and frustrated over failure of senior leaders of the ultrasecret group to take action, the count had complained to a confidant, "I'm tired of waiting for the generals. Now the colonels are going to take over!"

Winging toward Wolfsschanze, von Stauffenberg clung tightly to the briefcase he held on his lap. In it was a package containing a British-made bomb captured in France. Despite his physical infirmity, von Stauffenberg was confident that he could succeed in covertly shoving a bomb-loaded briefcase under a conference table at the Führer's feet. Only the count's body had been mutilated, not his brain nor his steel will.

This would be the perfect opportunity to act, the thirty-eight-year-old aristocrat knew. Many of the leaders of the Third Reich would be clustered around the Führer to greet Benito Mussolini, the bombastic Italian Duce and Hitler's longtime ally. The Junkers droned onward through the sultry summer skies.

On the same day that Count von Stauffenberg was keeping his appointment with destiny, hundreds of miles away in Normandy the *Oberbefehlshaber West* (Commander in Chief, West), Field Marshal Hans Guenther von Kluge (known to some Germans as "Clever Hans") was conferring with his army and corps commanders in a dense wood south of battered British-held Caen, the ancient capital of Normandy. The sixty-one-year-old, stocky, pale-faced "Clever Hans" had been a Hitler favorite when conducting a "victorious defense" while commanding the Army Group Center in Russia for two years. He had arrived in France on July 4 with spirits high and a firm resolve that the Allies could be defeated in Normandy. Within days, the hero of "victorious defense" had become totally disillusioned. The *Feldgrau* (German soldiers) were being mindlessly butchered in a hopeless cause. Von Kluge had entered a pact with Field Marshal Rommel to surrender to the Anglo-Americans independently of Hitler.

Now on the twentieth, torrential rains had drenched Normandy in the morning, but by afternoon the skies had broken, the downpour ceased, and von Kluge was able to place his unrolled battle maps on the hood of his Horch command car. Despite having just inflicted a bloody beating on British forces in General Bernard Montgomery's all-out effort to break through German lines in his race for Paris, the assembled Wehrmacht commanders were unable to conceal their gloom and despair. Contributing to the thick aura of pessimism was the haunting specter of Erwin Rommel, the heretofore seemingly indestructible warrior, hovering near death in a Luftwaffe hospital. The untimely fate of *der Junge Marschall* (the Boy Marshal) loomed as a harbinger of the catastrophe lurking just ahead for the Feldgrau of Normandy.

Oberstgruppenführer (SS Colonel General) Sepp Dietrich was a crony of Hitler's since the Munich beer hall brawls in the early days of the Nazi party, but he had since grown sour on the Führer and raged to von Kluge about the "mad" orders arriving daily from Wolfsschanze to "hold at all costs." General of Panzer Troops Heinz Eberhard, whose tankers and stubble-hoppers (as German infantrymen called themselves) had halted the British assault at Caen, was bitter in his denunciation of "them"—meaning Hitler and the high-ranking toadies at Wolfsschanze. Eberhard complained his units had suffered more than 45,000 casualties since D-Day, seven weeks before, and had received only 2,400 ill-trained replacements from a Reich that was, in its fifth year of war, scraping the bottom of the manpower barrel.

Major General Dietrich von Choltitz, the stiff-necked leader of LXXXIV Corps facing the Americans in the St.-Lô sector; SS Colonel General Paul Hausser, the gruff, outspoken commander of Seventh Army in Normandy; Sepp Dietrich; and Eberhard were in firm agreement: the German forces should pull back to the Seine immediately to avoid their total destruction in Normandy.

Privately, Field Marshal von Kluge held the identical view. It was strategic madness, an invitation to continued butchery of their troops, to stubbornly remain in place. But an overriding factor stayed von Kluge's hand until he could find the opportunity to surrender the German armed forces in Normandy: he could constantly feel the hot breath of Hitler on his neck. The Führer had grown increasingly concerned about the loyalty and resolution of his generals and was diligent in his search for any indication of "defeatist attitudes."

As raindrops trickled from overhanging leaves onto the visor of von Kluge's peaked officer's cap, the German commander in the West now sought to steel the drooping spirits of his senior battle leaders. "We will hold," von Kluge declared, "and if no miracle weapons can be found to improve our basic situation, then we'll just have to die like men on the battlefield."

The ringing exhortation was greeted with stonelike silence.

In his bitter reference to "miracle weapons," von Kluge was courting more than displeasure should his remarks reach the ears of

25

the Führer. For months Hitler had been stridently demanding that his beleaguered forces in Russia, Italy, and now in Normandy not give up "one foot of territory," because his battlefield secret weapons were on the way and would turn the tide against the Allies.

Field Marshal von Kluge climbed into his Horch and headed for Army Group B headquarters at La Roche-Guyon, north of Paris in a great bend of the Seine River. He was now wearing two hats: one as Commander in Chief, West and the other as Rommel's successor in command of Army Group B. Von Kluge had a cogent reason for taking over for Rommel: he could not afford to risk the possibility that Hitler might appoint a Rommel replacement who was deeply loyal to the Führer.

As von Kluge's Horch sped through the French countryside, his front-seat spotter constantly scanning the skies for the dreaded *Jabos* (fighter planes), he was unaware of Count von Stauffenberg's fateful mission to Wolfsschanze that day. But von Kluge himself had long flirted with the Schwarze Kapelle conspiracy. He had blown hot and cold on the aims of the secret clique in direct ratio to the Wehrmacht's (German Army's) fortunes on the battlefield. Twice during the past two years at his headquarters at Smolensk on the Russian front, von Kluge had been visited by emissaries of the Schwarze Kapelle who sought to woo him. Von Kluge listened patiently on both occasions, but was noncommittal. Neither time did he report the treasonable calls, a particularly unpardonable sin by one of his exalted rank and presumed deep devotion to Hitler. Von Kluge, a cagey old warrior and infighter, was covering all bets. When the bloodbath erupted between the Führer's ruling Nazi establishment and the plotters in the Schwarze Kapelle, von Kluge intended to make certain that he was aligned solidly with the "surviving" side—whichever that might be.

Elsewhere that July 20 on the other side of the lines, General Omar N. Bradley, the angular, soft-spoken Missourian who commanded the U.S. First Army, was in the operations tent of his headquarters complex of canvas and caravans shoehorned into an apple orchard behind Omaha Beach. Bradley and his G-3 (operations officer), Colonel Truman C. "Tubby" Thorson, were discussing details of Operation Cobra, a daring scheme which, if successful, would break the Americans out of the tangled hedgerows of Normandy and send tank-tipped flying columns as far south as Avranches, a coastal town thirty-five miles away at the point where the Cotentin Peninsula rounds into Brittany.

Rather than mount another maximum effort by infantrymen to forge out of Normandy, slashing yard by bloody yard through the hedgerows in frontal assault with four corps abreast, Cobra would concentrate enormous power at a tiny rectangle of countryside along the St.-Lô-Périers road, a few miles west of the key road center of St.-Lô. That town, the Cotentin Peninsula's largest, with a peacetime population of 11,000, had been captured on July 18 by the U.S. 29th Infantry Division after a bloodbath at its gates. St.-Lô was now a pulverized pile of rubble.

The targeted rectangle was three-and-a-half miles long and one-and-a-half miles deep. Cobra would kick off with hundreds of heavy bombers, supplemented by mediums and fighter bombers, pulverizing the rectangle with more than 60,000 bombs. Infantry of three divisions, closely packed along the St.-Lô-Périers road, would immediately advance into the bomb-saturated rectangle and clean up whatever resistance survived. Then swarms of tanks of the 2nd and 3rd Armored divisions would bolt through the opening and dash southward—all the way to Avranches, Bradley's staff hoped.

Bradley was deeply worried about "shorts" from the saturation bombing exploding among his waiting infantrymen. "This high-level bombing is a risky business," he had confided to his commanders. "There'll be no margin for error, or a rain of bombs will fall on our own troops. But the potential gain is worth the risk."

In order to minimize the possibility of American bombs hitting American foot soldiers, General Bradley's plan called for the heavies of the U.S. Eighth Air Force, flying from bases in England, to approach the targeted rectangle on a course *parallel* to the arrow-straight St.-Lô-Périers road so that any "shorts" dropped from 12,000 feet would land on the German side of the bomb-line, not on the American.

Cobra had been set for July 19, but murky weather and low clouds that would limit visibility forced postponement to July 21.

Bradley tried not to take counsel of his fears. But the specter of bombs raining onto his ground-assault troops continued to worry him deeply. "Those airmen do a lot of boasting," he confided to an aide. "But the truth of it is, they are not skilled in pinpoint bombing."

27

Only the day before, General Bradley had been involved in a heated confrontation with the "Air Barons" at Air Chief Marshal Trafford Leigh-Mallory's awesomely sumptuous headquarters at Bentley Priory near Stanhope, England. From its cavernous chambers, the Royal Air Force had directed the crucial Battle of Britain in 1940, which swept the Luftwaffe from the skies and prevented Hitler's impending invasion of the British Isles.

Bradley had flown to England to hammer out final details of the massive Cobra air bombardment with the air force's high command. The lineup of Air Barons facing Bradley and a few aides was formidable: the commander of Allied air forces, Leigh-Mallory—argumentative, abrasive, intensely disliked and distrusted by American leaders; Eisenhower's deputy, Air Marshal Arthur Tedder—alert, impatient, and a pipe-smoking addict; commander of the U.S. Eighth Air Force and hero of the Tokyo bombing raid, Lieutenant General James H. "Jimmy" Doolittle; Air Marshal Arthur Coningham—aggressive, with his large square jaw thrust out when confronting an adversary; commander of the U.S. Ninth Air Force Major General Lewis H. Brereton—diminutive, eyes peering coldly through horn-rimmed spectacles; and U.S. Army Air Corps commander in Europe, Lieutenant General Carl Spaatz—soft-spoken, reserved, and capable.

A middle-aged man took his place alongside the Air Barons. Clad in a rumpled, green-tweed suit that looked as though he had slept in it for weeks, the man was introduced simply as Solly Zuckerman. Only later would the curious Bradley and his aides learn that Zuckerman was a British civilian and a professor of anatomy at an English university. Whoever Solly Zuckerman was, Bradley and his ground officers mused inwardly, he must be of major importance: the Air Barons appeared to defer to him.

Hardly had the confrontation—Ground versus Air—begun than a squabble erupted. Bradley voiced his intense worry over "shorts" falling on American ground troops and insisted that the heavies fly a course parallel to the St.-Lô-Périers road. The air commanders lashed back with pointed objections: a parallel approach would expose the bomber stream to German flak over a much longer period. The air leaders held out for a perpendicular approach to the targeted rectangle.

The debate grew heated. Under no circumstances, the soft-spoken but now-riled Omar Bradley stressed, would he agree to a flight plan that called for hundreds of heavy bombers to fly in over the heads of his foot soldiers. The meeting broke up with the American ground commander in Normandy convinced that his *parallel* flight-approach had been accepted by the air generals. Bradley would soon learn how wrong this assumption had been.

As General Bradley and the Air Barons fired verbal flak at each other in England, U.S. Lieutenant General George S. Patton, Jr. was pacing about like a caged tiger at his Third Army headquarters in an apple orchard near Nehou in the Cotentin Peninsula, far behind the front lines. Patton was itching to get into action; he had been "in the doghouse" since the previous autumn when he had slapped a soldier in Sicily whom he suspected of malingering.

Outspoken, opinionated, profane—and the Allied general the Germans feared most—Patton had arrived "secretly" in Normandy on July 6, only to be met by several hundred cheering American soldiers at a landing strip behind Omaha Beach. They had heard of his "secret" arrival. The silver-haired, ramrod-straight, fifty-nine-year-old general told his well-wishers, "I'm going to lead you to Berlin, and when we get there I am going to personally shoot that goddamned paper-hanging son of a bitch [Hitler]!" Howls of laughter echoed across the hedgerowed landscape.

Now for two weeks the armor commander had been languishing at Nehou with only a paper army, a Third Army headquarters, while someone else did the fighting. He had been given no specific assignment and in his frustration growled to aides, "My destiny in this war is to sit here on my ass and watch the cider apples grow!"

Patton was what news reporters called "good copy." He could be counted on to spit out some offhand remark that, a few hours later, would appear in bold headlines back in the States. Now an eager group of reporters gathered around the Third Army commander, aware of his deep frustrations and anger over the stalemate.

Flicking the ash off his cigar, Patton cautioned the newsmen, "No notes, no quotes." This time he was determined to "put a zipper on my big mouth."

Asked what he would do to break the stalemate if he were in command in Normandy, Patton could not resist a candid reply. "I'd line up my tanks on a narrow front and in a couple of days we'd go through the Krauts like shit through a goddamned goose. We'd head for Avranches and from there bust out into Brittany and all over France," he said.

Patton, as was his wont, paused briefly for dramatic effect, then added, "Of course, that would be too bold for some. We'd never do it with that little fart in charge."

Reporters knew the identity of "that little fart"—British General Bernard Montgomery, the nonsmoking teetotaler who was commander of combined Anglo-American ground forces in Normandy. Patton, and Montgomery had long been arch foes, hardly able to exchange civilities when meeting.

The Cotentin and its treacherous *bocage*, the wooded area where Americans had been fighting and dying for several weeks, was intimately known to Patton. In 1913, he and his wife, Beatrice, had reconnoitered almost every foot of the Cotentin Peninsula by roadster while on their second honeymoon, from the port of Cherbourg at the northern tip all the way south to Avranches. "We might have to fight here some day," the young career officer had prophetically explained to his young wife thirty-one years before.

As launching of Cobra grew ever closer, George Patton relieved his frustrations by lashing out at American generals in his personal diary:

> "Neither Ike [Eisenhower] nor Brad has the stuff. Ike is bound hand and foot by the British and doesn't know it, poor fool . . . Bradley and Hodges are such nothings. . . . I could break through in three days, if I commanded."

It was just after 6:00 P.M. on July 20 when Field Marshal von Kluge's Horch pulled up to his château at La Roche-Guyon after his exhausting and gloom-ridden conference with his battle commanders in the rainy wood south of Caen. Striding wearily into his office, the pudgy general's eyes promptly focused on a document marked *Blitz Geheim* (literally, lightning secret) that had arrived only minutes before and had been placed on his desk. Hurriedly tearing open the envelope, von Kluge slumped into a chair, a thunderstruck expression etched on his pale face. The Schwarze Kapelle had struck. Adolf Hitler was dead.

Tiny beads of perspiration broke out on von Kluge's forehead and his hands trembled slightly as he began reading details in the astonishing message: Colonel General Ludwig Beck, who had resigned in a huff in 1938 in a bitter dispute with Hitler over the Führer's proposed occupation by force of defenseless Czechoslovakia, had been proclaimed Acting Chancellor of Germany, and Major General Erwin Witzleben, commander of the Berlin garrison, had assumed full powers of commander in chief of Germany's armed forces. Von Kluge was directed to immediately arrest or execute SS generals in France.

A nervous Guenther von Kluge put down the document. He was in a quandry. Which way should he leap? Was Hitler *really* dead? At that moment he received an urgent telephone call: General Beck, long the spiritual leader of the Schwarze Kapelle, was on the line from the headquarters of the Home Army on the Bendlerstrasse in Berlin, the nerve center of the conspiracy. Beck pleaded with the commander in chief, West, to support the revolt. "Are you with our aims and do you place yourself under my orders [as Acting Chancellor]?" the former chief of the German General Staff demanded to know.

Von Kluge parried the question and told Beck, "I'll have to consult with my staff here and call back in a half hour." That call would never be made.

Now dark thoughts raced through von Kluge's mind. Had the Gestapo monitored Beck's call? Had the dreaded secret police forced the Schwarze Kapelle leader to make the call in order to trap von Kluge in the conspiracy? Would von Kluge's failure to immediately offer his full support to the conspiracy at this crucial point result in his being marked as a *fuhrertreu* (zealously loyal to the Führer) and therefore marked for execution by the Schwarze Kapelle?

FOR TWO HOURS von Kluge discussed the momentous developments with his chief of staff, Lieutenant General Guenther Blumentritt. He observed that his first action should be to secure an armistice with the Americans and British in Normandy, then call a halt to the flying-bomb launchings along the Pas-de-Calais.

Again von Kluge's telephone jangled impatiently. It was Lieutenant General Bodo Zimmerman calling from OB-West headquarters at St.-Germain. He told a shaken von Kluge that he had just talked to Field Marshal Wilhelm Keitel, chief of the *Oberkommando der Wehrmacht* (OKW, the armed forces high command), at Wolfsschanze.

"Keitel said that the Führer was the target of a bomb blast, but is alive and only slightly injured," General Zimmerman related. "Keitel stressed that we are to take orders from no one but him or Himmler [the Gestapo and SS chief]."

An ashen-faced von Kluge thoughtfully replaced the receiver. He shuddered inwardly to think he had almost leaped too soon to the side of the Schwarze Kapelle conspirators.

Von Kluge soon determined for certain that Adolf Hitler was alive. He turned resignedly to Blumentritt and remarked, "When I was in contact with these people there was still hope [for Germany]. Today I am without hope, for hope is now without meaning." The butchery of the beleaguered Feldgrau in the hedgerows of Normandy would continue unabated.

It was nearly midnight in the quiet environs of picturesque La Roche-Guyon, untouched by war, when Field Marshal von Kluge dictated an urgent message:

"To the Führer and the Supreme Commander. Thanks to a merciful act of Providence, the infamous and murderous attempt against your life, Führer, has miscarried. On behalf of the three branches of the Armed Forces entrusted to my command, I send you my congratulations and assure you, my Führer, of our unalterable loyalty."

Shortly after dawn, the Allied Supreme Commander, General Eisenhower, who had arrived in France the day before to observe the launching of Cobra, was told by an excited aide of the aborted attempt on Hitler's life. Elated, Eisenhower exclaimed, "Holy smoke! There seems to be a revolt going on among the Krauts. What does this mean?"

Told that for three weeks Allied intelligence sources had been picking up reports of an assassination attempt, Eisenhower beamed, "Well, it sure looks good for Cobra!"

In the initial burst of euphoria over a quick end to the Normandy bloodbath, the supreme commander failed to grasp a crucial factor: Wehrmacht commanders in France now would fight with the desperation of cornered rats to *prove* their total loyalty to Adolf Hitler.

2

Cobra Sharpens
Its Fangs

LATE IN THE evening of July 21, Lieutenant Colonel Andrew
Barr, a Securities and Exchange Commission official in civilian life
and now intelligence officer of the 3rd Armored Division, and three
of his staff had shoehorned their way into the back of a half-track
that had been altered to form a small office with raised bows en-
abling one to stand without stooping. Inside was a built-in desk with
map drawers underneath, a typewriter to one side, and a mapboard
on the other. There was a scarcity of sitting space.

The office half-track was part of the forward echelon of Major
General Leroy H. Watson's armored division bivouacked in lush
green fields surrounded by the inevitable hedgerows, a considerable
distance to the rear of the St.-Lô-Périers road. Inside the half-track
with Colonel Barr were his assistant G-2 (intelligence) officer, Major
Haynes W. Dugan; senior noncom, Master Sergeant Frank A. Koukl;
and Corporal Dereath N. Palmer. Barr had just opened a discussion
of the latest reports on the German order of battle.

It was a beautiful summer evening. There had been little gunfire
at the front, none in the 3rd Armored bivouac area. Most of those in
the half-track were looking ahead to the evening meal.

Suddenly the tranquility was shattered. Barr, Dugan, and the
others heard a vehicle being driven at high speed on the nearby road
and peeked out to see two American soldiers from another division
racing toward them. A sergeant was standing beside the driver,
madly firing a carbine into the air and shouting at the top of his

voice, "Gas! Gas!" It was a familiar call. All had heard it many times in Stateside training but had laughed it off. Now it was for real. Had a desperate Adolf Hitler launched a poison-gas attack against the powerful American army coiled to break out of the Normandy *bocage*?

Pandemonium erupted.

The four 3rd Armored men in the half-track all tried to get out the narrow door at the same time. Discipline—and rank—prevailed. Colonel Barr leaped out first with Major Dugan on his heels, quickly followed by Sergeant Koukl and Corporal Palmer. The frantic search for long-forgotten gas masks was on.

Colonel Barr, meticulous as always, went immediately to his mask and hurriedly clamped it on his face. Major Dugan also located his easily; he kept it next to the front seat of the half-track, his usual riding place. Koukl found a mask, but Palmer did not.

"Koukl," Palmer called out with a tinge of panic. "Have you seen my mask?"

From behind his mask Sergeant Koukl shook his head negatively.

"I know it was there," Palmer shouted back.

The scene was being repeated all over the large bivouac area of the 3rd Armored Division.

Lieutenant Colonel Wesley A. Sweat, division operations officer, was on the latrine at the time the wild-eyed soldiers raced by in the weapons carrier, like modern Paul Reveres spreading the word of impending doom. Hastily grabbing his pants, Sweat headed for his gas mask when, with both hands occupied, he struck a slick patch of mud and performed a pratfall. He scrambled to his feet and continued onward.

At the time of the gas alarm, an officers' meeting was being held at Combat Command-A (CC-A) headquarters. The participants promptly scattered, searching desperately for their masks. Several of the officers leaped into jeeps to race for their own command posts (CPs) to locate their elusive face coverings. One of these was Lieutenant Colonel Carlton P. Russell, commander of the 3rd Battalion, 36th Armored Infantry Regiment of the 3rd Armored Division. As Russell and his driver sped off, another careening jeep just missed crashing into their vehicle and moments later smashed into a third rapidly departing jeep. Several other vehicles collided in the mad scramble.

While the frantic rush was on for gas masks in the forward echelon of the 3rd Armored Division, Major Dugan, the assistant G-2, put his training as a civilian reporter into play: he called someone to find out what was going on. Climbing into his half-track, he picked up the phone and was happy to hear a cool head at the VII Corps message center, a Captain Wilson who was Dugan's opposite number there.

Speaking with distortion through his gas mask, Dugan blurted out, "There's a hell of a gas scare around here. Anything to it?"

Captain Wilson laughed and replied, "Negative. Some of our troops had been exploding captured German ammo and the fumes caused discoloration of the gas-detecting paint on some of our vehicles."

With a sigh of relief, Dugan hung up the telephone. But just to be on the safe side, he continued to wear his gas mask. So did his comrades.

WILD SHOOTING AND restrained pandemonium were rampant throughout rear areas in the American sector. Many units caught up in the poison-gas hysteria went haywire, even berserk. Military policemen and sentries throughout the night fired indiscriminately. At the headquarters of Major General Elwood R. "Pete" Quesada's fighter-bomber command, west of Caen, one MP shot his pistol six times into the air while shouting "Gas! Gas!" An officer rushed up to the MP.

"Why'n hell did you empty your clip?" the officer demanded.

"Well, sir," the MP replied, "I know you only fire three times to give a gas alarm, but I never fired this pistol before . . . and I was nervous as hell."

"Then why did you fire it? Did you detect gas?"

"No, but everyone else was shooting, so I joined in."

At Isigny, excited American military policemen halted vehicles to warn occupants that a German poison-gas attack was in progress. At Carentan, medical orderlies hurriedly slipped gas masks onto patients at a clearing station. Tens of thousands of American soldiers wandered about in the darkness wearing the unbearably hot, restrictive, and uncomfortable masks.

At about midnight, after a hurried investigation, the First Army chemical officer reported the gas alarm false. Word was sent out to all units and slowly, even apprehensively, gas masks were removed. A stillness returned to the rear areas.

Shortly after 1:15 A.M., only one hour later, guards at Pete Quesada's fighter-bomber area heard the cry of "Gas!" from the direction of St.-Lô. Immediately the short tranquility was shattered as rifles and pistols were fired into the air. Again pandemonium swept through the American sector like a raging fire across a dry prairie. Colonel Benjamin A. "Monk" Dickson, Bradley's intelligence officer at First Army, hurriedly dispatched five public-address vans along the main supply routes, broadcasting that the gas alarm was false. Little was achieved. Gas masks were kept on, shouts of "Gas!" rang out, and shooting continued until a hot, July sun finally peeked across the lush Normandy countryside.

ON JULY 20, foul weather had again forced postponement of Cobra, this time indefinitely on an hour-to-hour basis. Cobra was now in the hands of the weathercasters who would give the signal, on the basis of their imprecise science, when the skies would clear sufficiently for the saturation-pounding from the air.

In England, without consulting General Bradley, a fateful alteration had been made in the massive bombing that would launch Cobra: General Doolittle, the hero of the daring B-25 bombing raid on Tokyo shortly after Pearl Harbor and now commander of the U.S. Eighth Air Force, decided to ignore the wishes of the American ground commander in Normandy. Doolittle's 2,246 bombers would approach the impact area directly over the heads of Americans on the ground. The peppery air commander's principle concern was the safety of his flight crews. He felt that a parallel course to the St.-Lô-Périers road would result in excessive casualties among his airmen.

On the eve of momentous operations in Normandy, sixty-one-year-old, silver-haired U.S. Lieutenant General Lesley J. McNair, the organizational genius who in three years had expanded a tiny core of professionals into a mighty army of several million men, was stewing in southeast England over his "combat assignment." McNair, who had been chief of the Army Ground Forces in Washington, had been rushed to the European theater of operations a week previously by Chief of Staff George C. Marshall. He had been told only that he would receive a key post.

McNair, anticipating a field army or even army group command in Normandy, eagerly reported to the Supreme Commander at Southwick House. When General Eisenhower told McNair that he would succeed General Patton as commander of a phony First Army Group, supposedly massed in southeast England for a powerful cross-Channel smash against the Pas-de-Calais, General McNair was deeply chagrined and white with anger. Heated words followed between the two generals.

Word quickly spread among correspondents at Supreme Head-quarters Allied Expeditionary Force (SHAEF) advance headquarters at Southwick House outside Portsmouth. "Ike and McNair have had one hell of a fight!" But good soldier that he was, a disappointed Les McNair took up the wooden sword of his paper-tiger command, resigned to letting others do the fighting. No one had any way of knowing that McNair would be dead in a few days, killed in action in Normandy.

General McNair had been rushed to England to replace Patton at the urgent request of the XX-Committee (Double-cross Committee), an ingenious group of brilliant and devious British minds whose function it was to confound and confuse the Wehrmacht about Allied intentions and capabilities. Through a massive deception plan code-named Fortitude, the XX-Committee had bamboozled Hitler and his counterintelligence apparatus on D-Day into expect-ing a second, even more powerful, Allied landing at the Pas-de-Calais by the phony Army Group Patton. To meet this looming threat, Hitler had ordered his first-rate Fifteenth Army to remain in place along the Pas-de-Calais for six weeks, even as the German Seventh Army fought for its life in Normandy, only a day's motor march to the west.

Patton's presence in Normandy, instead of in southeast England, soon became known by the Germans through left-behind spies. The armored leader was to have been "under wraps," but concealing his presence was a task akin to hiding an approaching tornado. To continue the massive *ruse de guerre* and to prevent Hitler from shifting his Pas-de-Calais divisions to oppose Goodwood and Cobra, a replacement whose professional credentials would be accepted by the Germans had to take over command of the fictitious army group in southeast England. That man was Lesley McNair.

Through double agents controlled by the XX-Committee, German counterintelligence learned that Patton had "stuck his foot in his mouth" once again and been "demoted" and that General McNair, one of the U.S. Army's most brilliant officers, had been rushed over to replace the errant "bad boy." The German divisions along the Pas-de-Calais continued to brace for an assault by Army Group McNair as Cobra sharpened its fangs.

MEANWHILE, THE MIGHTY pent-up American assault force, from General Bradley on down to the machine gunner on outpost along the St.-Lô-Périers road, fidgeted nervously. Omar the Tentmaker, as the correspondents had dubbed the well-liked First Army commander, had made every conceivable preparation. Now all he could do was wait . . . and wait . . . and wait some more. This gave him time to think—thoughts of what would be the consequences if Cobra, like Goodwood, were to fail.

BRADLEY AND OTHER ground commanders had long been fully aware that the Air Barons were stridently claiming that Nazi Germany and its armed forces could be brought to their knees by bombing alone. If Cobra were to fail in the wake of Montgomery's maximum effort at Caen being halted, it was quite possible that Bradley, and even Eisenhower, would be sacked and sent home to desk jobs, branded as failures. Even worse, the Allied air marshals and generals might assume a dominant role in the war against Hitler, and the massive Anglo-American force bottled up in the hedgerows and rolling fields of Normandy might be ordered to linger in place indefinitely.

Outwardly, Omar Bradley was his normal, composed, optimistic self. Inwardly he was deeply concerned. Sheepishly, he asked a close aide at night to "find me a couple of sleeping pills."

TWO DAYS AFTER the bungled effort to murder Hitler, von Kluge called Colonel General Alfred Jodl, Hitler's trusted aide and OKW operations chief, whose primary function was to translate Hitler's strategic orders into writing. Jodl had been at Hitler's side since 1940, and was noted in the officer corps principally for his uncanny talent for being able to tell the Führer bad, often catastrophic, news from the battlefield in such a way that the impact upon Hitler was minimized.

"The whole Normandy front is an *ungeheuerer Kladderadatsch* (monstrous mess]," the commander in the west told a nervous Jodl. Von Kluge asked him if the Oberkommando der Wehrmacht (in effect, meaning Hitler) "fully appreciates the tremendous consumption of our forces on big battle days." Jodl, as was his custom in delicate discussion, listened—but offered little response.

Von Kluge said that his infantry "cannot hold much longer." He said that he wanted the Führer to know that the Normandy battle picture was "very serious."

"If a hole breaks open, I have to patch it," von Kluge stressed. "And I have few troops to patch it with. Tell that to the Führer."

An increasingly desperate von Kluge replaced the receiver. He doubted if Jodl would even mention his call to Hitler.

Von Kluge was wrong. A few hours later a response arrived from the Führer: *"Starre Verteidigung!"* (Stand fast!)

Hitler felt he could win the war against the Anglo-Americans if only his Feldgrau continued to hold on. His flying-bomb campaign was wreaking havoc in England. Only the preceding day a V-1 had plummeted down during the noon rush on a shop-lined street in teeming London. Its 2,031 pounds of explosive blew apart a crowded restaurant and filled the air with knife-edged shards of splintered glass. The enormous blast tore off the top of a bus jammed with civilians and ripped open another packed bus, tossing passengers high into the air, their clothes afire. Hours later the screams and moans of those buried alive under piles of rubble could still be heard. The searchers were digging out scores of the dead in their quest for survivors. The toll from that one missile was enormous.

Time was what the Führer needed. Time. The battered, outnumbered, and outgunned *Feldgrau* had to hang on in Normandy. The survival of the Third Reich—and of Adolf Hitler—well could be at stake.

On the sultry morning of July 23, Lieutenant General Fritz Bayerlein, the grizzled, tough commander of the crack Panzer Lehr Division, was sipping coffee with an aide at his CP three miles south of the St.-Lô-Périers road. Bayerlein had fought in countless battles, having been Field Marshal Erwin Rommel's chief of staff in the North African campaigns. Bayerlein was unflappable. Little disturbed him.

"Where do you think the Allies will try to break out?" the aide casually inquired. "We're pretty thin here."

Bayerlein took a swig of his dark brew and replied, "Oh, I don't think we've got anything to worry about. They'll try to break out with the British over at Caen."

Unknown to General Bayerlein, his decimated grenadiers and panzers were at that moment on the precise rectangle of ground that would soon be deluged with 60,000 Allied bombs. Some 5,000 troops of the Panzer Lehr were directly in the path of the Cobra juggernaut.

At Army Group B headquarters at La Roche-Guyon, an increasingly apprensive Field Marshal von Kluge put in a call to Obergruppenfuehrer (SS Colonel General) Paul Hausser at his Seventh Army headquarters. A few weeks before, when appointed to his post by Hitler, Hausser had become the first Schutzstaffel (SS) general to command a field army. Von Kluge was expecting the impending all-out Allied assault to erupt at Caen, but he was also keeping a sharp eye on General Bradley in the St.-Lô sector.

"Pull your Panzer Lehr back from the front lines and replace it with infantry," the Commander in Chief, West, ordered. "Infantry can't be beat in the hedgerows. Put your tanks in army reserve, and then we will have a force to counterattack—in case there should be a breakthrough."

For reasons that are unclear, General Hausser simply ignored this direct order. Bayerlein's grenadiers and tanks would remain in place along the St.-Lô-Périers road.

VON KLUGE'S FIRM belief that the looming Allied maximum effort to break out of Normandy would strike in the British sector at Caen was reinforced by a massive deception campaign. British and American warships were sent into the waters off Le Havre, east of Caen. As anticipated, this was promptly reported to German intelligence. The Allies also greatly increased air reconnaissance in the vicinity of Caen, a telltale factor also noted by the Wehrmacht. And finally, a rash of French underground sabotage actions suddenly erupted along the northern coast of France. German intelligence also was fed clues that indicated a large Allied airborne landing south of Caen.

MEANWHILE, IN THE final few days before Cobra, feverish activity, cloaked in the most intense security precautions, was taking place behind American lines. A "secret weapon" was being fashioned to spring on unsuspecting German infantry burrowed into the earthen hedgerows. The "secret weapon" was simple in conception, yet would play a major role in the planned breakthrough. Scores of Sherman tanks were being fitted with long, heavy-steel, tusklike prongs welded to the front.

During all the fighting in the *bocage*, American Shermans had been thwarted by the thick walls of the hedgerows, and lethal German 88-millimeter guns and infantrymen armed with Panzerfauste had taken an alarming toll. There were only two ways for the Shermans to advance in the *bocage*: lumber toward the narrow gap in each hedgerow through which Norman farmers had for centuries pushed wheelbarrows or driven cattle and horses, or scramble up and over the earthen walls. German guns covered the gap, and as soon as a Sherman appeared there it was knocked out by a high-velocity shell from the next hedgerow. If American tanks tried to go over the top of the dirt embankments, their thin bellies were exposed and most burst into flaming torches when struck by German shells or shoulder-launched rockets.

Earlier in the month, Sergeant Curtis G. Culin of the 102nd Cavalry Reconnaissance Squadron had conceived the idea for crashing tanks through the hedgerows. The tusklike prongs protruded out to the front, and when a Sherman smashed into an earthen obstacle the steel prongs pinned the tank and kept it from bellying-up over the wall; then it would crash on through under its own power, guns blazing and the brush and dirt from the hedgerow draped over the tracked vehicle to provide natural camouflage.

General Bradley was delighted with Sergeant Culin's invention. German obstacles from the Normandy landing beaches were uprooted to provide steel for the mass production of tusks. Welders worked around the clock. Orders were issued not to use any of the tusk-equipped Shermans until Cobra, so that the Germans would be completely surprised by American tanks crashing directly through the earthen barriers. The new "secret weapon" was called "Rhinoceros" or "Rhino" for short.

Morale among American tankers skyrocketed with Rhino. Now, when they rumbled into action, the armored crews would know that they were not advancing to likely mutilation or death.

At his battle headquarters outside the village of Goucherie, five miles north of the St.-Lô-Périers road (the Cobra bomb-line), the youthful VII Corps commander, Major General J. Lawton "Lightning Joe" Collins, was poring over maps with several aides. Collins, who at age forty-eight was the army's youngest corps commander, had been entrusted by General Bradley with the key Cobra assignment: breaking through German defenses and racing southward.

Joe Collins, who received his moniker for swiftly driving the Japanese off Guadalcanal in the Pacific the previous year, after his division relieved the marines, would employ tactics identical to those used in an American football game. His "linemen" would be three veteran infantry divisions who would grapple face-to-face with the opposition at the line of scrimmage (the St.-Lô-Périers road) and gouge open a hole. Collins' linemen were Major General Raymond O. "Tubby" Barton's 4th (Ivy) Infantry Division, Major General Manton S. Eddy's 9th Infantry Division (the Old Reliables), and Major General Leland S. Hobbs's 30th (Old Hickory) Infantry Division.

Once the linemen had opened the hole at the line of scrimmage, Collins would hand the ball to his swift backfield runners who would dash through the opening and head for the opposition's goal line. The ball carriers would be Major General Edward H. Brooks's 2nd (Hell on Wheels) Armored Division, General Leroy "Wap" Watson's 3rd Armored Division, and Major General Clarence R. Huebner's motorized 1st Infantry Division (the Big Red One). As in football, how far the ball carriers ran would depend upon the reaction and defensive spirit of the opposition.

One of those concerned with the defensive spirit of his "team" in Normandy was Adolf Hitler. In the wake of his miraculous escape from the bomb blast that had killed and wounded several officers next to him and left his operations building at Wolfsschanze a shambles, on July 22 the Führer fired off a terse, yet explicit, message to Wehrmacht commanders: "Anyone who gives up an inch of ground will be shot."

A second urgent message from Hitler was clearly aimed at Field Marshal von Kluge and possibly other top battle leaders in Normandy: "Anyone who speaks to me of peace without victory will lose his head, no matter who he is or what his position."

Reading this, von Kluge may have realized that his days on earth were numbered. Hitler, through the Gestapo, had already learned that von Kluge and Field Marshal Rommel had a connection to the assassination conspiracy.

TO THE BELEAGUERED German combat troops in Normandy the assassination plot was not of crucial significance. As the Gestapo was arresting and executing ringleaders of the Schwarze Kapelle in Berlin within hours of the bomb blast, a typical German *schutze* (private)—call him Hans Kiel—facing the Americans along the St.-Lô-Périers road kept right on fighting as though nothing had happened.

Schutze Kiel's world was that of the hedgerows. Of moment-to-moment survival. His face was always in the mud. He cringed at the bottom of his foxhole as American artillery shells constantly screamed in and rocked him with their explosions. His stomach was always tied in knots. His taut nerves danced on end when he heard the piercing cries of comrades mutilated by jagged, white-hot shards of steel that sliced faces in half and ripped off arms and legs, leaving gushers of blood spurting from the stumps. Kiel, frequently deluged to the skin by sheets of cold rain, had to subsist largely on cold field rations.

Kiel did not have the time, nor was he in a mental state to concern himself with matters beyond the fringe of his own little perimeter. He and his comrades were in a world all their own, a world of endless struggle to stay alive. But Schutze Kiel and other Feldgrau silently went on doing their duty, though subconsciously they were aware that an enormous catastrophe was looming in Normandy. They would fight on in a hopeless situation—with tenacity, skill, and courage.

On the evening of July 23, Allied meteorologists in Great Britain were feverishly analyzing weather data and checking outlying reporting stations in the Atlantic in an effort to predict climatic conditions over Normandy for the following day. English Channel weather had long been notorious for its capriciousness. The meteorologists were uneasy. It could be murky over Normandy in the morning, but the skies just might clear by noon. Then again, they might not.

At Bentley Priory outside Stanhope, Air Chief Marshal Leigh-Mallory, air advisor to the supreme commander, was wrestling with a crucial decision. He had the authority to set the date and time for launching Cobra. On the basis of the weathercasters' ambiguous prediction, Leigh-Mallory, impatient over the lengthy delay as were all Allied commanders, set H-Hour for 1:00 P.M. on the following day, July 24.

Eighty minutes before H-Hour, 350 fighter bombers of Pete Quesada's IX Tactical Air Command would pound a 250-yard strip in the targeted rectangle on the south side of the St.-Lô-Périers road after infantrymen had pulled back some 1,200 yards as a safety measure. Twenty minutes later, 1,812 Liberators and Flying Fortresses of Jimmy Doolittle's Eighth Air Force would pulverize the three and a half-mile-long rectangle to a depth of one-and-a-half miles with 3,300 tons of high explosives and fragmentation bombs.

For one hour Doolittle's heavies would pound the target, after which 350 more Mustang and Thunderbolt fighter-bombers would swoop in to bomb and strafe the narrow 250-yard strip just to the south of the road. Just then the withdrawn American infantrymen were to return to their former positions fronting the road to be ready to jump off when the last bomb had fallen. While "Lightning Joe" Collins's foot soldiers were edging back up to the road, 396 mediums of the IX Bomber Command would pound the southern half of the rectangle for forty-five minutes.

As the assault infantrymen began crossing the St. Lô-Périers road 1,100 big guns, massed almost hub-to-hub, would open a thunderous barrage into the rectangle against suspected enemy strongpoints —if any had survived the awesome rain of bombs.

THE WHEELS OF the gigantic Cobra machinery had been set in motion. Battalion, company, and platoon commanders of the assaulting 4th, 9th, and 30th Infantry divisions were briefed as the late-setting Normandy sun dipped down over the western horizon. No patrols were sent out. Those briefed on Cobra might be captured and tip off the enemy. There was last-minute letter writing. Huddled under a poncho in an apple orchard, mortar Sergeant Robert Murphy of Tubby Barton's 4th Division scrawled a note to his parents back in New Orleans: "There's something Big up. You'll know about it by the time you get this letter. This waiting is hell on all of us. The Krauts over there probably feel the same."

Nearby in a damp foxhole, another of Barton's 4.2-inch mortarmen, twenty-one-year-old Sergeant Karl Kaupert, was also penning a note to his parents in Milwaukee. Kaupert was born in Berlin, came to the States as an infant, and spoke German fluently. He had gained a reputation among his comrades as a "cool cookie" under fire. Kaupert wrote: "GIs, tanks, big guns everywhere. The hedge-

44

rows around each field are lined with them. The Luftwaffe comes over at night and drops bombs at random. I don't see how they can miss hitting something. This is a powder keg ready to explode."

Waiting for the signal to move out, Major William A. Castille, intelligence officer of Combat Command-B (CC-B) of Watson's 3rd Armored Division, was outwardly calm. Inside he conjectured as to how his relatively green outfit would respond in its first major test now looming just ahead. During 3rd Armored's baptism of fire three weeks before in support of the 29th Infantry Division, bearded, grimy infantrymen frequently commented to Castille on his shiny new Justin tanker's boots. Now on the eve of Cobra the armored major idly reflected upon the popularity of his glossy footware with the long-suffering infantrymen and how they had repeatedly cast coveted glances at the boots. He was struck with a curious thought: "If I get killed, I will probably be buried in my stockinged feet!"

Along the narrow, hedgerow-lined roads to the rear, thousands of American foot soldiers were moving up closer to the front. Elements of Hobbs's 30th Infantry Division were marching in almost total silence, grim-faced, tight-lipped, widely spaced against sudden shelling. Most had the haunted, fixed stare of those moving into desperate battle, their thoughts focused on whether they would be alive, and in one piece, in a few hours. There were only the sounds of heavy wheezing and puffing under the burden of heavy combat gear.

Many of Hobbs's men were replacements, frightened nearly witless over the unknown ordeal into which they would soon be plunged. The "old" men were scared, too; their eyes and ears had seen and heard it all. Most of the new men had been with the 30th only two or three days. Some did not even know the names of their platoon sergeants and company officers. A large number of the youthful replacements—"cannon fodder," the Big Wheels called them privately—were only ten days away from the peaceful confines of Camp Walters, Texas. Some had been in the army only twenty weeks.

Onward they trudged into the gathering twilight. Even in the most hideous specters conjured up by tormented minds did these men of the Old Hickory Division visualize that their greatest danger would not be from German gunfire but from American bombs.

At his apple-orchard, tent headquarters in the center of the Cotentin Peninsula on the eve of Cobra, General George Patton was

45

plunged into the depths of despair. One of the monumental battles of the war was about to erupt and he, a man born to fight—who had shown his mettle in North Africa and Sicily—was to be left behind. In the eighteen days he had been stewing and fretting since arriving under wraps in Normandy, Patton had convinced himself that there was a conspiracy afoot to keep him out of the conflict. He named the culprits: Omar Bradley and Bernard Montgomery.

Patton's depressed mood was not relieved, even when a top aide to General Eisenhower assured him, saying, "Hell, George, no one's trying to keep you out. Everybody's most eager indeed to get you and Third Army operational."

Contributing to Patton's blue mood and frustration was the fact that he felt that Bradley had stolen the Cobra concept from him. On July 2, while Bradley's army was slugging its way through the *bocage* country, General Patton had submitted to the First Army commander a bold plan for breaking out of the Normandy stalemate: concentrate tanks, backed by infantry, on a narrow front; punch a hole in the German line; and send armor racing south down a good road network to Avranches. This July 2 report, Patton was certain, served as a basis for Cobra.

3

Devastation
from the Sky

GENERAL FRITZ BAYERLEIN, commander of the Panzer Lehr Division, dug in along the St.-Lô-Périers road, emerged shortly after dawn on July 24 from his château command post. His eyes promptly searched the skies, and he was encouraged to note the thick cloud cover. That would meant that the swarms of dreaded Allied fighter-bombers would be curtailed.

Returning inside for his early morning coffee, Bayerlein was told by an aide that Dietrich von Choltitz's LXXXIV Corps had reported to Seventh Army during the night that there were indications of a concentration of American armor north of the St.-Lô-Périers road. "Nonsense," Seventh Army had replied. "The Allies will hit in the Caen sector."

It was a quiet morning in Bayerlein's sector. Here and there sounded an occasional rifle crack or the short burst of a chattering machine gun. A light artillery barrage, a brief mortar stonk, the angry bark of a Browning automatic rifle.

The front along the St.-Lô-Périers road seemed haunted. A fine mist caressed the lush greenery. Here and there crows and sparrows cawed and flew gracefully from bush to tree. Crickets in the tall grass chirped. Except for the few troops firing sporadically, the battlefield was deserted. Most of the Norman residents had abandoned their humble homes and fled. The few civilians who remained took refuge in the cellars of isolated farm houses. At either end of the small area soon to be saturated by American bombs stood the now ghostlike

47

hamlets of Amigny-la-Chapelle and Le Mesnil-Eury, their tiny clusters of houses gray and foreboding. The village priest had remained behind in Amigny-la-Chapelle to be present if needed by his few parishioners who were scattered about the battle zone.

A few German infantrymen, their clothing still damp from the early morning mist, cautiously poked through houses and outbuildings of the deserted hamlets after emerging from cramped, wet foxholes. They were searching for eggs, bacon, or other food delicacies that might have been overlooked by the departing farm families. or for cider and Calvados, the latter known to the Feldgrau and dogfaces alike as "white lightning." A few belts of Calvados could make the unbearable days and nights a tad more tolerable.

At midmorning, several American and British aircraft were winging through murky skies over the English Channel, bound from England to Normandy. They were loaded with a galaxy of top Allied brass who wanted a front-row seat to view the launching of Cobra, one of history's most awesome military spectacles. Air Chief Marshal Trafford Leigh-Mallory glanced out the window of his Royal Air Force medium bomber every few minutes. He had given the "Go!" signal for Cobra the previous night. Now he was having second thoughts as his aircraft burrowed through the overcast.

Diminutive General Lew Brereton, the taciturn commander of the U.S. Ninth Air Force, was flying the same course in a transport plane, along with Major General Matthew B. Ridgway, commander of the U.S. 82nd Airborne Division, which had been withdrawn to England after spearheading the American assault on Normandy on D-Day. Brereton scribbled in his diary:

"Every precaution has been taken to minimize danger to our own [ground] troops. The infantry will withdraw 1,500 yards north of the St.-Lô-Périers road. . . . Red smoke shells will be fired by our artillery to mark the bomb-line for the fighter-bombers, [which will be] first to attack. All our vehicles will be marked with yellow or cerise panels."

Brereton's understanding of the Cobra plan was wrong in one crucial respect: Joe Collins's infantry would not be pulled back 1,500 yards, but only 600 to 1,000 yards. The corps commanders' frontline battle leaders had vigorously protested giving up ground their men had paid such a high price to purchase; they feared the Germans would promptly move forward into the vacuum.

By 10:00 A.M. General Bradley's headquarters was jammed with a glittering array of "visiting firemen" from England, the United States, and even Mexico. The presence of General Les McNair, commander of the phony Army Group McNair (formerly Army Group Patton) in southeastern England raised the eyebrows of those privy to the Fortitude deception ploy. If the Wehrmacht learned that McNair was not with his troops in England, would it not jeopardize the German-held belief that McNair's fictitious 32 divisions were poised to assault the Pas-de-Calais at the same time Cobra struck?

The Parade of the Generals departed Bradley's CP complex behind Omaha Beach at 10:50 A.M., bound for front-line observation posts, or near the front line. Lieutenant General Courtney H. Hodges, the quiet, reserved deputy to Bradley, was in the first jeep, accompanied by Lieutenant General William H. Simpson, commander of the new U.S. Ninth Army, which would not be committed until later. Following in another jeep were two air corps generals, major generals Ralph Royce and Brereton, and an observer from the Mexican air force, General Hector Avila. Major generals Guy B. Henry from the War Department in Washington and Ridgway, plus an assortment of lesser generals followed. A reinforced platoon of civilian war correspondents brought up the rear of the cavalcade.

H-Hour for the saturation bombing by 2,246 aircraft was less than ninety minutes away by the time the generals arrived in the combat areas. It was a worried group. A heavy cloud cover had socked in the target area. General Bradley and Air Chief Marshal Leigh-Mallory tensely awaited developments at the First Army CP behind Omaha Beach. General Collins stepped outside his headquarters building at Goucherie every few minutes to gaze searchingly at the murky skies.

At about 11:00 A.M. the telephone rang at General Fritz Bayerlein's thick-walled château CP at Canisy. A battalion commander of the 901st Panzer Grenadier Regiment along the St.-Lô-Périers road was on the line: "American infantry [across the road] are abandoning their positions. They are withdrawing everywhere."

Bayerlein, commander of the Panzer Lehr Division, and his aides were puzzled. They joked that the Americans had "lost their nerve."

Now General Bayerlein was all the more convinced that the all-out effort by the Allies to break loose from Normandy would not hit in the American sector at St.-Lô but in the British zone at Caen. But if the Americans did come, he was ready for them. Bayerlein, his command decimated by weeks of relentless hedgerow warfare, was unable to hold a continuous line. He concentrated on defending the main roads and junctions. He had employed his panzers in depth down the two roads that ran to Marigny and St.-Gilles, concealing them along hedgerow-lined lanes.

At 11:40 A.M. Leigh-Mallory, at Bradley's First Army CP, put in an urgent call to his command in England: "Cancel the Cobra bombing!" It was too late. Three hundred and eighty-five heavies were plowing through the overcast toward the tiny rectangle of ground along the St.-Lô-Périers road. Frantic efforts were launched to scrub the air assault by contacting the Flying Fortresses and Liberators in the air. It was a difficult task, perhaps a hopeless one. In the meantime, all over southern England, other heavies were taking off for Normandy.

Thousands of grimy, bearded, American infantrymen, pulled back from the bomb-line, milled about and gazed into the cloud-flecked skies as they heard the roar of approaching aircraft. It was twelve noon. General Pete Quesada's Thunderbolt and Mustang fighter-bombers, swarms of them, had arrived over the target rectangle on a *parallel* course precisely on time. Word of the bombing's scrubbing had not reached the fighter pilots.

The fighter-bombers in foursomes circled the target briefly, then one by one peeled off and roared downward. There was a mighty explosion, the earth shook, and a black plume of smoke spiraled into the gray sky. One of the first bombs had struck an American ammunition dump by mistake. Another Thunderbolt flight loosed a bomb salvo that exploded less than 500 yards from where the group of American generals was viewing the air spectacle. All of the generals flopped to the ground.

For forty-five minutes the Mustangs and Thunderbolts bombed and machine-gunned the three-and-a-half-mile-long rectangle of Norman landscape as German grenadiers and tankers cringed under the impact. As the final fighter-bomber departed, an eerie lull settled over the killing grounds.

Minutes later, the first of Jimmy Doolittle's heavies arrived, fired blue smoke signals to mark the target, and in seconds the air was saturated with the curious whining sound of hundreds of bomb clusters fluttering earthward. The American generals heard the shriek of missiles heading directly toward them, and as they dropped

50

face downward the bombs exploded some 300 yards away, right on top of elements of the 120th Infantry Regiment of Hobbs's 30th Division. Many infantrymen were killed and scores wounded by the single cluster.

An excited and furious General Lew Brereton, the Ninth Air Force commander, looked at his watch and shouted to an aide above the din of exploding bombs and roaring aircraft engines, "It's exactly 12:50. Make a note of that! We'll check on that bunch!"

Ground generals with Brereton were at once alarmed and angry. The bomber stream was not approaching the target on a *parallel* course, but on a perpendicular route directly over the heads of Joe Collins's infantrymen packed below.

Lesley McNair, the Chief of Army Ground Forces, whose lot it had been to "command" the phony Army Group McNair, had gone on ahead of his fellow generals to get a closer look at the bombing from a battalion observation post. McNair had been wounded previously when struck by a bomb fragment while visiting the front in the North African fighting. Now he barely escaped death again. He had impaired hearing and had not heard the cluster of bombs whistling toward him. An alert aide shoved McNair into a ditch just as the bombs exploded.

Succeeding flights of Flying Fortresses and Liberators continued to rain down bombs, most detonating among Germans in the rectangle, others killing and maiming American troops. At Pete Quesada's headquarters west of Caen, a wing commander of the Ninth Fighter Command, Colonel William Macauley, was startled to receive a report of "shorts" landing among Collins's infantrymen. He was out of touch with his chief, General Quesada, who was at the front.

Acting on his own initiative, he tried to reach the bombers over a frequency he felt they would hear. "Stop the bombing! Stop the bombing!" he shouted repeatedly into the transmitter. The frantic message got through to many heavies, and the big Liberators and Flying Fortresses turned away before reaching the target and headed back to England.

Colonel Macauley slumped into a chair in nervous exhaustion. He had turned back the tidal wave of explosives before hundreds, perhaps thousands more American foot soldiers had been killed by bombardiers unable to see clearly through the haze. But had he jeopardized Cobra? He, a relatively lowly colonel, had taken it upon himself to halt the mighty bombing operation.

AT THEIR OBSERVATION post, the bevy of American generals were puzzled over the abrupt termination of the massive air bombardment. They were unaware of the disaster resulting from the "shorts" that rained down on the 30th Infantry Division or of the action by the obscure Colonel Macauley in turning away the heavies. General Hobbs, commander of the Old Hickory Division, charged up to General Hodges, Bradley's deputy at First Army. Hobbs, a classmate and close friend of Bradley's, was white-hot with anger. He was furious at the bombing failure that had killed 25 of his men, wounded 130 others, and had shaken the morale of his troops to the marrow of their bones.

"The goddamned air corps came north-south, not east-west along the road as planned," he shouted at General Hodges.

Back at his Omaha Beach command post, Omar Bradley was shocked and raging with untypical vehemence over the bombing fiasco. What he had feared for days and had haunted his nights had occurred—"shorts" from American bombers had rained down on his massed foot soldiers. He had understood that the flight approach was to be *parallel* to the road, but the heavies flew in on a perpendicular course directly over the heads of the assault troops. Aides said they had never seen the soft-spoken Bradley so angry.

"They broke faith with the plan," Bradley told outsiders. To confidants, his opinion of the air generals was far more precise: "They're goddamned liars!"

It was not just Bradley, Collins, Hobbs, and other ground commanders who were furious. General Quesada, the boyish-looking leader of American fighter-bombers in Normandy, fired off a message of indignant protest to his air bosses in England—a message that fell just short of insubordination. He demanded to know whether "another plan had actually been employed"; Quesada's Thunderbolts and Mustangs had made a lateral approach to the target, as they were supposed to.

Expecting an attack by American infantry in the wake of the bombing, German artillery pounded Collins's positions north of the St.-Lô-Périers road. In the meantime, as front-line American battle commanders had feared, the Germans had moved into the vacuum created when the 4th, 9th, and 30th divisions had pulled back from the bomb-line.

At his headquarters at La Roche-Guyon, Guenther von Kluge received garbled reports that his front-line positions had been heavily bombed. He presumed the strike had been in General Heinz Eberhard's Panzer Group-West sector, in front of the British at Caen. Von Kluge placed a hurried phone call to Eberhard.

"What's happened up there?" von Kluge asked in alarm. It was at Caen that he expected the Allies to try to break out and where he had congregated the bulk of his armor.

"Nothing new," Eberhard replied calmly. "Everything's very quiet here."

Learning that it was the Panzer Lehr Division at St.-Lô that had been bombed, von Kluge called General Hausser at Seventh Army in Le Mans. "Give me a quick rundown on the facts," a nervous von Kluge demanded.

Hausser complied in a calm tone. "Strong air activity on my right flank, attacks in the form of bomb carpets behind the MLR [main line of resistance]. Only limited [ground] attacks; no concerted assault recognizable."

"In other words," von Kluge stated, hoping Hausser could devine American intentions, "as weather improves we can expect increasingly severe fighting around St.-Lô and westward. Isn't that about right?"

Hausser agreed. "Between St.-Lô and the sea."

Von Kluge persisted, "I ask you again, do you get the impression that you're heading for heavy fighting?"

"We've got to expect it somewhere," was the casual reply. Hausser showed no undue worry or concern.

"Without any doubt," von Kluge stated, as though talking to himself, "there's something new in all this air activity. We have got to expect a heavy enemy offensive somewhere."

The Commander in Chief, West, worried both about whether the Gestapo would link him with the Schwarze Kapelle and about what the Führer's reaction would be if the Allies were to burst out of Normandy and spill out over France, felt that the air bombardment west of St.-Lô was only a feint. All indications were that General Bernard Montgomery would launch the main offensive at Caen and toward Paris. Late in the afternoon, Field Marshal von Kluge climbed into his Horch and set out for the Caen sector to be on hand when the British struck the next day. He was too cagey an old warrior to fall for the American *ruse de querre* at St.-Lô.

Word of the Cobra cancellation reached General Collins at his CP in Goucherie at about 12:30 P.M. The VII Corps commander promptly ordered his front-line assault units to launch a limited-objective attack at 1:00 P.M. to regain the ground along the St.-Lô-Périers road into which the Germans had moved after the American pullback from the bomb-line. Elements of the 4th, 9th, and 30th divisions jumped off and ran into savage German resistance.

LED BY THE redoubtable Colonel Harry A. "Paddy" Flint, his customary, black-silk scarf knotted at the neck, and carrying an ancient Springfield bolt-action rifle, the 39th Infantry Regiment of the 9th Division struck a buzz saw almost at once. Germans, armed with an array of Schmeisser machine pistols and machine guns, had established several strongpoints in front of the 39th Infantry and refused to budge. The attack ground to a halt.

There was no doubt about it: at age fifty-six, cavalry-trained Paddy Flint, a poker-playing and drinking buddy of General George Patton, was far overage to command an infantry regiment in battle. Yet there he was, a happy, dust-caked fugitive from a dozen cushy— and safe—supply and liaison jobs. Profane, gruff-voiced, fearless, revered by his fighting men, Colonel Flint had begged his now-high-ranking West Point classmates to "get me away from all these goddamned paper shufflers." He was given a regiment.

In Normandy, as in North Africa and Sicily, Flint's short, aging, horse-bowed legs sometimes were not as sturdy as his fighting heart. When they let him down, Flint would simply take a seat, even at an outpost in view of the Germans, to get his strength back. He never worried about the enemy marksmen picking him off. "Those goddamned Krauts are the world's worst rifle shots!" he proclaimed. It was soldier's talk that Eisenhower, a West Point plebe when the colonel was a first classman (senior), had personally seen to it that Flint got the up-front command—and kept him there. Paddy Flint was delighted to be in the thick of things.

"Normandy," he declared, "is my graduation exercise as a foot-slogger."

Now Flint was about to receive his diploma. All he had to do was

54

to push up to the St.-Lô-Périers road and then lead his 39th Infantry on across, the next day, he hoped. But his men were falling like flies around him from the German automatic-weapons fire. And mortar rounds began exploding among the stalled regiment.

"I'm going up and see what'n hell's holding us up," Flint told an aide. He took a rifle platoon forward and soon found the trouble. Said Paddy over a walkie-talkie, "I've found the goddamned bottleneck. Some dug-in Krauts with Schmeissers. We'll start the bastards cooking."

Flint called for a Sherman tank, hopped aboard it on his creaking legs, dodged a rain of bullets aimed at him as the tracked vehicle sprayed the hedgerows. "Goddamned Krauts never could hit anything!" Paddy spit out.

The tank driver was wounded. Flint crawled off the Sherman and went forward on foot. A sharp crack rang out from a hedgerow to the front, and the indestructible Paddy Flint went down, hit in the head by a sniper's bullet—"a goddamned lucky shot!", the colonel would have called it. Aid men soon rushed up, loaded Paddy onto a stretcher. Said a private as the party started for the rear, "Remember, Paddy, you can't kill an Irishman—you can only make him mad." Colonel Flint smiled weakly. He would die the next day.

Flint's men struggled for eight hours to wipe out the German strongpoint and reach the objective, the St.-Lô-Périers road. The bloodletting had been great: the 39th Infantry suffered 77 casualties. A battalion of the 47th Infantry Regiment of the 9th Division fought until dark to seize a single hedgerow. Two battalions of the 8th Infantry Regiment of the 4th Division suffered 27 killed and 70 wounded in slashing through hedgerows a few yards at a time. By nightfall, the 8th Infantry reached a point 100 yards short of the road. There the exhausted dogfaces dug in.

The errant bombs that had fallen on elements of Hobbs's 30th Infantry Division dazed and demoralized the fighting men. Officers labored feverishly to rally and hurriedly organize the decimated units, and within an hour of the bombing disaster, men of the Old Hickory Division were advancing through the hedgerows and fighting their way to the St.-Lô-Périers road.

General Omar Bradley was left in a deep quandry by the abortion of Cobra. The Germans obviously had been alerted by the bombing that some kind of activity was imminent in the St.-Lô sector, and Bradley feared the enemy would rapidly shift reserves and reorganize defenses. There was no time to be lost. First Army had to strike, and strike with its full power, if Cobra was to have a chance to succeed.

Bradley contacted Air Marshal Leigh-Mallory: could the air forces lay on the bombardment again in the morning, only this time with the heavies flying a course *parallel* to the St.-LôPériers road so that any more "shorts" would fall on the German side?

"Impossible!" snorted Leigh-Mallory. There would not be time to rebrief thousands of airmen and to rearrange the flight plans, all in less than twenty-four hours. What's more, if Bradley, the ground commander, insisted on a *parallel* approach by the Flying Fortresses and Liberators, Leigh-Mallory would cancel the air bombardment for Cobra altogether.

In that event, Bradley knew, American ground troops would be left bogged down in the hedgerows and swamps not far from the D-Day landing beaches—indefinitely. Perhaps the Air Barons would take over the dominant role in the war and try to bring Nazi Germany down through air power alone. The First Army commander, accepting the air marshal's protest of insufficient time to implement a new flight plan in less than twenty-four hours, pondered the situation momentarily. Could Leigh-Mallory mount the *same* operation in the morning with his heavies flying in from the north over the heads of Lightning Joe Collins's massed assault troops? Leigh-Mallory replied condescendingly that that could be done. Cobra would be repeated the following day, July 25. The heavies would arrive over the St.-Lô-Périers road at 11:00 A.M.

"It's risky business," a worried Omar Bradley anguished to his aides. "But it's got to be done."

AT HIS CP at Canisy at daybreak on the twenty-fifth, General Fritz Bayerlein had mixed emotions. The skies appeared to be clearing, which meant American Jabos would again be overhead for the daily pounding that the Wehrmacht had received since D-Day. On the other hand, Rommel's former chief of staff was confident that should the Americans attack, his Panzer Lehr grenadiers and tankers could repulse them. Bayerlein had a low opinion of American infantry.

THERE WAS REASON for Bayerlein's confidence on this bright summer morning. He was convinced that his Panzer Lehr had withstood a major American attack, without losing a foot of ground south of the St.-Lô-Périers road, even though his division had suffered more than 350 casualties and had 10 tanks knocked out the previous day. Overnight, Bayerlein had received 200 replacements, most of them green. But burrowed into hedgerows with rifles and Schmeisser automatic pistols, these inexperienced men could take a heavy toll of American attackers out in the open.

AT 8:45 A.M., Major General Hoyt S. Vandenberg, Air Marshal Leigh-Mallory's American deputy, and Vandenberg's chief of staff, Brigadier General Frederic S. Smith, hopped aboard a fast medium bomber at an airfield outside London. The aircraft raced down the runway in the early-morning haze, lifted off, and set a course for Normandy. This time Vandenberg was determined to check for himself what climatic conditions were like over the St.-Lô-Périers road. There the two American air generals cruised over the battle-lines, reported that although there were cloud puffs drifting lazily over the rectangle of Norman countryside, bombadiers should be able to visually sight the impact area. Meanwhile, 1,580 Liberators and Flying Fortresses carrying high-explosive bombs, and 398 mediums loaded with 500-pound general-purpose bombs and 260-pound fragmentation bombs, had been taking off from airfields in southern England. They formed up over the green countryside and headed for Normandy in a stream 100 miles long.

At First Army headquarters early that morning, the Parade of Generals formed up again in a long string of jeeps, with the war correspondents bringing up the rear. The caravan was bound for the same observation post as the day before, about a mile and a half behind the St.-Lô-Périers road bomb-line, in the hamlet of Vents. Arriving at 8:35 A.M., General Hodges led the group into the kitchen of a cottage, where coffee was sipped as the high American officers, plus one Mexican air force general, awaited the appearance of the mighty sky armada. The euphoria of the previous day had vanished.

General McNair insisted on moving up closer and joined forward elements of a battalion of Hobbs's 30th Infantry Division. With his record of narrow escapes, McNair seemed to lead a charmed life.

General Bradley, whose lot it had been to order a repeat performance of the air bombardment knowing that catastrophe might strike again, arrived at Collins's CP at 10:30 A.M., a half hour before the heavies were to appear overhead. Collins and Bradley went into a little café, in Goucherie, partially destroyed by previous shelling, five miles behind the St. Lô-Périers road. They, too, sipped coffee . . . and waited . . . and waited some more.

At 9:36 A.M., there were cries of Jabo! at German outposts along the St.-Lô-Périers road as the first flights of Thunderbolt and Mustang fighter-bombers roared in over the battleground. Loaded with 500-pound bombs under their wings, fragmentation bombs, and napalm—the thick liquid that bursts into fiery balls on impact—there were 596 of the squat Thunderbolts and sleek, swift Mustangs. For more than an hour they bombed and strafed German positions along a 250-yard strip that ran for three-and-a-half miles along the road.

North of the bomb-line, thousands of American foot soldiers had again pulled back 600 to 1,200 yards. Some were jammed shoulder to shoulder in grassy green fields pock-marked with black-rimmed shell holes; others lined the narrow dirt roads while still others pressed together against the tangled vegetation of the hedgerows. All gaped skyward at the fighter-bombers as the planes pounced on the Germans. Piled beside the infantrymen were their cumbersome accoutrements of war: rifles, BARs, machine guns, bazookas, mortar barrels and shells, ammunition boxes, packs. The dogfaces had received strict orders: "Get in foxholes or stay under cover." Few did. Surely the "fly-boys" wouldn't repeat the "shorts" of the previous day.

The final foursome of Thunderbolts dropped their lethal eggs, banked, and headed for home. South of the St.-Lô-Périers road, battered Feldgrau feverishly dug into piles of rubble and Norman earth to recover the bodies of the dead and wounded buried by the *Ami* 500-pounders.

SOUTH OF THE St.-Lô-Périers road, German infantrymen and tankers tensely braced for the ground attack they felt certain would quickly follow the heavy pounding by the fighter-bombers. Lieutenant Hans Uehler of 7th Company, 902nd **Panzer** Grenadier Regiment, was relieved on counting noses in his heavy-weapons platoon to find that only one man had been wounded that morning. Why did the American infantry not come? Why had the killing ground become so quiet? Not even the *Ami* artillery was firing.

58

Suddenly, the tranquility was shattered. A lookout shouted, "Enemy aircraft! Enemy aircraft!" It was a familiar warning call, yet neither Uehler nor other German fighting men in Normandy ever grew accustomed to it. The call meant death and destruction were imminent.

Lieutenant Uehler whipped out his binoculars and peered into the sky toward the north. He was thunderstruck by what he saw, and a chill surged through his body. He and his men had been bombed repeatedly since D-Day, but the approaching American bomber armada was the mightiest aerial spectacle that he had ever seen. As far as Uehler could see through his binoculars, there was an endless stream of four-motored aircraft—and they were heading directly for *him*.

The lieutenant turned to look at those of his men who were nearby. His eyes met their dull stares, cold with terror. He presumed his eyes looked the same to them.

As Uehler again peered through his binoculars, a shout rang out behind him: "Look! There are the blue flares!" Each German veteran knew the meaning of those flares: American pathfinders were marking targets for oncoming bombers. And the blue flares were directly overhead—the Panzer Lehr Division was the target. Uehler, a courageous officer, felt cold perspiration break out on his forehead. His stomach knotted and churned.

Now the skies were filled with the mighty drone of the first waves of Flying Fortresses and Liberators, in groups of twelve. German dual-purpose, 88-millimeter guns, their snouts pointed skyward, opened fire. Black puffs of smoke broke out among the lead American bombers. A Flying Fortress faltered, tried to regain formation, then started a long earthward glide, nearly out of control. Three white parachutes blossomed from the stricken bomber. No more chutes appeared. A second Fortress was struck squarely by a shell. In seconds it was a ball of fire, plunging to earth. This time there were no parachutes.

Soon there was the eerie, whistling noise of hundreds of bombs plummeting through space, then a steady drumfire as they exploded on the terrified Germans like a string of gigantic firecrackers. More bombs followed—thousands of them. The ground shook and quivered. Over the narrow target, a choking pall of smoke and dust hovered. The pungent odor of cordite penetrated German nostrils with a sickening sensation.

Entire trench systems and their occupants were wiped out. Tanks were crushed, bodies tossed high into the air, minefields exploded, messengers were blown off motorcycles, artillery and machine-gun positions disappeared. One of Lieutenant Uehler's 20-millimeter automatic guns, deeply dug in, was hurled 50 feet into the air, then plunged to earth a twisted, blackened chunk of metal. Grenadiers, clinging desperately to the bottom of foxholes, were driven out of their senses by the torrential rain of bombs. They bled profusely from the mouth, ears, and nose. Many leaped from cover and scrambled around in circles, babbling incoherently. Other Germans stood stonelike in the open, numbed by the deluge of death and destruction, eyes glazed and staring sightlessly.

At Panzer Lehr headquarters at Canisy, just south of the targeted rectangle, General Fritz Bayerlein was raging with frustration. His flak guns had barely opened up when they were knocked out by bombs. After an hour, he was a commander without a command, out of communication with everyone, even by radio. Looking off toward what had been his front lines, all Bayerlein could see was an enormous cloud of dust. One factor was now obvious to him: this was the opening round of the all-out Allied effort to break out of Normandy. Here at St.-Lô, the issue would be decided—not in the British sector at Caen as predicted by Field Marshal von Kluge and by Hausser at Seventh Army.

On came the endless bomber stream, as if it were a conveyor belt. The tortured, pockmarked earth shook and rumbled endlessly under the colossal cascade of bombs. It was as though a gigantic supernatural force had taken hold of miles of Norman countryside and was shaking it furiously in vengeful anger. Five miles behind the St.-Lô-Périers road on the American side, officers of the 1st Infantry Division artillery were watching the bombardment from an open upstairs window of a farmhouse. The concussion of the bombs caused the men's shirtsleeves to quiver. Outside in the barnyard, cattle and pigs shook their heads constantly: the bomb blast was hurting their ears. At the little café in Goucherie, five miles from the bomb-line, generals Omar Bradley and Joe Collins saw the starched lace curtains ruffling constantly from blast waves.

Massed behind the St.-Lô-Périers road, American foot soldiers by now were in an almost gala mood. "I'm glad my father wasn't born in Germany!" a machine gunner called out joyously. "Hitler, count your goddamned goose-steppers!" shouted another. "Give those goddamned Kraut bastards hell!" yelled a third.

Standing along a dirt road some 800 yards behind the bomb-line, Corporal Walter Makara, a 4th Infantry Division mortarman from New Hampshire, observed to his companion, Sergeant Kurt Schroeder, a lanky, thirty-nine-year-old from Milwaukee, "Kurt, I almost feel sorry for those Krauts over there!"

"You do?" snapped Shroeder in mock amazement.

"I said *almost*," Makara replied with a smile.

Makara and Schroeder held the same view as all the waiting assault troops of the 4th, 9th, and 30th infantry divisions: they would soon have to advance into the rectangle, so the more bombs dropped on the Germans there the fewer of the enemy would be around to oppose them.

Slowly, almost imperceptibly, the mild breezes shifted and the enormous dust and smoke cloud that had blanketed the German side of the St.-Lô-Périers road began to drift back over American lines. Soon the arrow-straight road was covered with the thick pall, and bombardiers at 12,000-15,000 feet could not distinguish the red smoke of artillery markers from the bright flashes of hundreds of exploding bombs.

A group of heavies unloaded and dropped their cargo in a draw just in front of elements of the 30th Infantry Division, a few hundred yards on the American side of the road. Renewed apprehension gripped the Old Hickories. The next wave came in closer with their bombs . . . and the following wave even closer. By now the great dust clouds had reached the 30th Division's forward elements. Orange grenades, recognition signals, were frantically put out. They did no good, obscured by the dust pall. Terror-stricken, the dogfaces clawed into the dirt as they heard the shriek of bombs falling directly onto them. A tremendous roar erupted as scores of bombs exploded around Leland Hobbs's men. Bodies and pieces of bodies cascaded into the air. Screams pierced the pall. One man ran about shouting to no one in particular, "They're trying to kill all of us!"

Fragmentation bombs and high explosives from 35 Flying Fortresses and Liberators and bombs of 42 mediums fell within American lines. The entire command group of the 3rd Battalion, 47th Infantry Regiment was wiped out, save the battalion commander.

61

Thirty men in the battalion were killed or wounded. All four assault companies of the 8th Infantry, 4th Division, were hit by bombs. The fire direction center of the 957th Field Artillery Battalion was smashed.

General Hobbs, up front with his forward elements as was his custom, clung to the ground helplessly as bombs exploded around him. A quick glance saw dirt geysers shoot into the air and bodies of his Old Hickories blown high out of slit trenches, falling to earth like limp rag dolls. Bede Irvin, an Associated Press photographer, was snapping his shutter when a bomb fragment cut him in two. Lee McCardell of the *Baltimore Sun* was next to Bede and escaped serious injury. General Hodges, First Army deputy commander, heard the falling bombs, threw himself into a roadside ditch as explosives shook the ground around him. Picking himself up moments later, Hodges saw no sign of the other generals in his observation party. They had apparently fled—anywhere away from the conveyor-belt stream of bombers.

At the small café at Goucherie, Omar Bradley was a deeply worried man. So many reports of "shorts" had flooded in that he felt most of his assault troops had been wiped out. The First Army commander already had known, however, that bombs were raining down on his foot soldiers—the starched lace café curtains, only fluttering earlier, were now rustling violently from the closer blast waves. Bradley confided to Joe Collins that Cobra would probably have to be canceled, this time permanently.

At 11:32 A.M., the holocaust along the St.-Lô-Périers road ended. For the first time in hours the tortured Norman countryside ceased to rumble. The deafening explosions and shriek of falling bombs had vanished. Only the thick pall of dust and smoke remained. Four thousand tons of high explosives, fragmentation bombs, and napalm had rained down on Germans and Americans alike—most of it landing on the Feldgrau. It had been a tremendous slaughter.

General Fritz Bayerlein's Panzer Lehr Division had been nearly wiped out. Early that morning he had some 5,000 troops dug in on the Americans' targeted rectangle of ground. Perhaps 1,000 of them had been killed, more than twice that many wounded, hundreds of others reduced to babbling incoherency. Only a few of Bayerlein's tanks survived the carnage.

Shortly after the massive bombing, General Paul Hausser, commander of Seventh Army, arrived at a battle headquarters far to the rear of the St.-Lô-Périers road. He was seated in the cellar of an ancient stone tower as a shaken Fritz Bayerlein reported to him, having made the trip on a motorcycle that had escaped destruction. Hausser, the SS general, demanded a report on conditions at the front. A young officer had been sent forward by Bayerlein, and at that moment he burst into the basement.

"Here," Bayerlein said to his army commander, "you can have it first hand."

The generals listened in grim silence as the lieutenant declared, "I did not find a single strongpoint that was intact. The main line of resistance has vanished. Where it used to be is now a sector of death."

4

"They're Turning
Our Armor Loose!"

WHITE-FACED WITH anger, Leland Hobbs rushed up to General
Courtney Hodges, even as the thick cloud of smoke and dust was
drifting over the American positions. His eyes were red from the
smoke and from tears of rage and anguish. Ninety percent of the
errant bombs had fallen on his Old Hickories.

"We're good soldiers, Courtney," Hobbs gasped, "but there's
absolutely no excuse. No goddamned excuse at all. The air corps was
instructed not to drop unless they could see the goddamned highway. . . ."

There was nothing the First Army deputy commander could say.
He said nothing.

Hodges began searching for his fellow generals who had been
with him as observers at the hamlet of Vents and had scattered
during the "short" bombings. He located all, except for General
McNair. No one had seen McNair, who had seemed to lead a
charmed life.

McNair's aide was located. He did not know where the general was
either. The last he had seen of him, McNair had jumped into a
foxhole when the "shorts" began to scream in. The foxhole was
found by the aide, and men with entrenching tools started digging
furiously into it—the hole apparently had been hit by a bomb and
the missing former Chief of Army Ground Forces might have been
buried there. The digging proved to be futile.

Later, word was received at General Bradley's headquarters: the remains of a lieutenant general were lying alongside a narrow dirt road. There was not much left of the officer who was chiefly responsible for building the mighty United States Army in only three years and who had eagerly looked forward to a battle command in France. He apparently had been tossed a long distance by a bomb. The only means of identification were a shoulder patch and three silver stars.

General McNair, the noncombat officer who died in combat, would be buried secretly in Normandy the following day. Secrecy was vital to maintain the German-held illusion that the Allies still had 32 divisions massed in southeastern England to cross the Channel and smash at the Pas-de-Calais. McNair's wife would be told only that he had been killed. Nothing would be passed on to the media.

At Joe Collins's CP at Goucherie, the peppery VII Corps leader and his boss Omar Bradley sat helplessly and waited for cut communications to be restored in order to learn the extent of the bombing "shorts" on American assault troops. They hoped for the best—feared the worst. The ground attack might have to be canceled.

Collins soon could reach his three assault divisions. Hobbs's 30th Division was the hardest hit, he learned—61 killed and 374 wounded by "shorts." The 47th Infantry Regiment of the 9th Division suffered 14 killed and 33 wounded. As tragic as the errant bombing was, Bradley and Collins could breath a large measure of relief: the assault formations hadn't been hurt as badly as they feared. Altogether, Collins's VII Corps suffered 601 casualties, including 111 killed.

There was another crucial factor that the United States Army did not consider in its reckoning of battle casualties: intense shock effect. The battered 30th Division reported 164 cases of combat exhaustion —those soldiers were so dazed that they could not perform their duties in a normal way.

Collins fired off a message to his three assault divisions: "Attack as planned!"

Rallied by company commanders, platoon leaders, and platoon sergeants, the men of Barton's 4th, Eddy's 9th, and Hobbs's 30th shouldered their packs, picked up rifles, BARs, machine guns, and light mortars, and moved off in attack formation toward the St.-Lô-Périers road positions from which they had pulled back earlier that day. Off in the distance to their front, swarms of Thunderbolt and

Mustang fighter-bombers swooped menacingly over the slaughter grounds, strafing and bombing anything German that moved. Trudging along with the haunted look of all infantrymen going into close-quarter battle, the perspiring, wheezing dogfaces could not resist an inner admiration for their foe in gray-green uniforms across the road. Despite the devastation that had struck the Germans, here and there an enemy gun barked defiantly, and a few isolated machine gunners fired futilely at diving fighter-bombers.

Dazed, demoralized, and many still terrified from the ordeal of the "shorts," Joe Collins's assault troops reached the St.-Lô-Périers road and prepared to cross. They expected little or no opposition. Instead they were met with surprisingly dogged resistance from surviving Feldgrau of Panzer Lehr and fanatical *Fallschirmjaeger* (paratroopers) of the 5th Parachute Division on the right of Bayerlein's men, who had escaped most of the bombing. Cobra's ground attack was off to a wobbly start.

Not only had the "shorts" shaken up the troops, but the bombing infused uncharacteristic caution into American division commanders. That afternoon, General Clarence Huebner, the rugged leader of the 1st Infantry Division, observed to aides, "It [the "shorts" bombing] was the most terrifying thing I have ever endured."

Leading elements of the three assault divisions methodically wiped out German outposts south of the road. Soldiers of Hobbs's 30th Division were edging down a narrow, hedgerow-lined road when they heard the nearby roar of powerful engines. Instinctively they leaped into ditches and behind hedgerows to escape streams of bullets aimed at them by a swarm of American fighter-bombers that zoomed over the cursing Old Hickories at treetop level.

Collins's attack bogged down, far short of the first day's objectives. Gloom was thick over Bradley's First Army headquarters. General Eisenhower, who had flown over from England to be on hand for the momentous breakthrough, was visibly depressed—and furious at the Air Barons. He vowed never again to employ heavy-bombers in close support of ground troops. Grim-faced and solemn, Eisenhower flew back to his headquarters late that afternoon. On the flight, he unlimbered his mule skinner's vocabulary to flay the hide off the air corps.

Depressed as he was, General Eisenhower knew there was still a war to be fought. That night his attractive chauffeur and confidante, sultry Kay Summersby, penned in her diary: "Attack got off this morning. Not going too well. The air bombed our troops. E. says that we must press on with the attack and get going."

LATE ON THE afternoon of July 25, a disappointed General Joe Collins studied his predicament at his CP at Goucherie. Instead of plunging through a vacuum created by one of history's most concentrated air bombardments, the 4th, 9th, and 30th Infantry divisions had to battle vicious German resistance. They had failed to reach their two key objectives, the road centers of Marigny and St.-Gilles, less than three miles south of the St.-Lô-Périers road.

Collins had planned not to unleash his armored divisions until the three infantry divisions had cracked the Germans' main line of resistance and seized the rubble piles of Marigny and St.-Gilles. But where were the enemy's principal defensive positions? Had the aborted bombing of July 24 warned the Germans; had they pulled back their main line of resistance? Lack of coordination on the enemy side led Collins to believe that the Germans had been damaged far more seriously by the massive air bombardment than the GIs, fighting their way through the hedgerows, had realized. The VII Corps commander reached a conclusion based on military instinct: his three divisions had broken through the German defensive crust and were being opposed by *isolated* groups of especially tough enemy soldiers.

Joe Collins, a bold commander, decided to gamble—taking a calculated risk, the military called it. He would not wait for Marigny and St.-Gilles to be captured by his infantry as planned. He would turn his armor loose in the morning, July 26, to exploit the penetration. He would throw into the breach Clarence Huebner's veteran 1st Infantry Division, with Colonel Truman E. Boudinot's CC-B of the 3rd Armored Division attached, and Ted Brooks's 2nd Armored Division with Colonel Charles T. Lanham's 22nd Regimental Combat Team attached.

Skies were clearing early on the morning of the twenty-sixth when weary, bearded dogfaces outside Marigny and St.-Gilles heard a roar in the distance. They peered skyward and witnessed a sight that again turned them ashen: flying majestically toward them from the north was a stream of American medium bombers of Lew Brereton's

9th Air Force in England, on their way to unload over Marigny. Stomachs churning, mouths dry, the American foot soldiers clung to the bottom of holes and tensed for the "shorts" they were convinced were coming.

Along scattered German strongpoints, the cry rang out: "Enemy aircraft! Enemy aircraft!" The German infantry paratroopers scrambled for cover and leaped into deep foxholes. The devastation they had miraculously survived the day before was going to be visited upon them again.

On came the precise formations of American mediums, large specks in the bright sky with the sun glistening off fusilages—400 of the big birds. Nearing Marigny, bomb-bay doors opened and soon Feldgrau and GIs alike heard the fluttering of bomb clusters. Wave after wave unloaded over the target, turning the rubble piles into gray powder. American artillery followed with a thunderous barrage all along the front of the 4th, 9th, and 30th divisions. Only an occasional German gun responded.

Outside smoking Marigny, Robert Murphy, a curly-haired platoon sergeant in the 87th Mortar Battalion, heard the roar of powerful diesel engines to the rear. He and others rushed to the nearby gravel road in time to see a long string of American tanks clanking forward. "Goddamn," the New Orleans native shouted, "they're turning our armor loose!" Murphy whipped off his helmet, a habit when he became enthused.

"Hell, I know it!" responded red-haired Corporal James Groves, a teenager. "General Eisenhower called me last night and asked me what he should do after the bombing. I told him 'Ike, you ignorant bastard, turn our armor loose!'"

Murphy, Groves, and other mortarmen looked on as the belching Sherman tanks of the 3rd Armored Division rumbled past. The iron vehicles were menacing in appearance, with their snub-nosed 75-millimeter guns, .50-caliber machine guns, and long, snakelike antennae whipping madly in the breeze. Plumes of choking dust spiraled skyward in the wake of each Sherman, and soon the entire landscape along the road was a long blanket of smog. The collective roar of the engines was deafening as it echoed across the cratered Norman countryside.

Soon the mortarmen watching the parade of American muscle

looked as though large amounts of flour had been sifted over them. Dust churned up by the tanks clung to the perspiration on their faces and hands like stucco would to a wall.

Cupping his hands to mouth to be heard above the engines' roar and the grinding of steel treads, Corporal Groves shouted, "Where ya headin'?"

A baby-faced 3rd Armored lieutenant, his head and shoulders protruding from the turret of a Sherman, called back with a grin and a wave, "All the goddamned way to Berlin!"

Trudging forward in two files, one to either side of the road with the Shermans and light tanks lumbering along in the middle, were solemn-faced foot soldiers of Huebner's Big Red One. Burdened with the customary heavy gear and weapons, these infantrymen would team up with the tankers in an effort to crush remaining German resistance and drive onward.

Meanwhile, Brigadier General Maurice Rose's CC-A of the 2nd Armored Division had also jumped off, passed through the infantry, and quickly overrun scattered enemy strongpoints, soon rolling into St.-Gilles. The exploitation phase of Cobra had begun.

Combat Command Boudinot of the 3rd Armored Division ran into a force of German paratroopers determined to hang onto the ruins of Marigny; bitter fighting erupted. Outside the town, Battery B of the 391st Armored Field Artillery Battalion was furiously firing its six self-propelled guns when it received an urgent request for help. Elements of the 4th Cavalry Squadron were engaged in a savage fight with a larger force of Germans and in danger of being overrun. Could the artillerymen grab rifles and rush to the aid of the mechanized cavalrymen? They could.

Leaving a skeleton crew with five guns under a sergeant to continue the original firing mission in support of 3rd Armored tankers, the remainder of the artillery force rushed to the scene of the firefight and joined up with the cavalrymen to wipe out the enemy force. It was the first taste by American soldiers of the Indian-country warfare that would become the norm during the next few weeks.

That night Captain Philip Shaw, commander of Battery B, 486th Armored Antiaircraft Battalion, and two of his men detected the dim outlines of a tank on the other side of their hedgerow. Somehow the tank looked different. They stole through the blackness to where

70

they could gain a better view and were startled: a German Panther was parked right in their position.

Captain Shaw and his men obtained several TNT charges, crawled up to the Panther (the tank crew was inside), and calmly placed the explosives in the bogey wheels, then hurriedly withdrew. Minutes later there was a loud explosion across the hedgerow. The sound of a diesel motor starting up echoed over the landscape as the crippled Panther started forward. Moving like a panther himself, Shaw raced across the dark terrain, scrambled up onto the tracked vehicle, and dropped hand grenades down the open turret. There were sc.eams from inside, then only the sound of the engine. One German tanker, apparently only wounded, leaped out of the turret and tried to flee. He was attacked and killed by an alert antiaircraft man who had grabbed the first weapon available to him: an axe.

Late in the afternoon, General Bayerlein dashed out of his CP in the château at Canisy and hopped into the sidecar of a motorcycle. There was gunfire just down the road. The driver revved the motor, sped out of town just as the first Shermans of General Rose's CC-A, 2nd Armored Division, rumbled into Canisy. Reaching Dagny, three miles to the south, Bayerlein set up his battle headquarters.

It had been the longest day of Bayerlein's life. He had to stand by helplessly as his elite, but badly hurt, Panzer Lehr Division virtually vanished under a cascade of American bombs. He was exhausted, hungry, thirsty, and had not washed or shaved in several days. His once-immaculate uniform was now caked with dirt and badly wrinkled.

A staff car drove up outside and a stern-faced lieutenant colonel strode briskly into Bayerlein's office. Clad in a spotless dress uniform with the red stripes of the general staff running down the sides of his trousers, boots shined to a high gloss, the visitor felt ill at ease in the presence of the disheveled Bayerlein and a few of his officers.

The visitor said that he had been sent by Field Marshal von Kluge with a direct order: the St.-Lô-Périers road was to be held at all costs.

An oppressive silence engulfed the room. The tension was thick enough to slice with a knife. Two Panzer Lehr officers stared out the window. Bayerlein's face flushed with anger. Finally he spoke in a low voice tinged with sarcasm: "Hold at all costs? May I ask with what?"

71

As though Bayerlein had not asked the question, the staff officer replied firmly, "Herr General, I am passing on to you a direct order from Feldmarschall von Kluge. You are to hold out. Not a single man is to leave his position along the St.-Lô-Périers road."

For long seconds Bayerlein glared at the neatly tailored visitor. Then he moved into the face of von Kluge's emissary and shouted, "You may report to the Feldmarschall, Herr Oberstleutnant, that not a single one of my men has left his post. They're all holding their ground. They're dead! Do you understand? *Dead!*"

As darkness cloaked the killing grounds on the twenty-sixth, General Maurice Rose of the 2nd Armored's CC-A was exhorting his men onward into the night. Earlier Rose had received crisp, simple instructions from General Brooks, his boss: "Get moving, and keep moving!"

Rose pushed his column of tanks, other armored vehicles, and infantry in trucks on south of Canisy, Bayerlein's former CP. At pockets of resistance, the foot soldiers would hop down, engage the enemy, and tanks would move in to wipe out the remaining force. Then it was back into the trucks, and the column would push forward.

As the night wore on, unit officers complained to General Rose that their men were exhausted, having been fighting and moving for nearly twenty-four hours. They wanted to halt, at least to rest for a period. The reply by the stern, no-nonsense Maurice Rose, son of a rabbi, was always the same: "Keep going!"

Rose felt that the entire breakout depended upon his combat command's moving forward, and he intended to do just that—regardless of fatigue, losses, or blackness of night, which led to incredible confusion at times.

In the inky darkness, one half-track repeatedly violated road discipline by passing vehicles and working its way toward the head of the column. Each time the half-track darted around a tank or a truck packed with exhausted infantrymen, the black sky was turned blue with American curses. But the half-track persisted. "What's that bastard's big rush?" a loud voice called out from a truck. Reaching the head of the column, the half-track clanked around the lead tank. "Hell, I'm supposed to be leading this column!" an enraged captain shouted.

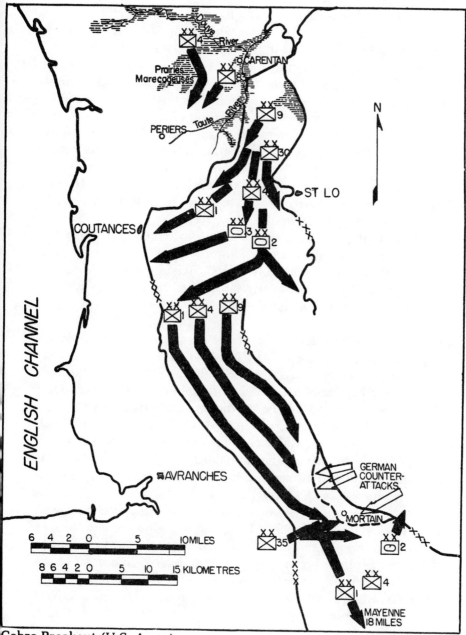

Cobra Breakout (U.S. Army)

Hardly had the words left the captain's mouth than someone yelled, "They're Krauts!" Several tanks opened fire on the German half-track, and in seconds it was a flaming funeral pyre.

It was shortly after 3:00 A.M. when Rose's CC-A reached its objective, a key road junction just north of the village of le Mesnil-Herman. There the column halted. As foot soldiers and tankers, utterly drained physically and emotionally, dropped to the ground in instant slumber, General Rose flashed a signal to General Collins at Goucherie: "Objective seized. Awaiting orders."

Collins, who had exhorted his commanders to push ahead through the night, was receiving similar reports from other assault units. The 8th Infantry Regiment of Barton's 4th Division had spearheads seven miles south of the St.-Lô-Périers road. Hobbs's 30th Division had moved forward against diminishing opposition and seized two bridges over the Vire River.

Elated by these reports, Collins was now convinced Cobra had broken through the German main line of resistance. He put in a call to General Watson of the 3rd Armored Division, in reserve near St. Jean-de-Daye: "Get ready to attack southward. I'm committing the remainder of 3rd Armored at dawn."

MEANWHILE, ON THE right (west) of Collins's assault divisions, Major General Troy H. Middleton's VIII Corps had been attacking all day to pin down German forces, while Collins's principal spearheads were to push southwest to Coutances, thereby moving in behind and trapping enemy forces facing Middleton. The VIII Corps was having its troubles. With Brigadier General Donald A. Stroh's 8th Infantry Division and Major General Eugene M. Landrum's 90th Infantry Division carrying the main burden, Middleton's Corps was confronted with difficult terrain, extensive minefields, and the tenacious men of the 2nd SS Panzer Division.

Troy Middleton, fifty-five, had joined the army as a private in 1910, worked up to colonel in 1939, and retired to become Dean of Administration at Louisiana State University. He was recalled in 1941, later promoted to major general and given command of the 45th (Thunderbird) Infantry Division. The Thunderbirds, a National Guard outfit whose members were from Oklahoma and New Mexico, performed so well in Sicily and Italy that Middleton, a unique combination of toughness and brains, was given a corps for the Normandy invasion.

Middleton had been disappointed with both the 8th and 90th divisions. He had sacked the previous 8th Division commanding general as well as two regimental colonels. And now he was looking for a replacement for Landrum, whom Middleton felt was not providing the needed spark for the 90th Division. The bespectacled Middleton was not employing these two divisions in the forefront of his attack through choice. It was a matter of necessity. The VIII Corps terrain provided dry ground only to the front of these two lackluster divisions.

At midnight on the twenty-sixth, General Joe Collins's principal concern was Huebner's Big Red One and Colonel Boudinot's attached Combat Command-B of the 3rd Armored, stalled outside Marigny, just two miles south of the St.-Lô-Périers road on the right shoulder of the breakthrough. Huebner was to have quickly seized Marigny, then sent Boudinot's tankers racing southwest down the fine macadam road to Coutances, slashing across the rear of German forces facing northward against Middleton's VIII Corps. Now Huebner's force was bogged down.

THE GERMAN SEVENTH Army, which had been pounded from the air and by artillery and assaulted repeatedly by two American corps, was rapidly being plunged into total disarray. But, unless Collins's armor could break loose, slash deeply into and behind the disintegrating enemy force, General Paul Hausser might have time to rally Seventh Army and reestablish a cohesive front.

5

Shoot-out at
St.-Benôit

AS A HOT sun began peaking over the bocage of Normandy on July 27, General Maurice Rose's tankers outside the crossroads at le Mesnil-Herman were roused from exhausted slumber. As they yawned and stretched, "refreshed" after two hours of sleep, cries of, "Climb aboard, we're movin' out!" echoed across the bivouac. Curses, loud and prolonged, split the sultry air. "Can't someone else win this goddamned war for a change?" an outraged tank driver bellowed.

Soon powerful motors roared and belched, foot soldiers wearily scrambled into open trucks, and CC-A of the 2nd Armored Division renewed its thrust southward. Rose had learned early in his career: "When you've got the enemy on the run, keep him on the run." That he intended to do.

Unknown to Rose or any of his men, less than a mile to his front and directly in the path of the American tanks was the unprotected CP of Lieutenant General Hellmuth Kraiss, commander of the 352nd Infantry Division, which had nearly driven the U.S. 1st Infantry Division back into the sea at Omaha Beach on D-Day. During the night, a reconnaissance unit of Kraiss's 12th Panzerjaeger Regiment, led by Captain Goethe, had been rushed to the le Mesnil-Herman crossroads to block or stall Rose's column. If Goethe and his men failed, General Kraiss and his entire staff would be in danger of becoming prisoners or killed, leaving the largely intact 352nd Division without direction.

As the forward elements of CC-A started to pass the crossroads, Captain Goethe's panzers, self-propelled guns, and 20-millimeter flak wagons opened fire and poured a heavy fusillade into the oncoming American vehicles. For the first time since jumping off at the St.-Lô-Périers road the previous day, General Rose and his men had run into heavy opposition. Shermans began to return the fire, and the intense battle raged for several hours. Six of Rose's medium tanks lay smoking, blackened wrecks, but Goethe knew he was far outnumbered and outgunned and that General Kraiss had escaped together with his staff. So the German captain broke off and withdrew to the rear. Combat Command-A, more cautious now, pushed on forward.

AT 7:00 A.M. that morning, VII Corps's big guns roared and a thunderous barrage pounded the smoking rubble of Marigny for twenty minutes. Then grim-faced dogfaces of Colonel George C. Smith's 18th Infantry Regiment scrambled out of foxholes and launched an attack to seize the town. They found it deserted. During the night, Colonel Frido Count von Schulenberg's stubborn fighting men of the 13th Parachute Regiment, who had hung on grimly for two days under bombardment by air and heavy weapons in order to deny that crucial road junction to the Americans, had slipped out of town and taken up strong defensive positions to the south on Hill 100.

With Marigny secure, Colonel Boudinot's CC-B of the 3rd Armored was turned loose immediately, and with its reconnaissance battalion of light armor in the forefront it began charging down N-172, the excellent road to Coutances. Scattered roadblocks were rapidly brushed aside. But the advance down N-172 turned into a confusing melee. CC-B trucks hauling up ammunition and supplies had to be escorted by tanks. German messengers on motorcycles, officers in Volkswagens, ambulances loaded with bloodied Feldgrau, and Wehrmacht colonels in staff cars regularly blundered into Boudinot's spearhead and were either killed or captured.

Until early afternoon, the 3rd Armored advance toward Coutances had been little more than an exciting road march. Then the going got slower and more difficult. Colonel Boudinot's long, slim finger of armored vehicles and trucks stretched back for several miles and was no wider than a hedgerow or two on either side of N-172.

Hodgepodge German units that had been facing Middleton's VIII Corps to the north had fallen back, and they began to pour fire into the advancing CC-B column from both flanks. To the front of the Americans, other assorted Wehrmacht units were whipped into a semblance of a cohesive force and brought Boudinot's leading elements under intense fire.

Early that morning, another thunderous artillery barrage erupted in front of Troy Middleton's attacking divisions on First Army's right. Patrols moved out and discovered that the Germans had pulled back in the night under cover of heavy fog and rain. Jumping off in pursuit of the fleeing enemy, Middleton's men were shackled by what the corps commander called "the worst minefields I have ever seen"—Teller mines, box mines, Schu mines, Bouncing Bettys, antitank mines—all shrewdly sown in roads, pathways, and gulleys over which foot soldiers, tanks, and vehicles would have to pass.

At the same time that Middleton's men were preparing to attack, excitement and bustle reigned in the bivouac of the main body of Leroy Watson's 3rd Armored Division, which had been in reserve around St.-Jean de-Daye (St. John's D-Day, to the troops), waiting for the "Go!" signal from General Collins to help exploit the breakthrough by the assault infantry divisions along the St.-Lô-Périers road. That signal had been received during the night.

Rumbling out of the assembly area in a deafening roar of engines, grinding of steel treads, and sharp crackling of communications radios was Task Force X, under command of Colonel Leander L. "Chubby" Doan—a tall, angular Texas polo player who was regarded by his men as a tough, dashing leader. Task Force X would be the sharp point of the 3rd Armored spearhead. A highly mobile unit, Doan's mechanized battle group consisted of Sherman medium tanks, light tanks, half-tracks, trucks, self-propelled 105-millimeter guns, tank destroyers (known as TDs), and so-called armored infantry (who were exactly like unarmored infantry and, in common with all foot soldiers, had to do the close-in, dirty work when the chips were down).

In command of the lead platoon of armored infantry was Lieutenant Joseph W. Herrick. He liked to refer to himself as just a plain dogface or doughfoot. Joe was quite a bit older than others in his grade—and much more experienced in the military and war. He had served thirteen years in the army, was a veteran of both the Philippines and China, where he had often fought against guerrillas and bandits of assorted stripe.

Despite Herrick's extensive combat experience, the army—perhaps characteristically, if its members could be believed—assigned Herrick as a vehicle test officer in the States. He had made such a nuisance of himself demanding to be transferred overseas into a combat outfit that his superiors, possibly to silence him, finally assigned him to the infantry, and he joined the 3rd Armored just in time for its move to Normandy.

Task Force X crossed the fateful St.-Lô-Périers road and pushed onward. It passed through the 8th Infantry Regiment of the 4th Division, which had helped gouge out the gaping hole in German lines and was now weary and battered. Minutes later, a short distance down the road, came the hysterical rattle of German Schmeisser automatic pistols (known to Americans as burp guns because of their rapid fire), and bullets zipped into and past the advancing column. Now came eerie fluttering sounds, followed by sharp explosions—mortar shells were dropping on Task Force X.

The armored column screeched to a halt. Lieutenant Herrick leaped from his vehicle and dived into a ditch. Up at the front of the column he heard the cry: "Infantry! Infantry! Where in hell is the goddamned infantry?" Obviously, there was a nasty job to be done.

In the middle of the road beyond the lead tank, Herrick spotted a boot. In the boot was a foot. A shapeless mass was huddled in the ditch alongside the boot. The lieutenant turned his gaze away. Herrick edged forward to the crest of a low hill and found one of his sergeants peeking through a tangled hedgerow. "A Kraut patrol, holed up down there, Lieutenant," the sergeant observed calmly, pointing a dirt-smudged finger toward a group of buildings flanking a single-track railroad that wound through the shallow valley below. Lieutenant Herrick checked his map. It was St.-Benôit.

Moments later Herrick sensed someone approaching and turned to see his commanding officer, Lieutenant Colonel Carlton P. Russell of the 3rd Battalion, 36th Armored Infantry Regiment. A hurried council of war was held, and it was agreed that the German platoon had rapidly disappeared in the face of the advancing armored column. "Those Krauts are probably halfway to Paris by now," was an observation.

Colonel Russell said to Herrick, "We've got to keep moving. Joe, take your platoon down to that railroad spur east of St.-Benôit"—he pointed a finger—"and blow out a culvert to let our tanks through." Herrick and his men moved out. The lieutenant had an uneasy feeling: he doubted if the German platoon was "halfway to Paris by now."

Herrick and his men stalked on, weapons at-the-ready. They had nearly reached the railroad track when six Germans jumped out of the tall weeds like gophers and took off toward the nearby village of St.-Benôit. Several rifles and a BAR spewed bullets, and two of the fleeing Germans went down. The rest ducked behind the railroad embankment. Herrick took a quick look at the dead enemy soldiers—they were SS troops, not the kind to flee to Paris, he thought.

A machine gun in the village chattered and bullets whipped past Herrick and his men, showering them with leaves. The lieutenant and Sergeant Carson dived for a foxhole filled with water. Take any hole, they thought, it doesn't matter—it will always be filled with water.

Fire from St.-Benôit ceased. Herrick caught a glimpse of waving white flags. "Keep down, goddamn it!" he shouted to his men. Old soldier that he was, the lieutenant knew treachery might be on the minds of the adversaries in the village.

Suddenly there was a loud roar to the rear, and a pair of 3rd Armored Shermans clanked into the field behind Herrick. The tankers took no time to ask questions. They opened up on the village with their .50-caliber turret guns and 75-millimeter cannon. White flags and Germans disappeared in a cloud of dust.

Now the defenders of St.-Benôit had a sudden change of heart. Surrender was out of the question. In seconds Lieutenant Herrick and his men, clinging to the base of a thick earthen hedgerow, were being raked by withering bursts of rifle and machine-gun fire, as mortar and artillery shells exploded around them and demolished the hedges like a ravaging forest fire. Herrick cursed the "hare-brained, trigger-happy" tank crews who had dashed onto the scene just as the Germans were trying to give up.

Herrick thought the two Shermans would return the enemy fire. But he heard a revving of motors and turned to see the iron monsters beat a path for the protection of the road, which was below the terrain level of the village. Herrick and his soldiers cursed long and loud.

The lieutenant glanced at his men crouched along the hedgerow. Sergeant Beck, the platoon sergeant, caught Herrick's eye, leaped to his feet, and ran toward the platoon leader for orders. A fine soldier, Herrick thought. Beck was halfway when an 88-millimeter shell hissed in. The sergeant's legs took several steps, even after the top half of his body had disappeared.

Now the German fire from the village grew more intense. Herrick felt his helmet being snatched off his head. It was Sergeant Carson, kneeling there beside him and screaming. The top half of Carson's head had been peeled away by a shell. He kept screaming and shouting, "Give me my hat! Goddamn it, give me my hat—my hat—my hat—I've got to have my hat!"

Herrick found himself instinctively struggling with the crazed Carson for possession of the helmet. He felt foolish—and sick. Carson was such a great guy and fine soldier. The wounded man let loose, scrambled to his feet, and began walking about in tight circles, clawing at the bloody pulp that minutes before had been his head. He kept screaming. As bullets hissed past, Lieutenant Herrick leaped to his feet and tackled him; then Sergeant Lubbock, a big man, sat on the mutilated man. Moments later, the screaming halted. Carson was dead.

The German fire slackened and the lieutenant gave the order for his men to pull back to the road. It was not an isolated enemy platoon in St.-Benôit as first thought, but a much larger force. The GIs began to crawl and slither along the ground. Many of the figures were still as Herrick moved past them. He felt like prodding each one and telling him, "Come on! Get up! We're pulling out!" but he knew it would be of no use.

Back at the road, Corporal Jarman, the big boy of the platoon, thrust out his bloody wrist, where once his hand had been, for Herrick to shake. Herrick shook it. Jarman knew that he would be leaving the platoon forever, that his war was over. He would survive and could learn to eat with the "other" hand. Jarman felt luckier than his fellow infantrymen. They would continue as fugitives from the law of averages, and death would almost certainly overtake them sooner or later.

Little Rasmussen wandered listlessly up and down the road, his clothes charred and his skin blackened, in excruciating pain. In his hands he clutched a bazooka that had been bent into a horseshoe. A bullet had set off the ammunition pack on his back. Good soldier, Rasmussen—since basic training, it had been hammered into him, "Don't ever let loose of your weapon."

Lieutenant Herrick and Sergeant Lubbock returned six times to the fire-swept field and brought the wounded back to the road.

A call was received from Colonel Russell, the battalion commander: "Joe, we've got to have St.-Benôit. You've got fifteen minutes to re-form and attack." The pressure was on up and down the American chain of command: Keep moving! Keep moving! The Krauts're off balance and in disarray! Keep moving!

Herrick and his platoon's survivors edged across open fields, crawled over hedgerow, and cautiously entered St.-Benôit. The village was deserted. The lieutenant radioed Colonel Russell: "The Krauts are gone. They must have added two and two and figured we'd eventually throw our tanks against them." A brief pause and Herrick added, "I'm glad the goddamned Heinies can add!"

Dusk was beginning to gather when Herrick received another call from Colonel Russell: "Tell your boys we've got to get one more hedgerow. Just one more. Then we can call it a day."

"Goddamn!" the weary, dirt-caked Herrick thought. One more hedgerow. It was always one more hedgerow. But he knew the heat was on Colonel Russell from on high. He was not blaming his battalion commander.

The platoon moved out to seize "one more hedgerow." Lying between two supporting Shermans, Herrick was soon stone-deaf from the muzzle blasts. American artillery shells kept plowing into tree branches overhead, and white-hot, jagged pieces of metal intended for dug-in Germans sprayed Herrick and his men instead. Sergeant Terhune let out a piercing squeal as a tree-burst hit right over the platoon. Terhune's suspenders to his ammo belt were severed, and his field jacket ripped open. A red stain, bright and ugly, spread across his brown shirt. He was frightened.

Sergeant Terhune was rushed off to an aid station. An hour later he returned to the platoon, a sheepish grin on his face, and a welt across his back that looked as if it had been raised with a whip. "What happened?" his comrades asked. "Damned if I know!" was the reply. Terhune began firing away at the unseen enemy burrowed into hedgerows to the front.

One of the Shermans that was threatening to burst Lieutenant Herrick's eardrums was struck by a shell from a German Panther. It fell silent, it's crew dead inside. Herrick and Corporal Wade grabbed a bazooka and went after the Panther, stalking it through the jungle-like vegetation as though it were a huge cat. They got it with a rocket shot, broadside. That was the surest way to kill a Panther. The American bazooka rocket always bounced off the thick-plated front of German Panzers.

Herrick and Wade kept under cover, waiting to see if any of the crew members were still alive. Seconds later a German popped out of the tank turret, leaped down, and took off across a field. The two Americans banged away at him, but never touched him. The fleeing German disappeared into the gathering darkness. "The bastard has a charmed life—or you and I need glasses!" Herrick muttered to his companion.

At about noon that day, July 27, a heated confrontation erupted at the headquarters of the German II Parachute Corps, outside Saint-Vigor, five miles east of Percy. The verbal combatants were Lieutenant Colonel Klaus von Kluge, son of the field marshal, and General of Paratroops Eugen Meindl, commanding the corps. The harassed, frustrated, deeply worried Meindl had become white with anger on simply learning that young von Kluge had been sent as his father's emissary to "find out what the situation is." What did the field marshal's spy want? Meindl conjectured to himself. More "hold to the last man" orders that had gotten the Wehrmacht in Normandy into the chaotic mess it was now in?

General Meindl was correct. He had been sent to strongly remind the parachute corps commander to "hold out, stand fast."

Meindl was in a foul mood when he arrived at his battle headquarters to find von Kluge's "spy" waiting. During a harrowing drive from Seventh Army headquarters at Le Mans to his own CP, Meindl had been forced to scramble out of his Volkswagen and into ditches thirty-one times to escape marauding fighter bombers.

"Hold out! Stand fast!" Meindl snapped to young von Kluge, biting off each word. "Convey to your father exactly what I am going to say to you: The time has come when Normandy can no longer be held, because our troops are exhausted. This is the fault mainly of orders to hold out in hopeless situations."

General Meindl, his face flushed with anger and frustration, asked if the field marshal fully understood the hopelessness of fighting when the Americans had total command of the air. "All that's left for grenadiers to do is to lie down and sacrifice their lives," Meindl exclaimed. "It's heartbreaking to have to stand by and watch."

THAT NIGHT COLONEL August Freiherr von der Heydte, the intellectual, tough commander of the German 6th Parachute Regiment, was agonizing in his dimly lit CP near Percy. Baron von der Heydte's young paratroopers—the average age had been seventeen and a half—had battled parachutists of the U.S. 82nd Airborne Division at St.-Mère-Église, the first French town to be liberated, on the morning of D-Day. Without artillery, tank or air support, the German teenagers had nearly fought their way into that town.

Since then, the 6th Parachute Regiment had seen almost continuous action and had taken severe losses. Since the launching of Cobra it had been hacked to pieces. Now at the close of July 27, with rampaging American tanks driving southward, von der Heydte asked for a tally of his total strength. Out of 1,000 paratroopers who had answered the bell on D-Day, only 40 were left.

A DISHEVELED LITTLE group of German soldiers had gathered in a farmhouse not far from Percy late in the afternoon of the twenty-seventh. It was the remnants of the once-elite Panzer Lehr Division: General Fritz Bayerlein, 7 officers, and fourteen enlisted men. Their armament consisted of a few pistols and rifles. Bayerlein hoped to round up more of his men, who were scattered over much of western Normandy, but by dusk American tanks arrived just down the road from his battle headquarters and began pumping shells into the old farmhouse.

One by one, during lulls in the direct fire from American guns, the men of the Panzer Lehr dashed out the front door and into cornfields and patches of woods with the "hunters'" shells exploding at their feet. Bayerlein was the last to leave. He bolted out the door of the now-burning farmhouse and fell on his face in a potato patch as a shell exploded beside him. Shaken but unhurt, Bayerlein scrambled to his feet. As darkness enveloped the killing grounds, the commander of the famous Panzer Lehr Division was trudging forlornly down a dusty back road toward Percy—alone.

That night of the twenty-seventh, General Omar Bradley had a new concern: the Germans were fleeing the trap Cobra had set for them. Troy Middleton's VIII Corps had taken fewer than 100 prisoners that day as the enemy to his front pulled back rapidly. In Joe Collins's VII Corps, the Big Red One had captured only 553 men in its three days in action following the bombardment. Worse, German Seventh Army commander Paul Hausser had recognized that armored spearheads were cutting in behind his forces facing Middleton and had rushed whatever units he could get his hands on to confront Colonel Truman Boudinot's CC-B of the 3rd Armored in its drive to seize Coutances. Hausser had to hold that key road center as long as possible. It was the escape valve for Wehrmacht formations. As a result, Boudinot's tankers came to an abrupt halt east of Coutances.

AROUND MIDNIGHT, GENERAL Bradley conferred with Middleton by phone. Middleton agreed: the quarry appeared to be slipping away. The two commanders reached a crucial decision. Despite the fiendish minefields confronting Middleton, at dawn he would unleash Major General John S. Wood's 4th Armored Division to attack south along the Périers-Coutances road, as far as Monthucon. There General Wood would coordinate future advances with Colonel Boudinot of the 3rd Armored's CC-B before either of the columns converging on Coutances tried to crash into that city. At the same time, General Middleton would instruct Major General Robert S. Grow's 6th Armored Division to pass through the leading assault infantry; the armor was to bypass Coutances on the west and take out for the coastal town of Granville to the south.

As General Bradley removed his combat boots to steal a few hours of sleep before dawn he was gripped by cautious optimism: perhaps Cobra was going to pay off in monumental dividends beyond his wildest dreams, if only his tanks and foot soldiers continued to exploit the turmoil within the German forces. Toward that end, he knew, at daybreak four American armored divisions would be plunging generally southward in tank-infantry task forces—Collins's 2nd and 3rd Armored and Middleton's 4th and 6th

Armored. Maybe, just maybe, their momentum might even carry them on past the primary objective—Avranches at the base of the Cotentin Peninsula.

In the meantime on the twenty-seventh, as Normandy was ablaze, Great Britain's senior soldier, Field Marshal Alan Brooke, Chief of the Imperial General Staff, was a highly agitated man. For three days now criticism had been publicly heaped upon the head of Brooke's protégé, Bernard Montgomery, the wiry little commander of the 21st Army Group at Caen. Much of the abuse came from American media, but even the British press was hinting the same thing. So was Prime Minister Churchill. The criticism: General Montgomery was sitting idle at Caen while the Americans were doing all the fighting and suffering most of the casualties.

That day Brooke sent a signal to Montgomery: "[Eisenhower] seems to think that the British army could and should be more offensive . . . It is equally clear that he considers that [Lieutenant General Miles] Dempsey should be doing more . . . It is equally clear that Ike has the very vaguest conception of war."

Brooke continued: "Now, as a result of all this talking and the actual situation on your front, I feel personally quite certain that Dempsey (commander of British 2nd Army) must attack at the earliest possible moment on a large scale. We must not allow German forces to move from his front to Bradley's front or we shall give more cause than ever for criticism."

That same night Montgomery replied: "Everything will be thrown in. Gave orders to Dempsey . . . that attack is to be pressed with utmost vigor and all caution thrown to the winds and any casualties accepted . . . Americans are going great guns, and with Second Army drive south . . . I think results may be good."

6

The Mystery Man
of Normandy

EARLY ON THE morning of Thursday, July 28, Field Marshal Hans Guenther von Kluge, the "master of victorious defense" on the Russian front, was on the phone to General Alfred Jodl at Wolfsschanze. The leaking German dam in Normandy had cracked wide open under the enormous tidal wave of American bombs, shells, and bullets.

"Herr Jodl," von Kluge cried, "everything here is *eine Riesensauerei* (one gigantic mess)!"

Indeed it was. No longer did a front exist. Now it was a wild melee between fleeing bands of exhausted, disspirited, confused Feldgrau and surging American task forces of tanks and infantry. Gone were the Wehrmacht's symbols of yesteryear—the highly polished black boots, the battle streamers and the bugles, the Spartan discipline, the swagger. General Paul Hausser's Seventh Army had turned into a rabble.

Adolf Hitler had by now become convinced that Army Group McNair in southeastern England was a hoax. Fortitude—the massive, ingenious Allied deception ploy—had finally worn thin. In his desperation, nearly eight weeks after D-Day, the Führer authorized von Kluge to pull a few divisions away from the Fifteenth Army along the Pas-de-Calais and rush them to Normandy to help stem the American tide, now threatening to become an all-consuming flood. But most of the Channel forces had to remain in place, just in case the Allies decided to launch an amphibious operation to seize the V-1 launching sites.

Hitler, who had compared himself as a master strategist with Napoleon and Frederick the Great, made plans to establish a battle headquarters in eastern France from where he would personally call all the shots in the Normandy campaign. The Führer, in the wake of the bungled attempt to kill him, now saw a traitor behind each tree—particularly among his generals. He thoroughly distrusted von Kluge, who had committed the sin of "allowing" the Americans to break loose in Normandy and who had been implicated in the assassination plot. Von Kluge's days would be numbered.

Hitler raved to his pair of toadies, Jodl and Keitel, that in the future he would supply his Commander in Chief, West, only enough information on future overall military plans as was needed to fight the war in France. The Führer had become increasingly aware that his strategic orders to field commanders were being read by the Anglo-American high command almost before they were received by the Germans for whom they were intended. Traitors in the signal corps or the general staff were responsible for this outrageous and potentially disastrous situation, Hitler stormed. He remained unaware that the "traitor" was actually an ingenious British device codenamed *Ultra*. Since the beginning of the war, those associated with Ultra had been intercepting, decrypting, and translating top-secret German electronic messages for distribution to a select handful of top Allied military and government leaders in the war's most carefully guarded secret. Ultra had broken the unbreakable code of Nazi Germany.

Ultra was located in an old, rambling, unpretentious mansion at Bletchley Park, outside London. Its presence cloaked by the most intense security measures, the facility was referred to in hushed tones merely as Station X. The few in Normandy being supplied a steady stream of German top-secret messages were generals Bradley and Montgomery, their chiefs of staff and their intelligence officers. General Collins, who spearheaded the great breakthrough, was not privy to the monumental secret of Ultra. Neither was Middleton nor other Allied corps commanders.

Meanwhile in London an important question was being thrashed out at the highest levels: should the Allies take up where the Schwarze Kapelle had failed and try to kill Adolf Hitler by aerial bombing? Through Ultra, the Führer's presence was constantly pinpointed, almost minute-by-minute. It was decided not to make the effort for fear of tipping off the Germans to the fact that their code had been broken. "Besides," observed Prime Minister Winston Churchill, flicking the ash off his long cigar, "they might put some other Nazi in there who is even worse than Hitler. With Hitler at the helm, we can't lose the war."

At dawn on this day, the twenty-eighth, Colonel Leander Doan's tankers and foot soldiers of Task Force X of the 3rd Armored Division set out down the road toward the village of Cerisy la Salle. The burdened infantrymen got a taste of how "the other half" lives—they scrambled aboard tanks to ride into battle. It was a hot seat, however. "You can toast bread on these goddamned engine gratings!" a dogface called out. "Yeah, and I've got a checkerboard imprint on my ass!" another responded.

A short distance down the road the leading tank pulled up to a sharp halt. Rifles cracked in the vegetation to the front. Tank officers held a hurried consultation. Someone better investigate what's up there. The "investigators" were, as usual, summoned. Shouts rang out from the front of the column, the familiar, "Infantry! Infantry! Where in the hell is the goddamned infantry!"

Lieutenant Joe Herrick, the veteran of numerous scraps in the Philippines and China, took a squad and edged forward through the tangled growth of a hedgerow. "I thought we were supposed to be out of these goddamned hedgerows by now!" a grunting dogface hissed in a stage whisper. Holing up where they could see and not be seen, Herrick and his men waited. In such delicate situations, virtually face-to-face with an unseen enemy, there was the ever-present urge to scratch, sneeze, cough, clear a dry throat, or break wind. It took enormous effort to restrain the urge.

Herrick waited for ten minutes. That was long enough. He started to give the order to flush out the nest with fire. But before anyone could pull a trigger, three Germans edged out of the underbrush with hands held high. Wise old head Herrick shouted at his men to stay put. He feared treachery. The leader of the three, a youthful blond corporal, strode confidently, even arrogantly, toward the American squad. The two Germans following suddenly bolted for the rear and were cut down by rifle fire that threw them into a ditch.

The corporal was happy to be alive and talked as though he and his captors were actually only opponents in a peacetime athletic encounter, and now that the game was over they would all join in good fellowship. Herrick's men gathered around the talkative German to give him a shakedown—a search for souvenirs. At that point, Lieutenant Colonel Russell, the battalion commander, arrived on the scene to find out what the holdup was. Russell became irate when the outgoing German insisted on riding on the hood of a jeep. Somewhere the corporal had learned that Americans occasionally transported a prisoner that way.

Russell responded to the request with some choice words and a sharp kick to the German's posterior. It was a very disappointed enemy soldier who started toward the rear—on foot and alone. His dignity, not to mention his backside, had been sorely bruised.

The Task Force X column started off down the road once more toward Cerisy la Salle. An officer in the lead tank was leaning halfway out his turret when there was a loud explosion and a grating crunch—a flat-trajectory round had scored a direct hit. The tank leader went straight up, did a lazy slow roll, and came down running, his legs pumping before they reached the road.

Riding on the rear deck of the third tank, Lieutenant Herrick was knocked to the ground when his vehicle took another direct hit. Tanks and infantry deployed in the hedgerows, and moments later a skirmish line of German grenadiers broke out of a wood about one hundred yards away and moved directly toward the Americans. A volley of fire sprayed the Feldgrau, who turned and scrambled back into the woods, leaving a score of dead sprawled about the field.

Now German shells began exploding around the stalled column. Lieutenant Herrick left his platoon deployed up front and went back in search of his battalion commander. If Colonel Russell had any answers, he wanted to hear them. The American column was apparently as confused as the shadowy German force around it. He found Russell herding some tanks into a field. As Herrick and the colonel talked, a tank received a bazooka hit and blew up. The Panzerfaust team had to be concealed in a brush-covered lane nearby.

Russell shouted, "Go get 'em, Herrick!"

"What with?" the lieutenant yelled back. "All my men are down the road."

Russell grabbed two men and shoved them toward Herrick: "Take these men—and give 'em hell!"

The three moved off toward the lane, with the lieutenant trying to figure out whom he was supposed to give hell to—the Germans or the two men.

Machine-gun bullets hissed in. Herrick and the two "volunteers" hit the ground. There were three holes in the lieutenant's field jacket, and several holes in the clothing of the other two. They were both dead.

When the firing ceased, Herrick crawled up the lane on his knees. Now he was drenched in perspiration. He passed an anti-tank rocket launcher lying in the road, the imprint of a man's body in the grass next to it. A little farther on was a German helmet, and footprints in the mud. Herrick stopped. "Hell," he said to himself, "I don't want a career as a hunter." He slipped off and returned to his platoon.

Word was passed down the line: Cerisy la Salle was too tough a nut for a single armored task force to seize. Foot-sloggers of the Big Red One would move in to do the job.

As Chubby Doan's Task Force X and other columns of the 3rd Armored's CC-A thrust southward, Combat Command-B of the 3rd had been halted by German resistance just short of Coutances in its drive down N-172 to the southwest. As a result, Joe Collins's corps lost the race into Coutances to Middleton's corps when John Wood's 4th Armored Division slammed on into the key road center at dusk. Failure of the 3rd Armored's CC-B and its attached infantry from the Big Red One to rapidly seize the town threatened to thwart General Bradley's plan to block German units fleeing south through Coutances from in front of Middleton's corps.

Now Bradley and Collins played the trump card they had up their sleeves. Brigadier General Isaac D. White's CC-B of the 2nd Armored Division, which had been trailing Maurice Rose's spearheading CC-A to Canisy, received urgent orders: quickly turn to the southwest, loop around Coutances to the south, and race for the Cotentin's west coast, halting nine miles short of the shoreline to allow a corridor for Middleton's corps to drive onward toward Avranches. Knocking out several hasty roadblocks along the way, White's tankers sped down a single road and by nightfall had reached the village of Notre-Dame-de-Cenilly, seven miles from Canisy and halfway to CC-B's primary objective, Lengronne. Early the next morning White dashed on to Lengronne.

General White had strung out a series of strongpoints along his path of advance, and now he received orders from Joe Collins: "Block any Germans trying to escape to the south." Once again an American spearhead had slashed in behind the fleeing enemy formations.

That morning, in the peace and quiet of a lovely Norman summer day far behind the blazing fight, a grumpy and frustrated General George Patton was heavily engaged in such dull chores as inspecting an evacuation hospital, a bakery, a supply dump, and a salvage plant. It was a humiliating experience for the man a major Stateside magazine only the previous fall had termed "one of the great fighting generals of history."

At midafternoon, Captain Elliott R. Taylor, an aide to Patton's chief of staff, burst in on the 3rd Army commander at the supply dump. He was visibly excited. "General, Sir," he gasped, struggling to regain his breath. "You're wanted on the scrambler at headquarters! It's *General Bradley!* He's been looking all over for you!"

"Hot damn!" Patton exploded, lashing his glossy boot with a riding crop. He raced back to his operations tent in the apple orchard at Nehou and put in an urgent call to the commander of First Army.

"George," Bradley said, rolling out a time-honored phrase, "this is it."

Patton's face flushed with excitement. But the elation quickly vanished. Bradley wasn't quite ready yet for Third Army to be made operational.

"You'll supervise operations in Middleton's zone as deputy First Army commander," Bradley stated. "You are to trail Middleton's columns and aid in unscrambling them should they become entangled." But, Bradley indicated, Patton was not to take command of the corps or actively influence the course of its operations.

It was a vague assignment. But Patton was so excited over getting into action that he did not quibble. Keeping George Patton from "actively influencing the course of VIII Corps operations" would be akin to hiding the rising sun from a barnyard rooster.

General Bradley also said that Patton's entering the fray, or even his presence in Normandy, would be kept a deep, dark secret "to keep the Germans guessing." Patton, who was not overburdened with personal humility and lived for the spotlight, didn't even dispute that point, even though every top American commander already knew that the Germans were fully aware that Patton was in Normandy.

George Patton's zealously loyal staff was furious on hearing of their boss's new assignment. Deputy army commander. A hollow title. A gimmick. Bradley, they were convinced, was merely afraid the dynamic Patton would steal the show. Why else would he throw a blackout curtain over the general the Wehrmacht feared most?

As for Patton himself, he was as excited as a kid with his first toy. He stomped gleefully around the apple orchard, goddamning the Germans with each step, strapped on his pair of ivory-handled revolvers and dashed off to the fighting front. He couldn't care less what his title was—even if it was hollow.

Unknown to Patton or his angry staff, General Bradley for weeks had had misgivings about calling the bold armored leader into the fight. Not because the reserved, self-effacing Bradley was "afraid that Patton would steal the show," but due to the First Army commander's apprehension over Patton's demonstrated "impetuous habits."

"I'm afraid that if I bring in George, I will spend half my time watching him and the other half watching the Germans," Bradley had confided to an aide a few weeks previously. He struggled with his personal dilemma: whether to have Patton in his command or get along without him. Bradley could not decide which was the lesser evil.

In the bloody slugging match in the hedgerows there had been no critical need for a bold, slashing cavalryman like George Patton. But now with the Wehrmacht in Normandy beginning to fall apart, and American armor in position to thoroughly slice up the German Seventh Army, the situation *demanded* a George Patton.

So Patton became what his staff called "The Mystery Man of Normandy."

That night George Patton closed a letter to wife Beatrice, back in Boston, with his personal creed for success on the battlefield: *"L'audace, l'audace, toujours l'audace!"*(Audacious, audacious, always audacious!)

Late on the afternoon of July 28, General Joe Collins was racing for Coutances as fast as his jeep could weave in and out of hundreds of American vehicles edging toward the key town. The VII Corps commander feared there would be a horrendous traffic jam in Coutances between Troy Middleton's 4th Armored Division coming down from the north and his own 3rd Armored Division when it finally broke into that city from the east. Collins's fears were justified. He found the wild confusion he had anticipated.

Both the 3rd and 4th Armored divisions were struggling to get onto the road leading south to Gavray that had originally been in

Collins's sector. The VII Corps commander promptly ordered his aide to clip in his portable phone to First Army. When General Bradley came on the line Collins explained the situation. "Wood [4th Armored] is already into Coutances and heading south, so he'll get the right-of-way," the First Army commander stated.

As tanks and foot soldiers, half-tracks and trucks, jeeps and ammunition carriers of the 3rd and 4th armored swirled around a main road junction at the edge of Coutances in a wild cacophony of blaring horns, revving engines, shouted orders and strident curses, Joe Collins was astonished to see that neither Leroy Watson, the 3rd Armored's commanding general, nor any of his senior leaders was at this crucial site. Since the launching of Cobra, Collins had grown increasingly concerned that the top leadership of 3rd Armored was not moving the division with the dash expected of it. Furious at the absence of General Watson, Collins again had his aide, Captain Jack Walsh, clip in his phone, this time to Watson's CP. The corps commander's anger grew more intense when he found the 3rd Armored general at his headquarters instead of being up with his spearhead elements. Collins ordered Watson to rush to Coutances at once and start unscrambling his snarled division from the 4th Armored.

Collins waited until Watson arrived on the scene, then rushed back to his own CP near Marigny. He hurried a call to General Bradley and outlined the situation he had found at the crucial Coutances crossroads and the absence of senior 3rd Armored commanders. "Watson's a fine man and a good soldier but out of place in an armored division," Collins stated. Then he asked that Watson be relieved.

Though Leroy Watson was a classmate of both Eisenhower and Bradley, the First Army commander granted Collins's request. "I'll send you an experienced tank commander as soon as one is available," Bradley declared. That man would be Brigadier General Maurice Rose, leader of Combat Command-A of Ted Brooks's 2nd Armored Division.*

---

*General Leroy Watson urged Eisenhower not to send him home but to give him an infantry battle command. Impressed by Watson's sincerity and realizing he was basically an infantry leader, the Supreme Commander assigned him as assistant commander of the 29th Infantry Division, and later Watson took over as commanding general of the 29th, due to his outstanding performance.

Late that evening, Omar Bradley dispatched a letter to General Eisenhower in England: "To say that the personnel of First Army Headquarters is riding high tonight is putting it mildly. Things on our front really look good . . . I can assure you we are taking every calculated risk, and we believe we have the Germans out of the ditches [hedgerows] and in complete demoralization."

As dusk approached on the twenty-eighth, mass confusion reigned among German forces fleeing southward. Communications were nonexistent. General Paul Hausser, commander of the once-proud Seventh Army, had to drop face downward in a muddy ditch when he was fired on by an American armored car. Colonel Tychensen, assistant commander of the 2nd SS Panzer Division, was shot and killed near his command post by an American patrol.

Seeking to re-form a defensive line across the base of the Cotentin Peninsula, Field Marshal von Kluge ordered LXXXIV Corps to occupy strong positions along a ten-mile stretch. These orders were given to General Hausser, who in turn passed them along to LXXXIV Corps. But due to snarled communications, only the corps rear could be reached. There a quartermaster officer hopped on a bicycle at about midnight and pedaled arduously through the blackness to reach the corps commander, General von Choltitz, at his battle headquarters. Totally out of touch with his fleeing units, a grim-faced Dietrich von Choltitz shrugged his shoulders in resignation and despair, and tossed von Kluge's urgent order onto his desk. There was nothing he could do.

UNKNOWN TO VON Choltitz or other German commanders, Brooks's 2nd Armored Division, reinforced by a battalion of Barton's 4th Infantry Division, had slashed in behind his disorganized elements and was lying in wait for Germans fleeing southward. Brooks's men were strung out for seven miles facing north in a series of strongpoints. Shortly before dawn, tense Americans at a crossroads three miles southwest of Notre-Dame-de-Cenilly heard the rumble of tanks approaching from the north. Mouths grew dry. Stomachs churned. Perspiration dotted foreheads. Fingers were on triggers as men of a company of armored infantry and a company of tanks waited nervously while the sound of motors to the front grew louder.

Edging forward in the blackness was a column of twenty-nine German tanks and vehicles, led by an 88-millimeter self-propelled gun. Suddenly a gun on one of the 2nd Armored's Shermans barked, shooting a bright orange flame into the sky, and dug-in Americans loosed a torrent of machine-gun and rifle fire into the oncoming force. German grenadiers leaped from trucks and scrambled for roadside ditches. The enemy gun in the lead and those on other tanks returned the fire. An intense shoot-out had erupted in the darkness, with crazy geometric patterns of tracer bullets criss crossing the black sky.

Strident shouts of German officers pierced the battle din, and Feldgrau began crawling forward in the ditches along both sides of the road. Five or six German tanks rumbled toward the Americans at the crossroads. Two Shermans went up in flames. The self-propelled gun overran 2nd Armored positions, but the men stuck to their foxholes and peppered the tracked vehicle with small-arms fire, killing its driver and gunner. The gun carriage blocked the road, effectively halting the charge of other panzers.

Now the German grenadiers closed with the American riflemen and for nearly two hours, until dawn, a bitter face-to-face fight raged. Screams rang out in the blackness. Grunts told that bayonets had found their mark. Curses in English and German spilled out. The fight for a once-nondescript Norman crossroads was a bloody one. At daybreak, the enemy force withdrew, leaving behind 17 dead and 151 wounded. The 88-millimeter self-propelled gun, which had furnished a welcomed roadblock for the hard-pressed 2nd Armored defenders, was undamaged. Its motor was still running and the gun loaded and ready for firing. The Americans suffered 52 casualties, along with the two knocked-out Shermans.

Another wild melee broke out about the same time, not far away, when about fifteen German tanks and several hundred grenadiers assaulted an outpost manned by a company of the 4th Infantry Division. The American company commander was killed almost at once and, outgunned and outnumbered, the remainder of the outpost defenders fell back half a mile into the positions of the 78th Armored Field Artillery Battalion. Two of the battalion's batteries opened direct fire on the large German force advancing through the darkness, and a third battery bombarded the enemy with indirect fire. Together with the guns of a platoon of tank destroyers, the artillery held the Germans at bay for thirty minutes, at which time a hastily summoned company of nearby armored infantry arrived.

As dawn broke, the Germans withdrew. Left behind were the blackened carcasses of seven Mark IV panzers and 126 dead grenadiers.

THE GERMAN FORCES engaged in the fierce battles with 2nd Armored tankers and foot soldiers during the early-morning hours of darkness were the leading elements of a large concentration seeking to break through to the south and escape the American trap. The stand of the 2nd Armored caused a tremendous backup of German panzers, trucks, armored cars, self-propelled guns, staff cars, towed artillery, horse-drawn conveyances, ambulances, and communications vehicles—packed bumper to bumper, three abreast, for more than three miles—in the vicinity of Roncey. With the arrival of dawn, nervous troops in the stalled column stared skyward in search of the ominous specks that would tell them that Jabos were approaching. How could the Amis miss spotting this enormous traffic jam, a fighter-bomber's paradise?

7

Massacre
at Roncey

AT DAYBREAK ON July 29, elements of Lieutenant Colonel Carlton Russell's 3rd Battalion, 36th Armored Infantry Regiment of the 3rd Armored's Task Force X deployed to assault Hill 363, on which the Germans were dug in. Already Mustangs were bombing and strafing the elevation, and artillery and mortar rounds were exploding on it with great shocks of black smoke and flame. The dogfaces were tired—and sleepy. All night the Luftwaffe had been over, dropping those hideous flares that seemed to sway in the sky for hours, illuminating vast reaches of the landscape as though it were noon. Then came the bombs. The German aircraft were seeking out the rampaging American spearheads.

Leading the assault on Hill 363, Lieutenant Joe Herrick's platoon ran into a stubborn group of Germans at the line of departure and a short, but spirited, firefight developed before the enemy force was wiped out. This isn't going by the book, Herrick thought. A line of departure is supposed to be a quiet place where one can think—or not think.

Across from Herrick sat a figure clad in a gray-green uniform, coal-bucket helmet clamped on his head, a bolt-action rifle across his knees. He scowled at the American lieutenant. Herrick scowled back. The German got the best of the contest due to the fact that the enemy soldier had three eyes and Herrick only two. The third one was a neat round hole in the center of his forehead. "I might look like that sometime," Herrick got to thinking. So he went over and turned the dead German around.

At 8:30 A.M., the American rifle platoon moved forward into a dense wood and started up the steep hill. A withering burst of automatic-weapons fire tore through the trees and around the dog-faces as they advanced. Now mortar shells began to explode nearby. The platoon was halted, face down, on a stretch of muddy terrain. Suddenly Lieutenant Herrick felt the warm stickiness of blood. His face and hands were covered with it. But he felt no pain—a factor that frightened him. Then Evans, a teenaged rifleman next to him, slid down the muck onto Herrick. A jagged piece of steel protruded from the boy's neck. It was Evans's spurting blood that had covered the platoon leader. A medic slithered over to Evans, examined him, and pronounced him dead.

The attack bogged down. Soon Colonel Russell was blistering the airwaves over a walkie-talkie—who or what was responsible for holding up the war? "We've got to get that hill!" Russell exclaimed, "Now get the lead out!"

"Okay, we're going to charge," Herrick told Platoon Sergeant Lubbock, who in turn yelled to the rear: "We're goin' to charge the bastards. If anyone's damn fool enough to follow, get in tow!" Nearly all of the platoon were damn fools.

Herrick and his men went on up the hill, slipping and sliding, cursing the tangle of underbrush and the relentless chatter of enemy machine guns raking their ranks. Several men went down. The advance faltered. Mortar rounds shook the earth around the Americans. The hill seemed to get higher and higher. Finally reaching the top, Herrick and his men, legs as wobbly as thin cornstalks from the exertion, prepared to close with the enemy. But the Germans had vanished, as though they had suddenly become bored with it all.

The platoon waited for what seemed several hours, yet heard nothing from the German battalion. "They've forgotten about us," a soldier exclaimed to no one in particular. "Probably think we were wiped out." A short time later, foot soldiers of the Big Red One pulled their way up the elevation to take over for Herrick and his men. The platoon came down the hill and marched seven miles into a village in the valley, where they rejoined Chubby Doan's Task Force X, the fine cutting edge of Collins's VII Corps's advance.

It was nearly dusk that day when litter bearers were picking up bodies off the slopes of Hill 363. One of these was Private Evans, the youth with the jagged piece of steel in his neck, who had been pronounced dead. He was very much alive. No one rejoiced more when word of this was received than the medic who had pronounced him dead on the basis of a cursory examination under heavy fire.

The medic's name was Jeff—a typical combat medic and the most-respected man in the platoon. In the States Jeff had been the butt of endless jokes. He was called a "pill roller," a "shanker mechanic," and a "corn surgeon." It was all in good fun, but to Jeff, it hurt. All that changed when the first German shell came screaming in, slicing off half a man's face. As the injured man shrieked and pleaded for help; the riflemen took cover, but Jeff ran to the man through exploding shells and machine-gun fire.

Jeff never complained. He was short on stature, long on guts. He ambled along at the rear of the platoon, loaded down with everything except weapons: bandages, pouches, extra canteens of water, vials of morphine, sulfa containers, a few basic surgical tools. On his helmet was painted a large red cross on a field of white—"aiming stakes," the men carrying the weapons called the mercy insignia. Sometimes the Germans respected a red cross, sometimes not.

Jeff never fired a shot. But wherever a shot was fired, he was there. He seemed to be every place at once, patching and tending and worrying himself sick, not about his own well-being but that of his wounded comrades. Somehow Jeff felt personally responsible if one of his "boys" died of wounds. It took a special kind of courage to be a combat medic—Jeff had it in abundance.*

MEANWHILE, THAT AFTERNOON a patrol of the 17th SS Panzer Division nabbed American Private Anthony Blazus, who happened to blunder into the enemy. Blazus was taken to nearby Roncey, where his captors joined a huge convoy of vehicles, three abreast, facing south, but not moving. Blazus had no way of knowing that Ted Brooks's 2nd Armored Division had formed a barrier to prevent the German's escape. Panzers and other vehicles stretched out along the road in each direction as far as Blazus could see.

At a crossroads, a German officer was directing traffic. He wore red tabs so Blazus knew he was a general. And the general was very

---

*When the law of averages caught up with Jeff five months later in the Battle of the Bulge, it happened just the way he would have wanted it to occur—bent over one of his grievously wounded "boys," a morphine syringe in one hand, a look of deep concern and compassion on his own boyish face.

drunk. Alternately, he gave directions to the retreating column and returned arm-extended "Hitler salutes" from his aides who were dashing about. Blazus, despite his predicament, had to restrain a smile. He thought Hitler salutes were given by German military men only in Hollywood movies.

Suddenly there was a roar from the sky, and swarms of American fighter-bombers were overhead. The general quickly staggered from the center of the road to find cover. Cowering in a ditch, Blazus watched in fear and fascination as the merciless Mustangs and Thunderbolts raced up and down the column, machine guns blazing and 500-pounders dropping, until the whole two miles was a red, blazing tangle of shattered German bodies and wrecked vehicles. Tanks were ripped apart, big guns smashed, trucks set ablaze, bodies slashed into pieces and tossed into the air. Private Blazus felt like cheering despite his cold terror, but he dared not do so.

FOR MORE THAN six hours, *Jabos* of Pete Quesada's IX Tactical Air Command rotated squadrons over the smoking column. A gleeful Thunderbolt pilot radioed his base: "I've been to two church socials and a country fair, but I never saw anything like this before!" American artillery, alerted to the juicy target, joined in. Every big gun within range plastered the stalled column. It was carnage on the grand scale.

Suddenly the planes vanished. Dusk was at hand. An eerie quiet descended over the long stretch of Norman road lined with the blackened hulks of scores of panzers, several hundred trucks, and field guns. Sprawled about were the limp bodies of large numbers of German troops who had been unable to flee to the safety of woods on either side of the road. It looked to Blazus as though every German was dead and each vehicle and tank destroyed. This must have been how Dante's Inferno was, flashed through the American's head. His knees were still quivering. He felt sick to his stomach and thought he would vomit. There were a few dazed Germans in a ditch nearby, staring numbly with that haunted look of those who have just escaped sure death. No one was paying any attention to him, so Blazus slowly pulled himself to his feet and slipped off into the nearby woods.

As General Bradley's spearheads continued to grind steadily southward on the evening of the twenty-ninth, Ted Brooks's 2nd

Armored was given the task of wiping out German forces remaining in the Cotentin Peninsula. Brooks's procedure for doing this was to erect a cage and let fleeing Germans beat against the bars. As expected, under cover of darkness that night the "bar beaters" tried to escape southward once more.

A force of about one hundred and fifty Germans stumbled into the bivouac area of the 62nd Armored Field Artillery Battalion near Lengronne, and as Americans roused from their sleep leaped for personal handguns, a firefight broke out. These Germans surrendered after a few minutes.

Shortly before midnight about 1,000 Feldgrau and nearly one hundred armored vehicles, survivors of the "Roncey massacre" a few hours before, edged toward St. Denis-le-Gast from the north. The enemy force broke through a tank-infantry defensive position. A Mark V tank poked its gun muzzle through a hedgerow, and fired point-blank at the command half-track of an American tank battalion. The half-track exploded in a ball of fire. The German panzers' guns roared again, and several other vehicles at the command post were set ablaze. Now the American positions disintegrated, and the enemy force rushed into St. Denis-le-Gast.

Meanwhile, Lieutenant Colonel Wilson D. Coleman of the 41st Armored Infantry Regiment was rallying his men who had pulled back under the heavy German tank pressure. In the swirl of the firefight in inky blackness, Coleman's unit had become totally disorganized. The battalion commander gathered up as many of his men as possible and started back toward St.-Denis-le-Gast and its road junction. For nearly two hours a confused battle took place at close range, with American armored infantry and Germans fighting it out in tiny groups, pairs, and even individually.

Colonel Coleman, a pistol in his hands, turned to shout an order to his men when he collapsed, a bullet through the head.

With the arrival of dawn, St.-Denis-le-Gast was back in American hands. German losses in the sharp skirmish had been heavy: 130 killed, 124 wounded, and more than 500 taken prisoner, as well as seven tanks and 18 vehicles destroyed. The Americans had suffered nearly 100 casualties and 12 vehicles knocked out.

Eleven German vehicles, many packed with grenadiers, had pushed their way through the village in the darkness and confusion. But instead of fleeing on to the south, the enemy column turned westward toward Lengronne. A short distance down the road, an American crew was manning an antitank gun guarding the road and the bivouac area of the 78th Armored Field Artillery Battalion. As the gun crew stood by in the dark, the German column drove on past, only a few feet from the weapon. The Americans apparently thought the convoy belonged to the 2nd Armored Division.

Edging ahead, the German column was well inside the 78th Armored Field Artillery Battalion positions when an American officer stepped into the road and shouted, "Halt!" When the enemy vehicles stopped, the American called out to the driver of the lead truck: "Password?" The German apparently did not understand and thought he was among friendly troops. He stuck his head out the window and yelled back, "*Was ist?* (What was that?)."

"Krauts!" an American voice shouted from the darkness. Germans leaped from trucks, took cover, and opened fire. American artillerymen hurriedly picked up rifles and carbines and started shooting back. Long bur-r-r-p-p-s from German Schmeissers laced the night air. The slower-paced American machine guns replied. Thousands of bullets hissed overhead, and streams of tracers lighted the scene and crisscrossed the sky. Utter confusion reigned. Here and there silhouetted figures darted about. Germans fired at Germans, Americans at Americans. Captain Naubert O. Simard rushed to an exposed machine gun, began raking the Wehrmacht vehicles. He was cut down with his finger on the trigger and the gun barrel hot.

Now both adversaries began to rally from the initial shock and chaos. American howitzers were lowered and fired at point-blank range at distances of less than 100 yards. The crew of a tank destroyer that had been parked near the road making emergency repairs swung its turret and began pumping shells into the rear of the stalled German column. Feldgrau fled for their lives. Their running figures, outlined starkly by flames from burning German vehicles, were excellent targets for the artillerymen.

Slowly, a calmness settled over the scene. Those Germans who could, melted into the darkness and the woods. With the first crack of dawn, the men of the 78th Armored Field Artillery Battalion began counting German corpses—there were ninety of them. They began hustling more than two hundred prisoners into a temporary confinement area. All eleven German vehicles were blackened, twisted hulks. The Americans had lost five killed and six wounded.

While this sharp encounter had been raging, a small number of American infantrymen and a handful of tanks were peering northward through the darkness at a roadblock on the Coutance-Gavray road near the village of Cambry. Ears perked up as the telltale sound of tank motors was heard to the front. The ominous noise in the dark grew louder, and shortly several panzers, guns blazing, charged the American roadblock and crashed through. These panzers were the spearhead of a force of twenty-five hundred Germans seeking to break through the 2nd Armored Divison "cage" to continue their flight to the south.

Sergeant Hulon B. Whittington of the 41st Armored Infantry Regiment had taken cover when the panzers opened fire. With bullets whistling past him, Whittington leaped to his feet and scrambled up onto a Sherman tank. Shouting through the turret to the crew, his voice nearly drowned out in the din of battle, Whittington directed the Sherman to a point where its crew could bring point-blank fire into the leading panzers. The first round from the 75-millimeter gun struck the lead enemy tank squarely, causing it to spin crazily and block the road. The German charge stalled.

A bitter firefight broke out among flaming vehicles. Artillery units in the area were alerted to the halted German column and opened fire, not bothering to zero in their guns. Shells screamed in as the enemy grenadiers milled about in confusion. At dawn the German force had disintegrated—four hundred and fifty Feldgrau sprawled about over the battleground, dead. More than one thousand Germans had been taken prisoner, and nearly one hundred vehicles, including several panzers, had been destroyed. Well dug in and organized against their confused and even panic-stricken foes, the Americans had lost 51 killed and 63 wounded.

AS DISORGANIZED REMNANTS of the German Seventh Army were bloodying their heads against the bars of Brooks' seven-mile-long cage in desperate efforts to break out to the south, along the west coast of the Cotentin Peninsula General George Patton was a human dynamo "supervising" Troy Middleton's VIII Corps, which had been advancing steadily down an eight-mile-wide corridor against mainly delaying obstacles and mines. Learning that Middleton had his four infantry divisions out in front, Patton issued his first order in Normandy: "I want Wood and Grow to lead the advance."

The deputy First Army commander of two days was not concerned with such a technicality as to whether a "supervisor" could issue such orders.

General John Wood, commander of the 4th Armored Division, was a rough-riding, hard-talking cavalryman-turned-tanker, who had much of Patton's dash and impetuosity. General Bob Grow, leader of the 6th Armored Division, was an earthy Iowan who went into the army from the Minnesota National Guard in 1916 and saw World War I combat in the artillery and cavalry.

If Patton had a "favorite" division, it had to be the 4th Armored, possibly due to the Third Army commander's affinity for the spirit of the hell-for-leather cavalryman, Wood (whom Patton called The Professor). Back in England Wood had been involved in a serious training accident, and later Patton wrote in his diary: "The Professor was in a bad state as a result of having been ridden over by a jeep, which would probably have killed any other man."

AS WOOD AND Grow passed through leading infantry elements and bolted southward abreast, Patton's focus was upon Avranches, the ancient coastal town at the base of the Cotentin Peninsula, where it turned into Brittany. Four weeks previously Patton had marked a bold red circle around Avranches on his Michelin road map, and his gaze seldom left it. It was at Avranches that the fleeing Germans might dig in their heels and snap back at their pursuing tormentors. But the city was more important to George Patton than that: Avranches was the gateway to Brittany, and when the town was seized Patton's 3rd Army was to become officially operational and spill out into Brittany.

With Middleton's spearheads racing for Avranches, Patton now recalled how he and Beatrice had stood on the 200-foot-high bluffs on which the town rested and gazed across the bay to the famous rock of Mont St.-Michel. Eight miles away, it was clearly visible in its towering, majestic beauty. That was thirty-one years ago; now Patton was returning as a liberator.

Avranches had carried its battle scars for centuries. The Norseman had come and gone in A.D. 889. Plantaganet camped there in 1141 during his conquest of Normandy, as did Edward III a hundred years later. Heavy fighting by the Huguenots took place there in the sixteenth century. In 1940, the mighty goose-stepping legions of

Adolf Hitler took over the old town of 7,000 residents. Now the Americans, with their swarms of belching, roaring tanks were converging on Avranches in several long columns, leaving towering plumes of dust in their wake.

By July 30, the eyes of American and German commanders alike were focused on Avranches. Lying between the Selune and See Rivers, the ancient city on the bluffs was the hub of a network of roads leading from the north and the east. South of Avranches, at the foot of a lengthy winding road leading down the bluffs toward St.-Michel, the roads formed a straight line running across the Selune to a fork where again the road separated—into prongs leading east, west, and south. From that springboard, Patton's columns could race in each direction in the Brittany Peninsula.

George Patton's mind was awhirl. He was bursting with ideas—and even some concerns. The current targets of his thoughts were two large dams at the mouth of the Selune River near Avranches. Why can't those dams be knocked out *now?* The flood to follow would abate in a week, and he'd be south of Avranches by then. Five days before the Cobra bombardment, Patton had asked General Quesada, the fight-bomber chief, to "knock out those goddamned dams." Quesada was noncommital. Now, in the midst of the massive push by two corps, Patton roused General Bradley from exhausted sleep with a middle-of-the-night phone call. "Hey, Brad," he cheerily began, "how about using some paratroops on those goddamned dams over the Selune? They'd be ideal for blowing them up!"

"What'd he say, General?" inquired an aide after Patton had hung up.

"He was not very congenial about the idea."

On the twenty-ninth, General Patton, still in his role as "supervisor" of VIII Corps, went looking for the 6th Armored Division. He found it stalled on what he called the "wrong" side of the Sienne River. Bob Grow, the division commander, was sitting alongside the road. Brigadier General James Taylor, leader of one of Grow's combat commands, was huddled around a map with a group of officers in the shadow of an old church. Patton leaped from his jeep and rushed up to the 6th Armored commander.

"What in hell are you doing, Grow, sitting in the road?" he demanded.

"Taylor is in charge of the advanced guard, General."

"I don't give a goddamn who's in charge. Have you been down to the river?"

"No, sir, Taylor is trying to find a place to ford it."

"Well, unless you do something, Grow, you'll be out on your ass looking for a job."

Leaving General Grow behind, Patton strode off to the river and waded in to test its depth. On the far side, off in the distance, he saw a group of Germans lounging under a windmill. They looked at Patton. He looked at them. No shots were fired.

"Okay, Grow," the First Army deputy commander scowled as he climbed out of the water. "Take them across. This goddamned sewer isn't more than two feet deep."

Early on the morning of July 30 in Joe Collins's VII Corps sector, Lieutenant Joe Herrick and his armored infantrymen of Task Force X were trudging along a dusty road. The "fly-boys" and the artillery had obviously already paid their respects to the fleeing Germans; the road was littered with debris. German gas masks in their round aluminum containers, coalbucket helmets, and the soiled letters that always began, *Mein Lieber Hans* (my dear Hans) or Herman or Fritz and that usually ended, *Mutter* (Mother). Often Hans or Herman or Fritz was lying beside the crumbled, water-soaked letter, dead eyes staring sightlessly into the sky.

Suddenly there was a mighty roar and Herrick and the other dogfaces in the column looked casually into the sky, expecting to see the familiar white star of the U.S. Army Air Corps on a fighter-bomber. A chill surged through them and they leaped for cover as a black ME-110 of the Luftwaffe zipped in low and sent streams of bullets along the entire length of the column. The German pilot was good. Americans lay sprawled in the road, dead or seriously wounded, and two tanks were badly damaged.

Now the Luftwaffe pilot banked and returned for an encore. Herrick reflected that the enemy flyer had more courage than brains. Every weapon in the long column opened fire on the sleek German Jabo. The pilot whipped his plane straight up as it began smoking, then a white parachute blossomed as the German bailed out of his mortally wounded fighter plane. His body jerked and kicked as small-arms fire from the angry Americans in the column converged on him. Lieutenant Herrick could hear him screaming, even after his 'chute was shredded and he was in free-fall, like a bomb. The German struck the ground with a thud.

SHORTLY AFTER DAWN on the twenty-ninth, John H. Thompson, the veteran war correspondent of the *Chicago Tribune*, and three fellow reporters jeeped into the village of Roncey where the evening before American fighter-bombers had blasted a mammoth Wehrmacht traffic jam and left it a pile of twisted metal. Thompson had covered the savage fighting in Tunisia and had seen the carnage inflicted upon green American forces at Kasserine Pass. He had parachuted into Sicily with the U.S. 82nd Airborne Division, narrowly escaped death at Omaha Beach with the 1st Infantry Division on D-Day, and reported on the destruction of Fortress Cherbourg from the front lines. Thompson had never witnessed such awesome carnage as he viewed on this morning at insignificant little Roncey.

Dismounting from the jeep, Thompson, who sported a bushy beard, picked his way through the smashed vehicles to where Lieutenant Charles Henderson, a military policeman, was directing traffic in the square.

"What a hell of a mess!" the reporter stated the obvious.

"Our engineers counted the hulks of 504 Kraut vehicles and 77 tanks," Lieutenant Henderson replied, continuing to wave traffic on through.

"If I hadn't seen this, I wouldn't believe it," Thompson observed in an awed tone.

Many of the vehicles were still smoking, and a thick pall hovered over the village. The pungent smell of death and burned flesh was sickening. Hundreds of bodies in gray-green uniforms were sprawled along the road, in the fields, and inside tanks and vehicles. Some cadavers sat upright, black and unidentifiable as human beings, having been turned into human torches only hours before.

Earlier that morning, armored bulldozers had been rushed to Roncey, and in twenty-two minutes had shoved 114 vehicles off the main street to permit American tanks, self-propelled guns, and tank destroyers to roll on through toward Gavray and Hambye. Many in the American column covered their nostrils against the stench.

Adding to the macabre scene were hundreds of bedraggled Germans filling a prisoner-of-war cage just off the square and overflowing into the street. All day long they came in, hands on tops of heads, helmets long since tossed aside, eyes glazed from the horror of the fighter-bomber assault. They were herded in by a few grimy American soldiers, or came in on their own under white flags. These were not the soldiers the Wehrmacht had conscripted from Russia, Poland, or middle Europe—*"ost"* troops who had manned the Normandy coastal defenses. Many were from the elite German formations—members of the 2nd SS *(Das Reich)* Panzer Division, the 17th SS Panzer Grenadier Division, and parachute outfits.

Up a narrow lane came the incongruity of war. French farmer folk in their best clothes, for this was Sunday, strolled along, gawking at the massed wreckage of the might of Nazi Germany. Little girls in starched blue and white dresses; old granddads with white beards and faces wrinkled by age and the hot Norman sun; young men, stiff and awkward in their unaccustomed store apparel, halted reporter Thompson and his three comrades to laugh and talk. Bowed under four years of the Nazi yoke, the Normans were delighted with the carnage.

One elderly woman wearing widow's black grabbed Thompson by the arm and over and over cried out: *"Bonjour, liberateur!* [Good day, liberator!]" Thompson felt a tinge of embarrassment over the adulation being heaped upon him by the old lady, but he feared she might be disappointed to learn that he had not helped create this enormous German destruction, so he grinned widely and remained silent.

Thompson strode on past the seemingly endless wreckage. Almost every vehicle had burned, its metal riddled with bullet holes. Two deep black kettles, one full of spaghetti and the other containing two hams, lay amid the litter of a kitchen truck. Beside the vehicle were several dead Germans, apparently cooks who had been preparing the evening meal when the Jabos struck. Rifles and helmets filled ditches. Everywhere lay overcoats, many bearing SS insignia.

In a farmyard were the wrecks of two German utility vehicles. A pair of French girls, about two or three years old, were sitting inside. One kept pushing her foot against the starter, which whirred noisily.

John Thompson and his fellow reporters were examining the ruins of an 88-millimeter gun when they glanced down the road at an approaching group of soldiers. They recognized the newcomers as German soldiers—18 of them. Quickly the newsmen breathed a sigh of relief when they saw the large white flag in the hands of the sergeant leading them. Dazed, weary, hungry, the tiny bedraggled group had had enough.

The four reporters laughed and glanced nervously at each other. There were no armed Americans in the immediate vicinity. Thompson shouted, "Halt!" They did. He asked if any spoke English. None did. The Chicago reporter had a curious thought: "If they change their mind and decide to jump us, our total armament is four pencils and two beer-bottle openers."

Glad to be alive, the Germans stood supinely as Thompson and his three associates frisked the enemy for weapons but found none. Known as "Beaver" since his days in North Africa, Thompson summoned up his best Prussian drill-instructor simulation, pointed up the road to the rear, and growled, *"Macht schnell!* [Hurry, hurry!]" The eighteen German soldiers started marching back dociley, hands still upraised.

AS NIGHT FELL on the thirtieth, Major Haynes Dugan, assistant intelligence officer of the 3rd Armored Division, was with forward elements that had been moving so fast they had nearly run off their maps. Dugan hopped into a jeep with a driver and set off in the blackness for division headquarters at Hambye to secure a new supply of maps. He was understandably nervous. This was Indian country. The tanks and armored infantry in trucks had lunged forward, but large bands of Germans were still marauding to the rear.

The road ran through the center of Villedieu-les-Poêles, which was thought to be still held by the enemy. Corporal John Pfeffer tried to stay on the road, though hardly able to see it, while Major Dugan kept a nervous finger on the .30-caliber machine gun, which was half-cocked. When the pair came to a crossroads and were unable to read the signs, Dugan shinnied up the pole and read them with the help of his cigarette lighter.

Dugan and Pfeffer circled around Villedieu-les-Poêles and reached the division CP. Securing armloads of maps, they hopped back into their jeep and, with Dugan again riding shotgun, ran the inky gauntlet back to the CP of General Doyle Hickey's Combat Command-A, arriving at 4:00 A.M. The field was virtually empty. The CP had pulled out, leaving behind a lone half-track. Using its radio, Major Dugan put in a call for the missing CP, wherever it might be. Inquiring as to its current location, Dugan received only a whispered reply: "Message received."

Dugan was furious. He called again. The same hushed reply: "Message received." Only later would he learn the reason for this curious behavior—a German tank and crew were parked on the other side of the hedgerow and the CP group was keeping as quiet as possible.

AT WOLFSSCHANZE ON the afternoon of July 30, General Alfred Jodl wrote in his diary: "I have advised the Führer of the imminent fall of Avranches. He reacted favorably to the idea for the eventual withdrawal [of the German army] from France."

Next Jodl called General Blumentritt, von Kluge's chief of staff, at St.-Germain, outside Paris. In guarded terms, Hitler's confidant told Blumentritt to be ready to receive an order for the pullback from France. General Walther Warlimont of the Oberkommando der Wehrmacht had been designated as liaison with von Kluge's headquarters for the mass withdrawal.

Warlimont hastily prepared to depart for Paris. But as he was ready to leave, Warlimont was summoned by the Führer who snapped, "Tell Feldmarschall von Kluge that his job is to look forward to the enemy, not backward!"

Hitler had changed his mind. A withdrawal was not to be undertaken. Instead, the Germans would counterattack and, with a little luck, inflict a major disaster upon the Americans in Normandy.

A German
Disaster
Takes Shape

8

Avranches: Indian Country Outpost

AVRANCHES ON SUNDAY morning, July 30, was a curious mixture of German soldiers—weary, ragged, and demoralized—rubbing shoulders with frightened townsfolk trying to go about their religious obligations as though unaware that a man-made tidal wave of steel and explosives was rushing toward them from the north. A long Wehrmacht convoy rumbled into town from the east, its trucks jammed with Feldgrau casting furtive glances into the sky for the appearance of the feared Jabos. Little girls in white veils and scrubbed boys in their best clothes filed through the battered streets on the way to First Communion. Church bells tolled from towers covered with the grime of centuries. Here and there a German soldier would knock on a door and ask for a drink of water; he and his comrades had been marching for nearly twenty-four hours straight, all the way from north of Granville. If the French family proved friendly, he would reach into his billfold and show them a soiled picture of his wife and small child back in the Fatherland.

In Avranches and in hamlets around its fringes, an occasional shell screamed in. Only the trained ear knew if it was American or German. There seemed to be no particular target. In war, men simply had to shoot guns. Early that morning, twelve worshippers in the little church of Ponts-sous-Avranches heard the frightening approach of a large-caliber shell. Moments later there was an enormous, deafening explosion. As the little Catholic congregation cringed, the women wailing and children screaming, the roof caved

117

in. A "Miracle of Avranches" had occurred. Not a single worshipper was injured.

Avranches had been virtually a pile of rubble since it was bombed heavily June 7, the day after D-Day. Rubble littered the streets in the center of town, and nearly 1,600 houses had been destroyed or rendered uninhabitable. Stunned townsfolk had neither the means nor the dedication to try to clean up the mess. "What's the use?" was the attitude of these hapless civilian pawns of war.

BY THE THIRTIETH, the battle picture at the base of the Cotentin Peninsula seemed a confused jumble to American and German commanders alike. A gigantic free-for-all raged. General Bradley, due to the fluid situation, was out of touch with his rampaging armored spearheads. Often he did not know where they were. His battle maps were marked on the basis of reports from American reconnaissance pilots—if a village had broken out with the tricolored French flag, Bradley knew his spearheads had reached or passed that point.

The Americans had done more than break out of the *bocage* by sheer weight of numbers and firepower. Their "broken-field runners"—the tank-infantry task forces—had knocked the Germans off balance, had chewed up the best part of six German divisions, and had at least two others fleeing for their lives. American tanks in large numbers were on the loose in France for the first time.

Over Radio Berlin that morning, a voice with a tinge of apprehension told the Herrenvolk: *"The Americans in Normandy have launched at least two thousand tanks against the heroic German forces who are fighting desperately."**

Except in the worst weather, American Thunderbolts and Mustangs were almost always over the spearheads, flying in half-hour shifts with two-way radio communication between tank commanders and pilots. Outside Gavray a column of 3rd Armored Division tanks was forced to a stop by German antitank guns. Vehicles clogged the road. Overhead, Lieutenant Leslie C. Boce was cruising in his Thunderbolt when he heard the voice of the tank commander down below: *"Won't some of you people come and help, goddamn it? Everybody gets air support but me."*

---

*The Americans employed about 600 tanks in the breakthrough, although more were coming in at Cherbourg.

Lieutenant Boce replied: "I'm on my way!"

Minutes later, spotting a Thunderbolt overhead, the tank commander called out over his radio, "Is that you above me?"

"Yes, what can I do for you?"

"There's some Kraut guns on my right. They've been holding up my column."

"Okay, I see them. We'll take care of the bastards."

Boce and his flight of Thunderbolts peeled off one by one and pounced onto the enemy guns, loosing 500-pounders, and returning to strafe the position. Then the air corps lieutenant called the tank commander: "How are we doing?"

"Great!" was the enthusiastic reply. "We're already moving forward!"

Not far away, a ponderous German Tiger tank, its 88-millimeter guns belching defiantly, was holding up another American tank column. Above, the leader of a Thunderbolt flight called the tank commander: "There's a Tiger 75 yards down the road firing on your leading elements."

"We know. Can you help?"

"Affirmative. But the Tiger is too close to you to bomb. We'll strafe the bastard."

Minutes later the Thunderbolt called the Sherman: "Bombed the Tiger. Didn't get direct hit but three near-misses. He is stopped cockeyed in the road. Try and proceed and we'll observe your progress."

"All quiet. Well done, pal!" the tank commander responded. The advancing column found the Tiger helpless on its side in a ditch, the crew having scrambled to the rear.

THREE MILES NORTH of Avranches early in the morning of July 30, SS General Paul Hausser, commander of Seventh Army; his chief of staff, Major General Rudolf-Christoph Freiherr von Gusdorf; together with the rest of the staff, were holding a battle conference in an old farmhouse 200 yards from a north-south road. A faint rumble, which later became a roar, was heard in the distance toward Granville. Apparently a German tank column was moving southward. An officer casually strolled to a window and was startled: the armored vehicles rolling by did not have the black-cross markings of the Wehrmacht, but the white-star insignia of the Americans. Rolling toward Avranches was the spearhead of Brigadier General

Holmes E. Dager's Combat Command-B of the 4th Armored Division, totally unaware that only 200 yards to one side of the road were congregated the top brass of the German Seventh Army.

Believing that they were the target of an armored assault, generals Hausser and von Gusdorf and their aides scrambled out the door. They were at once puzzled and relieved to see the Shermans roaring on past toward the south. Down on all fours, the German command group edged up to the road, then a few at a time dashed across it between serials of Dager's combat command. Later the disheveled German escapees commandeered vehicles and drove to Mortain.

Later that morning, a company of Wood's 4th Armored Division tanks arrived at the northern outskirts of Avranches. Finding no opposition, they clanked up the hill leading to the town on the bluffs and reached the center of Avranches. Soon German columns, in disarray but fully armed and capable of putting up a fight, started pouring into Avranches from the east. The commander of the handful of American tanks pulled back out of town to the north.

The Germans in the battered, muddy panzers, each camouflaged with branches from apple trees, had no intention of halting at Avranches, and kept going through the town and down the road on the other side with its winding curves and steep descent. Air reconnaissance reported seeing French civilians out in the road around Avranches, waving the tricolor furiously, a sure sign that the *Boche* (Germans) had gone on past. Troy Middleton, who commanded VIII Corps, rapidly contacted John Wood of the 4th Armored Division and Bob Grow of the 6th Armored.

"Avranches is there for the plucking," an excited Middleton bellowed, "Now turn on the heat!"

Holmes Dager's Combat Command-B of the 4th Armored Division revved tank motors and renewed the charge toward Avranches. Finding two bridges intact over the See River, Dager crossed and entered Avranches in strength. He promptly sent a small task force five miles east to secure a third bridge over the See at Tirepied. At the same time, Grow's 6th Armored Division was fast closing in on the ancient town overlooking the blue Bay of St.-Michel. The Gateway to Brittany was ajar, and the Americans had a firm grip on the latch.

In his plunge to Avranches, Dager and his tankers had far outdistanced supporting infantry whose job it was to mop up enemy forces bypassed by the armored spearheads. Fleeing Germans often drifted back in behind the advancing tanks, so at Avranches Dager had to place outposts around the fringes of the town facing north, east, and south, much in the manner of pioneers of the Old West circling wagon trains at night for protection against attack from any direction. General Dager's wagon train was secured on the west by the Atlantic Ocean. Avranches was an American outpost in Indian country.

One of Dager's tank companies was on guard at the See River bridge on the main coastal highway leading south from Granville and into Avranches, facing to the north. At 10:00 P.M., the rumble of a large convoy approaching from the direction of Granville reached the alert ears of the tankers. Probably American infantry catching up with the surging tanks, the men concluded. As the convoy drew near, creeping along in the darkness, the tankers could discern that the vehicles were German and had large red crosses on white backgrounds on each one. Obviously, the mercy vehicles were removing enemy wounded.

The first few trucks edged on past within a few yards of the watching Americans, crossed the bridge, and began moving into Avranches. A couple more vehicles advanced to the bridge. Suddenly, large numbers of troops leaped from the "Red Cross" vehicles and opened up withering bursts of small-arms fire at the startled Americans. Streams of tracers from Schmeisser automatic pistols laced the black sky. Bullets riccocheted off Sherman tanks, sending up fountains of fiery sparks. The 4th Armored men cut loose with their 75-millimeter guns, setting several German trucks ablaze and blocking the bridge. The enemy column ground to a halt. Confused Feldgrau back in the convoy leaped out of vehicles, tossed away weapons, and trotted toward the bridge with arms held high in surrender, their frightened faces ghostlike in the glare of the angry flames from the knocked-out trucks and panzers. Several hundred Germans were taken prisoners.

Probing into the red-cross-marked vehicles, Dager's tankers discovered that they were loaded with ammunition, guns, and other nonmedical supplies, in addition to the armed grenadiers.

Angry over the German ruse, the Americans roughly questioned the prisoners. From them it was learned that a larger, more heavily armed German convoy was coming down the coastal road from Granville.

Shortly after midnight, a high-velocity shell zipped into the American outpost at the bridge, announcing the arrival of the German column. The missile struck an ammunition truck and set it ablaze. The tank commander, his position illuminated by the light of the burning truck, without infantry support and his men outnumbered by sullen prisoners, reached an instant decision: he would pull out. Leaving behind several hundred German POWs and an unguarded bridge, the American tank company clanked off into the night.

Pouring over the river span in considerable numbers, the German force set up artillery pieces on a bluff in the northwest portion of Avranches from which point it could fire on the See River bridge and the Granville-Avranches road. Part of the enemy convoy pushed on through the blacked-out center of town toward the southern exits, where they bumped into armored infantrymen of Dager's CC-B, who were guarding that section of the American "wagon train."

The collision in the darkness took both Americans and Germans by surprise. Both adversaries soon recovered from the initial shock and an intense firefight erupted. Private William H. Whitson of CC-B jumped behind a .30-caliber machine gun and began pouring heavy bursts of fire into the German ranks. Soon enemy bodies began piling up before his smoking barrel, and several vehicles caught fire when he sent volleys into them. Whitson was in an exposed position, but refused to seek cover. With daylight nearing, the German force pulled back, and a strange calm settled over the landscape in south Avranches. Comrades looked at Bill Whitson's body slumped over his machine gun, a bullet hole through the head. Fifty dead Germans were found in front of his automatic weapon, and he had destroyed nineteen vehicles.

AT DAWN, COMBAT Command-A of the 4th Armored Division, led by hulking, gray-haired Colonel Bruce C. Clarke, was clattering southward along the road from Granville and reached the unguarded bridge over the See that had been abandoned a few hours before by a jittery tank company. Avranches was said to have been secured, so Clarke and his men presumed they were merely on a road march. Moments later there was a hissing sound followed by an explosion in front of Clarke's lead tank. Then another, and another. The tankers hurriedly buttoned up and pulled off the road.

Colonel Clarke and other commanders soon spotted their tormentors: the German high-velocity guns that had set up on the bluffs in northwest Avranches during the hours of darkness. Clarke quickly deployed his infantrymen, who waded across the See, scaled the bluff, and killed or captured the enemy gun crews.

With the German forces in western Normandy in total disarray, Field Marshal von Kluge knew there was only one way to halt the rampaging Americans—but only if Avranches and the crucial bridge over the Selune River at Pontaubault four miles to the south were in German hands. Five roads from the east and north funneled traffic into Avranches, where the roads were compressed into one main highway leading over the Pontaubault span. This could be an Allied bottleneck, but the Germans would have to locate the muscle to force the cork into it.

Von Kluge was able to find only one battle formation upon which he could call. Colonel Rudolf Bacherer's 77th Infantry Division had been badly chewed up earlier in the savage hedgerow fighting, and had been moved to an area west of Pontaubault for rest. The 77th was a division in name only: its strength was little more than a battalion. In the desperate situation in Normandy, with the Americans threatening to spill out into Brittany and over France, the Wehrmacht's hope for a battlefield miracle would rest on the shoulders of Colonel Bacherer and his men.

It was nearly midnight on the thirtieth when an urgent signal was received at Bacherer's headquarters from his immediate superior, General of Artillery Wilhelm Fahrmbacher, commander in Brittany. A grim-faced staff officer handed the message to Colonel Bacherer, a bold and resolute leader, who read it with disbelief:

"Avranches is to be taken and held at all costs. It is the keystone of our defense. On it hinges the decision in the West."

A pin could be heard dropping in Bacherer's CP as the 77th Division commander tossed the signal onto his desk without comment. All present realized the absurdity of the order: the outcome of the struggle for Normandy, and perhaps for all of France, had narrowed to a focus upon one bridge, a single road, and the battered remnants of one division.

It was not in Colonel Bacherer's makeup to dispute an order, no matter how bizarre it might be. He promptly scraped together every man and gun he could lay his hands on, including several decimated units of the 5th Parachute Division and 14 self-propelled guns belonging to another formation. Bacherer established checkpoints and collared each straggler or roaming group that wandered in. With this hodgepodge collection, Colonel Bacherer jumped off at dawn of July 31, quickly lunged through Pontaubault and over its suddenly crucial bridge, and struck at the southern outskirts of Avranches.

The weather was ideal for the Feldgrau—gray, low clouds, and drizzle. Not a single Jabo was overhead. The grenadiers, supported by the fourteen self-propelled guns, fought their way into Avranches, and for a time it appeared that Bacherer might pull off the impossible—driving the powerful American force out of the key town.

At noon the skies cleared. Germans, battling from house to house, started casting anxious glances into the sky. Soon cries rang out: "Jabos! Jabos!" Like gigantic vultures the Thunderbolts and Mustangs pounced on the self-propelled guns, and in less than an hour all 14 were reduced to junk, their crews sprawled about them in death. American Shermans rumbled forward and poured direct fire into the German infantrymen, and soon Bacherer's battle group scattered back out of Avranches to the south and west, with American fighter-bombers nipping at their heels every step of the way. Under a hail of American tank, artillery and mortar fire, and relentless pounding from the air, Kampfgruppe (battle group) Bacherer disintegrated.

Bacherer, now reduced to commanding a few ragtag platoons, refused to quit. There was still the bottleneck at Pontaubault. In the faces of the onrushing Shermans, he would try to blow up the only bridge leading into Brittany. In the meantime, a task force of Colonel Clarke's Combat Command-A of the 4th Armored Division had descended the winding road leading south out of Avranches and was racing for the crucial Pontaubault bridge.

As Bacherer's first demolition team approached the bridge, it was met with a hail of fire that cut down several Germans and forced the remainder to scatter. Bacherer sent another team to blow up the bridge. It was ambushed and all its members were taken prisoner. Clarke's tankers raced on over the Selune River bridge.

At dusk several Shermans were approaching Colonel Bacherer's battle command post. The 77th Infantry Division commander slipped off into the darkness on foot down a sunken lane with the remnants of his unit—a lieutenant and two privates.

PRISONERS-OF-WAR CAGES IN Middleton's VIII Corps were overflowing. In the scattered fighting around Avranches, 8,314 Germans had
been bagged—the largest number ever taken by an American corps
in two days. As bedraggled, weary German POWs streamed into
Middleton's positions, the corps leader told his commanders that the
flood of prisoners must not hamper the advance. "Send them to the
rear disarmed and without guards," General Middleton directed.
"And keep going!"

LATE IN THE morning of the thirty-first, Field Marshal von Kluge was
on the telephone from Hausser's Seventh Army command post at Le
Mans to General Blumentritt, von Kluge's chief of staff at OB-West
in St.-Germain outside Paris. "It's a madhouse here!" von Kluge
declared. "You can't imagine what it's like. Commanders are completely out of contact with their troops. Jodl and Warlimont
(Hitler's top advisors at Wolfsschanze) ought to come down to see
what is taking place."

Outlining the situation, the field marshal added, "So far, it
appears that only the spearheads of various [American] mobile units
are through to Avranches. But it is perfectly clear that everything else
will follow. Unless I can get infantry and antitank weapons there,
[we] cannot hold."

There was a moment of silence. Then Blumentritt stated, "[Wolfs-
schanze] wants to know the locations of the alternate and rearward
defenses under construction in Normandy."

Von Kluge could not conceal his anger and frustration. "All you
can do is laugh out loud," he declared in a derisive tone. "Don't they
read our dispatches? Haven't they been oriented? They"—meaning
Hitler—"must be living on the moon!" When criticizing the Führer,
it was always prudent to use the expression "they."

"Of course, of course," Blumentritt replied soothingly.

As though suddenly struck with divine guidance, von Kluge
exclaimed, "Someone has to tell the Führer that if the Americans get
through at Avranches they will be out of the woods and they'll be
able to do what they want." He added resignedly, "It's a crazy
situation!"

Meanwhile, knowing that the Germans were on the run, American commanders exhorted their infantrymen and tankers to continue to strike hard. On the evening of the thirty-first, General
Tubby Barton, leader of the 4th Infantry Division, which had suf-

fered enormous casualties in nearly ceaseless fighting since assaulting Utah Beach on D-Day, gathered his unit commanders together at his CP. "We face a defeated enemy," Barton declared, "an enemy terribly low on morale, terribly confused. I want you in the next advance to throw caution to the winds . . . destroying, capturing, or bypassing the enemy and pressing"—he paused to find the appropriate word—"pressing recklessly on to the objective."

That same afternoon, Colonel Chubby Doan, the hard-driving leader of the 3rd Armored Division's Task Force X, was riding at the head of his column when it rumbled into Brécey, a small town eight miles northeast of Avranches in General Joe Collins's VII Corps zone. So swift had been Doan's advance and so disorganized were German communications that almost a company of Feldgrau were casually lounging along the curb of Brécey's main street, idly talking and taking slugs of Calvados and wine. At the sight of the American tank column, the Germans leaped for their weapons. Colonel Doan began blasting away with his carbine and pistol, and gunfire erupted from the entire American column. Those Germans not killed or wounded soon scattered, and others surrendered.

Collins had spent the day at the battle CP of General Hickey's Combat Command-A, where he received word that Task Force X had secured Brécey and was preparing to coil up for the night to rest the exhausted tankers.

"Tell Doan to continue the attack across the See River and seize the ridge overlooking it," Collins instructed Hickey. The See was two miles south of Brécey.

When Colonel Doan's leading elements reached the river, the bridge was out. The task force commander, after testing the depth of the See, ordered foot soldiers moving up to carry rocks, there were plenty of them along the road, and dump them into the river to make a ford so that vehicles could cross. By now nightfall had arrived, but it was crystal clear and Task Force X pushed ahead until it had seized a ridge above the crossing.

Lieutenant Colonel Carlton Russell, leader of the 3rd Battalion of the 36th Armored Infantry in Doan's force, learned that part of his command had been cut off in Brécey, possibly missing a sharp turn in the town. Russell hopped into his jeep with a driver, along with the captain of an artillery battery that also had not arrived, and set out for Brécey to find the missing elements. Looking down a long hill into the square in the center of the town, Russell and his companions were startled to see several vehicles ablaze and artillery shells exploding.

Brécey had been cleared earlier by Task Force X, so the three Americans were puzzled over what could be taking place there. They left the jeep and walked toward the town. As they drew closer, Russell and his companions could see that the burning vehicles were American jeeps and that several soldiers were laboring frantically to put out the fires. Russell noted that one man was wearing a camouflaged outfit, the traditional field garb of the Wehrmacht. He walked up to the soldier and exclaimed, "You'd better pull off that camouflage suit, or someone's going to mistake you for a Kraut."

The soldier ceased beating at the flames and stood stone still. At that moment, by the light of the fire, Russell recognized the insignia on the man's collar: German insignia. The enemy had taken over the center of Brécey after Task Force X had passed through. All these men in the square were Germans. Russell quickly whipped out his Colt .45. Pantherlike, the German in the camouflaged garb leaped at Russell and with a savage swipe of his bolt-action rifle knocked the pistol from the American's hand. A sharp, searing pain surged up Russell's arm.

The colonel, now unarmed, pounced on the German and threw him to the cobbled square. Grunts and groans filled the night air as the two men wrestled for the German's rifle. Russell wrested it away. The two adversaries were so close that Russell could not shoot his foe, so he grabbed the rifle by the barrel and crashed the butt against the grenadier's head, knocking him cold.

Now several other Germans around the square began shooting at Colonel Russell, and he fired back with the enemy's rifle. He shot three of them. A bullet smashed the stock of the German rifle, but by that time Russell was out of ammunition. There was only one course of tactical action remaining—haul out of there as fast as his legs would carry him.

In the meantime, Russell's driver and the artillery captain, one with a tommy gun and the other with a carbine, had been blasting away at the shadowy figures around the square. Those Americans, too, were nearly out of ammunition. Each had managed to pick off one or more Germans. The artillery captain had been struck across the bridge of the nose by a bullet, and blood was spurting out from the wound. "Shavey," Russell's driver, escaped unscathed.

Several days previously, Russell had ripped a long tear in his trousers, and his white long johns showed through. Lying in firing position in the darkness, with the firefight at its height, Shavey and the artillery captain saw a shadowy figure ambling by. "Come on," the jeep driver called out, leaping to his feet, "it's the colonel." He had recognized Russell by the exposed strip of long johns.

The three men hightailed it out of town and to the top of the hill where they had left their jeep. There they spotted several American antitank guns and crews.

"Turn your guns around and start shooting into the square down there," Colonel Russell ordered. "You won't have to worry about who you hit—it's filled with Krauts!"

Back at the See River with the rest of Task Force X, Russell contacted his cut-off units by radio: "Get through Brecey the best way you can," he told them. "And join up with us as soon as you can. We're moving forward!"

9

Explosion
into Brittany

AS KAMPFGRUPPE BACHERER'S vehicles were burning brightly on the southern fringes of Avranches late in the afternoon of July
31, symbolic funeral pyres for the tattered remnants of the once
proud German Seventh Army, virtual pandemonium erupted in the
ancient town on the bluffs. Frenzied townsfolk lined both side of the
Rue de la Constitution, furiously waving tiny French flags and
tossing flowers and unrestrained cheers at the passing parade of
clanking American tanks and weary foot soldiers. The Rue de la
Constitution was the main artery leading through Avranches and on
to Pontaubault. Up ahead, American bulldozers were noisily shoving aside huge piles of debris that engulfed the street, hacking out a
path wide enough for convoys and long columns of infantry to pass
through.

The bulldozer was new to the wide-eyed French citizens—and it
fascinated them. They wondered about its name. Soon the word
boulldozere swept through the crowd. An elderly native with a
handlebar mustache and wearing a black beret, a cigarette dangling
from a corner of his mouth, edged up to an American officer and
inquired in broken English: "Pardon, sir, me, but where the bulls
this machine it is to doze?"

The column waiting to advance through the cleared channel
backed up for miles, northward past the See River bridges. Sherman
tanks, trucks loaded with supplies and ammunition, jeeps, half-
tracks, command cars, masses of artillery, tank-retrievers, cranes, and
long trailers carrying bridge-building equipment.

Flushed with excitement, natives rushed up to the passing Americans and pressed "money" into their dirty, perspiring hands—worthless German occupation currency removed from the pockets of dead Feldgrau sprawled about Avranches.

Earlier on the thirty-first, General Patton, known as Georgie to his staff, was winding up affairs at his Nehou CP, where he had fretted and anguished for more than three weeks. He strode briskly into the operations tent, wearing what his aides called Frown Number 3. Puffing on a long, black cigar, Patton listened silently to briefing by G-2 (intelligence) and G-3 (operations) officers. Then he rose to speak.

"Gentlemen, Third Army is scheduled to become officially operational at 1200 [noon] on August 1. . . . Doubtless from time to time there will be complaints that we are pushing people too hard. I don't give a good goddamn about such complaints . . . The harder we push, the more Germans we will kill [and] the fewer of our men will be killed."

Patton paused briefly to allow those words to be absorbed, then added, "Forget this goddamned business of worry about our [open] flanks. Let the goddamned German worry about *his* flanks . . . Some goddamned fool once said that flanks must be secured, and since then sons of bitches all over the world have been going crazy guarding their flanks."

Looking around at each staff aide, Patton concluded, *"L'audace, l'audace, toujours l'audace!* Remember that, gentlemen. From here on out, until we win—or die in the attempt—we will always be audacious!"

The Third Army commander leaped into his jeep, the three stars of his rank on red metal pendants on front and back of the vehicle, a steamship horn that could be heard for miles on the passenger side; he sped along roads lined with blackened German vehicles and other debris of war to the battle headquarters of Troy Middleton. There Patton paced about, smoking one cigar after the other, fretting because no word had been heard recently from his spearheads at Avranches.

"Goddamn it," Patton finally exploded. "Did Dager say anything about those two goddamned dams over the Selune?"

Told that he had not, Patton grumbled and resumed stomping around the operations tent.

Bradley had brushed off Patton's request for American paratroopers to jump and blow up the Selune dams. Pete Quesada, the fighter-bomber chief in Normandy, had deftly sidestepped a request to bomb the dams. These two water barriers were crucial to Third Army's advance. If the Germans were to destroy the dams in front of Patton's spearheads the entire region would be flooded for a week, forcing American tanks to sit idle until the water receded.

At 10:10 P.M., a message arrived from General Dager at Avranches: "Have just captured two dams on Selune River."

It was almost at the precise minute that The Professor, General John Wood, the dashing cavalryman commanding 4th Armored Division, called up excitedly. "Clarke has crossed Pontaubault bridge. It's hardly damaged. We're pouring on over. A few Kraut vehicles are in sight, but we're blowing hell out of them!"

"Hot damn!" Patton exclaimed, slapping his thigh in glee. "The road to Brest is wide open—tonight!" Brest was 200 miles west of Pontaubault.

Like Napoleon, the Third Army commander had always maintained that "war is really a very simple thing: you find some son of a bitch you outrank and tell him to go kick hell out of the enemy."

Patton immediately sat down with Middleton and proceeded to prove that "war is really a very simple thing." In a short time they had worked out a Brittany campaign: Wood's 4th Armored would dash for Rennes, Grow's 6th Armored would rush the 200 miles to the key port of Brest, the 5th Armored Division would race to Fougères, and the 79th Infantry Division would take out for nearby Mont-St.-Michel, the fairy-storylike conical monastery perched on a huge rock overlooking the Bay of St.-Michel and Avranches, a shimmering mass of battered houses eight miles in the distance.

A wide grin on his face, Patton stalked off to bed. Tomorrow would be a big day for Third Army—and for George Patton.

As the Third Army commander removed his boots and climbed onto an army cot at about midnight on July 31, hundreds of miles to the east at Wolfsschanze Adolf Hitler was lecturing stone-faced staff officers, including Field Marshal Keitel and generals Jodl and War-limont. Only eleven days previously, Hitler had miraculously escaped death in the Schwarze Kapelle bomb plot. Now, possibly due to the shattering of his spirit and soul, the Führer was seeing stark reality, the dire threat to the Third Reich itself in the form of racing American tank spearheads at Brécey and at Avranches.

Hitler now considered France, not Russia, as the *Schwergewicht* (focus) of the entire war. He lectured his subordinates for more than an hour. If France were lost, he told them, "we forfeit the starting point of the U-boat war, and in addition, we are getting many things from France that are vital to our war effort."

The Führer said that "we must place this [halting the Allies in Normandy] at the head of all our considerations. We have reached *ein gewisser Höhepunkt der Krise* [an undoubted climax of the crisis]."

As was customary during the Führer's lectures, the assembled generals were permitted to insert only occasional monosyllabic remarks. Even though a shadow of his former vibrant self, Hitler remained firmly in charge, issuing orders and directives, cowing his military leaders.

IT WAS 10:26 P.M. when Field Marshal von Kluge, at improvised headquarters of Seventh Army outside Le Mans, received a phone call from General Speidel, his chief of staff at Army Group-B at La Roche-Guyon. Speidel strongly urged von Kluge to transmit an order to General Dietrich von Choltitz, commander of LXXXIV Corps, who for two days had been out of touch with the remnants of his scattered fleeing troops. The order had just arrived from Wolfs-schanze. Von Choltitz was directed to hold positions north of Avranches at all costs, even if the corps were encircled, "so as to be in the best position to restore the situation." Von Kluge ignored the order: American spearheads had raced on past Avranches, and supporting infantry divisions were moving south of the old town on the bluffs.

The cagey Speidel had good reason for his urgent request to transmit the order, even though it was two days late and could not have been carried out had it been timely: in the wake of the bungled attempt to murder Hitler, nearly every Wehrmacht general was suspect as a plotter, and failure to transmit a direct order from the Führer could be taken as evidence of participation in a conspiracy to bring down the Nazi state.

ACROSS THE ENGLISH Channel at 10 Downing Street, the traditional home of Great Britain's prime ministers, Winston Churchill was playing dinner host to General Eisenhower. The Kansas farm boy, one time West Point football player, and amateur boxer with a knockout punch in either hand, had come a long way. His pacifist mother back in the Midwest was proud of Ike, even if he was engaged in a violent pursuit. Churchill, puffing thoughtfully on a long, black Havana cigar and idly fingering his champagne glass, was worried. The next day he was to address the House of Commons— but there was little momentous "British news" he could reveal. The Americans were making all the big black headlines, while General Montgomery and his 21st Army Group were still in position south of Caen, only some 12 miles inland from the D-Day landing beaches.

"Maybe I could tell them that [British Lieutenant General Frederick E.] Morgan was the 'father' of the Overlord plan, if you have no objections," Churchill observed.

"No objections whatsoever," the supreme commander replied congenially.

The clicking of champagne glasses could be heard far into the wee hours at staid old Number 10 Downing Street that night of July 31. The Normandy front had been cracked wide open, American spearheads were running wild, so spirits were high—in more ways than one.

While Joe Collins's and Troy Middleton's surging tankers and foot soldiers were generating worldwide headlines, some of the most vicious fighting of the Normandy campaign was raging on the left of the breakthrough. There, Major General Charles H. "Pete" Corlett's XIX Corps and Major General Leonard T. Gerow's V Corps had been assigned largely diversionary shows. It was up to them to pin down the Wehrmacht in the hedgerows in front of the major road center of Vire, to prevent von Kluge from shifting troops to confront the massive breakthrough at St.-Lô.

Corlett was especially bitter over his role in the scheme of things. He felt that his and Gerow's corpses had made Cobra possible by hacking their way through the hedgerows to capture the road hub of St.-Lô on July 18. As a "reward" for this tactical triumph, Corlett's and Gerow's troops were destined to fight and die outside of the heady glare of the spotlight, but they kept some of the finest battle formations in the German army off the backs of Collins and Middleton.

AUGUST 1 DAWNED hot and sultry. Along either side of a blacktopped road on the ridge south of Brécey, tankers and foot soldiers of

Colonel Chubby Doan's surging Task Force X were sleepily climbing out of hastily slit trenches and from under tanks, half-tracks, and jeep trailers. That night Doan had passed down a strict order: "No shooting unless we are attacked." The task force was deep in "Indian country" and did not want to tip off the enemy to its presence. It had only enough ammunition and supplies for one full-fledged fight, and Doan wanted to conserve these. Within minutes of arising, the colonel was sorely tempted to violate his own edict: a long column of German grenadiers was spotted marching to the south only a few hundred yards away, a great target for the massed guns of the task force. But he resisted the temptation; his job was to knife on forward at full speed.

A short time later, some of Doan's men spotted a Volkswagen on a hill in the distance, carrying four Germans. "I want that Volkswagen!" the task force commander called out sharply. A patrol was hurriedly formed and set out to grab the vehicle, but it had vanished. Later Lieutenant Colonel Carlton Russell, the infantry battalion commander who had had the hand-to-hand fight in Brécey's square the previous night, was walking across the bivouac road when he heard a vehicle, looked up, and saw the same Volkswagen racing toward him. He whipped a rifle off his shoulder, aimed it at the approaching car, and to his surprise it stopped. Four Germans in the vehicle threw hands into the air, as now several other Americans had leaped into the road and were leveling their weapons menacingly. Chubby Doan had his Volkswagen.

Russell's first order of business was to relieve the driver of his Luger pistol. Turnabout is fair play, the battalion commander was thinking. The night before, a German in the Brécey square had caused him to lose his Colt .45.

Minutes later a German motorcyclist barreled along the road and into the Task Force X bivouac area. He was promptly collared. The cyclist was a messenger, and in a pouch were orders for a German division to move into that same area in which Doan and his men were bivouacked. These vital orders had to be rushed to 3rd Armored Division headquarters, somewhere to the rear. Doan loaded a half-track with a squad of heavily armed men, lined the outside with German prisoners whom the task force had been hauling (to discourage enemy ambushes), and sent the tracked vehicle back through the fluid lines with the captured enemy orders.

Some ten miles west of Doan's Task Force X, a deafening roar, which began the previous afternoon, still hovered over the ruins of Avranches. Tanks, trucks, and other vehicles were pouring through the old town, heading for the crucial bridge at Pontaubault. Along the four-mile stretch between Avrances and Pontaubault, rolling stock was bumper to bumper. Traffic snarls developed. Curses rang out. Horns blared. Threats were shouted. On occasion, officers with drawn pistols leaped into a dispute to untangle jams.

At intersections, white-gloved MPs perspired, cursed, pleaded, cajoled, and threatened, as they furiously waved the deluge of vehicles forward along the narrow road. Ack-ack guns lined the entire four miles to the bridge over the Selune River. Overhead, flights of Thunderbolts and Mustangs, as well as a few twin-boomed Lightnings, roamed back and forth, keeping a sharp eye out for the Luftwaffe, which until now had darted in only for occasional nuisance raids.

To Americans and Germans alike, this was the most significant four-mile stretch of road in France. The uproar would continue for seventy-two hours, and the stream of traffic would surge onward. General Patton was trying to achieve the impossible: pass seven divisions—with more than 100,000 men and thousands of vehicles, plus all their supplies, guns, and equipment—along this single narrow road through Avranches and on over the bridge at Pontaubault in only three days.

"It can't be done!" logistics officers had told Patton.

"By God, it will be done!" he had shouted back.

L'audace, l'audace, tourjours l'audace! But Georgie Patton was not foolhardy. He realized that this tactic was highly unorthodox and fraught with peril. Third Army's boundaries, narrow, hemmed in by the ocean, were crammed with troops and vehicles. The maneuver could become a disaster if a monumental traffic jam developed and the Germans suddenly pounced upon him and his men in this gigantic sardine can. For three days Patton himself, his corps and division commanders, and top staff officers were posted at key points along the four miles of vital road. For seventy-two hours this group of American brass would play the role of traffic cops.

At Wolfsschanze in East Prussia that first day of August, Adolf Hitler continued to focus on Normandy. He fired off a message to Field Marshal von Kluge that he, the Führer, was taking over day-today command in the West. Von Kluge tossed the signal aside in a curious mixture of exasperation and laughter: Hitler had been calling all the shots since before the Allies landed on D-Day.

At Station X, the home of Ultra in Bletchley Park outside London, the message was decoded with great glee. What better bonanza could the Allies hope for than to have Hitler take operational control from his skilled professionals?

Later that morning Ultra intercepted several other top secret messages from the Führer to his commanders in France, signals that had a tone of desperation. "If withdrawal is ordered, all railways, locomotives, bridges, and workshops are to be destroyed," one of the messages read. This suited Allied commanders fine: for months Anglo-American air forces had been working toward the same end. Hitler also ordered commanders of fortress ports to "fight to the last man and last bullet to deny the ports to the Allies." Long before D-Day, the Führer had specified the key ports that were to be fortified in Brittany, Normandy, and elsewhere along the French coast; he designated them as fortresses.

That day, August 1, Omar Bradley leaped up another notch in the command structure to take control of the new 12th Army Group. Under him would be Patton's Third Army, which became operational the same time, and the First Army, whose reins would be turned over to Lieutenant General Courtney Hodges, who had been serving as deputy to Bradley. Nearly 400,000 men, organized into 21 combat divisions plus service troops, would be under General Bradley's 12th Army Group—the largest and most powerful force ever assembled under a field commander in the United States Army. Initial headquarters of 12th Army Group was at Coutances, the first major objective of Cobra.

Courtney Hodges had much in common with George Patton. Both were several years older than their bosses, Eisenhower and Bradley. Both had entered West Point at the same time (1904), and both had scholastic troubles. Hodges flunked out because of deficiencies in mathematics, enlisted in the army as a private, and received his commission as a second lieutenant a year after his West Point class graduated. Patton also had encountered academic difficulties, but was permitted to take his plebe year again. He received his commission in 1909, at the same time as Hodges. Both men served with General John J. "Black Jack" Pershing in the expedition into Mexico, and both were battalion commanders in France in World War I—Hodges in infantry, Patton in the new tank corps—and each was decorated with the Distinguished Service Cross.

There the similarity between Hodges of First Army and Patton of Third Army stopped. Courtney Hodges was as soft-spoken, reserved, and indifferent to public recognition as Patton was loud, profane, flamboyant, and eager for the glare of the spotlight.

ALL MORNING ON August 1, General Patton had been casting anxious glances at his watch. He was in a hurry for twelve noon to arrive. At his CP near Granville, only an aide, Colonel Paul D. Harkins, was present to help celebrate the birth of Third Army: all the other brass were serving as traffic cops along the crucial stretch of road between Avranches and the bridge at Pontaubault. Precisely at noon, Harkins broke out a bottle he had been saving for the occasion and passed it to Patton. The new commanding general of Third Army took a long pull—and gagged. He rolled out his heaviest vocabularly of invectives to describe the bottle of "alleged brandy."

The structural changes in command held one serious deficiency, most American generals agreed. Bernard Montgomery, the methodical commander of the British 21st Army Group, would continue in control of all Allied ground forces until September 1, at which time General Eisenhower would assume that role.

Organizational revamping in the stratosphere of the American army in Normandy had no immediate bearing on those carrying the ultimate burden, the infantrymen and tankers. Few would be aware of the new command setup. Fewer would care. War in all its drudgery and horror would continue unabated for those in the forefront of the fighting. Since Cobra was launched one week before, they had been fighting day and night. Always the order was the same: push ahead and keep on pushing . . . push . . . push . . . push! They stole a few winks when and where they could, in ditches, slit trenches, snuggled up to hedgerows, the bed of a truck, inside a stifling hot tank. Constant exhaustion was the norm. One company commander fell asleep standing up, talking on a field telephone.

They were shelled, mortared, machine-gunned, and ambushed. Fiendish mines were everywhere, mines capable of blowing a man into powder, knocking the treads off a tank, or killing its whole crew. There was no time to use mine detectors on a road or a field.

Mines were discovered by driving or walking over them. There were casualties, many casualties. But the spearheads pushed on. The psychological impact created by German mines was enormous. One had to be extremely watchful, knowing that each man's step, the turn of a vehicle wheel, or crunch of a tank tread might be the last one. It was the knowledge that this sudden peril was always possible that got a man.

The tanker could carry a few personal items, but the infantryman had no blankets against the cool Normandy nights. He left behind all extra clothes except his raincoat, which frequently leaked. In his pockets he might have a toothbrush and a razor. The articles did him no good: there was no time for shaving or washing. Some fighting men in the forefront carried their money, others gave it to friends in the rear to keep. Still others had no money. It didn't matter. There was nothing to buy, nor time to buy it. Always it was push ahead. The German is on the run; keep him on the run.

Hot meals did not exist. Some men carried D-ration chocolate. Cold C-rations were brought through Indian country in jeeps, if the jeeps weren't ambushed. The men had to eat their cold food in the dark, unable to see the can from which they were eating. They simply ate by feel. They made cold coffee from cold water. In territory shared with marauding bands of armed Germans, fires were out of the question. Even in the daytime, smoke from a cooking fire could attract an alert enemy eye.

Fear was a constant companion of the fighting man in the vanguard. Some concealed it better than others. But there was a fear among most that was even more profound than that of being killed or mutilated: the fear of discrediting oneself in the eyes of one's comrades during battle. That, to many, was the greatest fear of all.

Lurking incessantly in the back of the fighting man's mind was one overriding thought. It flooded his waking senses, haunted his sleep. He tried to force it from his consciousness, but it refused to depart. The infantryman and the tanker knew that they were fugitives from the law of averages, that their ultimate destiny would be death or mutilation at some disputed barricade.

EARLY IN THE afternoon of August 1, General Jodl was on the phone from Wolfsschanze to OB-West at St.-Germain outside Paris. "The Führer is aware of the movement of American armies," Jodl intoned.

"He thinks it would be excellent to let as many troops as possible pass through the Avranches bottleneck before we cut them off at that point. In that way we shall take far more in our trap."

General Blumentritt, von Kluge's chief of staff who took the call, listened in stunned silence. "Take far more in our trap?" With what?

HITLER REMAINED CONVINCED that the Anglo-American alliance was a brittle one that would collapse if administered a sudden and disastrous defeat, and that Great Britain, already rocked for weeks by the V-1 bombardment of London and weary after nearly five years of war, would seek a political settlement. Then he could keep France as a base for his forthcoming long-range bombers that could pound New York, Washington, and other American cities, and send a frightened United States scurrying to the peace table.

Without consulting von Kluge, Dietrich, Hausser, or other battle leaders in France, Hitler had ordered plans to be drawn up by the OKW in Berlin and at Wolfsschanze for inflicting a disastrous defeat upon American armies in Normandy. Planning was carried out under the most intense security precautions in order to strike the Americans with total surprise.

The master stroke would hit at a place called Mortain. If all went well, Patton's Third Army would be cut off south of Avranches and wither on the vine, unable to obtain the supplies and ammunition it needed to continue to fight.

Meanwhile, the Mystery Man of Normandy, Patton, was dashing about the four-mile bottleneck between Avranches and Pontaubault like a man possessed, driving his men onward. "Brad simply wants a bridgehead [over the Pontaubault span]," Patton had confided that morning to his chief of staff, General Hugh Gaffey. "What *I* want and intend to get are Brest and Angers." Even Gaffey, aware of Patton's habit of setting objectives beyond the reach of the troops involved, was taken aback. Brest, the crown jewel of Brittany, was 200 miles west of Avranches. Angers, the historic capital of the Anjou, was nearly 100 miles to the south.

Patton was not acting rashly. He was adhering to his concept for success in battle—audacity. Through Ultra, the Third Army leader knew that the Germans had virtually denuded Brittany of combat elements in order to fight the invaders in Normandy after D-Day. Over the vast expanse of Brittany, the Wehrmacht had only 10 understrength battalions of infantry, four motley and unreliable *Ost* (East) battalions of former Red Army soldiers, and some 50,000 immobile noncombat naval, air, and service troops, most of them congregated around the ports. However, the elite German 2nd Parachute Division, under tough, skilled General Herman B. Ramcke (known to his young fighting men as "Pappa" Ramcke) was positioned around Brest and could cause Patton's spearheads a great deal of trouble.

THE SUN HAD just peeked over Normandy that first day of August when Bob Grow was roused from exhausted slumber and ordered to get his 6th Armored Division up and on the road. Push through Pontaubault and on to Dinan, Grow was told. The general promptly set to work drawing up plans for the movement. He would get his three combat commands through the Avranches-Pontaubault bottleneck before pushing onward.

Early in the afternoon, General Grow was directing traffic at a key road junction when he noticed a jeep halting nearby. Out jumped George Patton who raced up to Grow, his face flushed with excitement. "Bob, I've bet Monty five pounds we'd be in Brest by Saturday night!"

Startled, the 6th Armored commander quickly toted up the days. This was Tuesday. Saturday was only five days away. An armored division race through enemy-held territory without flank protection and reach Brest in only five days? Grow swallowed hard.

Sensing Grow's concerns, General Patton placed his hand on the armored leader's shoulder, looked him squarely in the eye, and said softly but firmly, "Take Brest, Bob."

Once the initial shock wore off, General Grow was elated. "We've received a cavalry mission from a real cavalryman," he exuded to his aides. A short time later, 6th Armored tanks were charging toward the tip of the Breton peninsula.

IN THE EARLY evening of August 1, the 4th Armored's Combat Command-A under hulking Colonel Bruce Clarke roared up to the northern outskirts of Rennes, forty miles southwest of Avranches and about midway between the north and the south shores of the Brittany Peninsula. A city of more than 80,000 citizens, once described as the "ugliest town in France," Rennes was the capital of

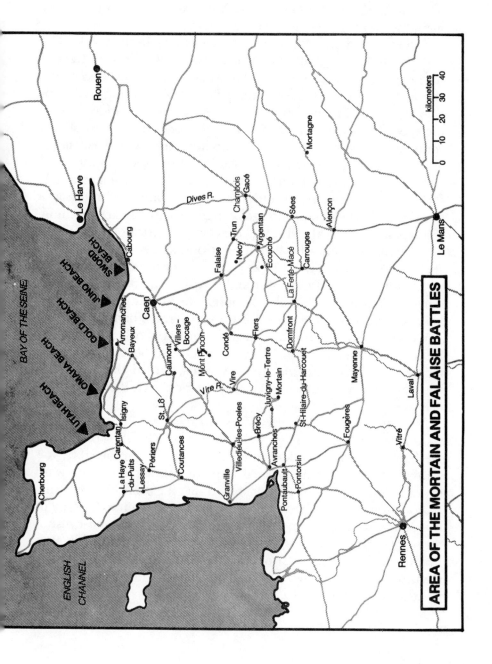

AREA OF THE MORTAIN AND FALAISE BATTLES

ENGLISH CHANNEL

BAY OF THE SEINE

UTAH BEACH
OMAHA BEACH
GOLD BEACH
JUNO BEACH
SWORD BEACH

Cherbourg
Le Harve
Rouen

L-a Haye
-du-Puits
Carentan
Isigny
Lessay
Périers
Coutances
Arromanches
Bayeux
Caumont
St. Lô
Cabourg
Caen
Villers–
Bocage
Mont Pinçon
Condé
Falaise
Nécy
Trun
Chambois
Gacé
Dives R.
Argentan
Sées
Mortagne
Écouché
La Ferté-Macé
Carrouges
Alençon
Le Mans
Granville
Villedieu-les-Poéles
Brécy
Vire
Vire R.
Flers
Juvigny-le-Tertre
Mortain
Domfront
St-Hilaire-du-Harcouet
Mayenne
Laval
Avranches
Pontaubault
Pontorsin
Fougères
Vitré
Rennes

kilometers
0 10 20 30 40

Brittany and the commercial center that linked the peninsula with the heart of France. Rennes was the hub of a road network, with ten main highways converging there.

Earlier that afternoon, lashed on by General John Wood, CC-A had rocketed out of Pontaubault and dashed all the way to Rennes. In 1940, the mighty German Wehrmacht had introduced to a shocked world a new type of warfare, *Blitzkrieg* (lightning war), and a young general named Erwin Rommel had gained wide fame for the speed with which he had led his armored divison through a confused French army. Now, four years later, John Wood had moved with even greater alacrity. Wood had out-Rommeled Rommel.

At Rennes, Bruce Clarke's combat command ground to a halt, stopped cold by two Luftwaffe companies manning 88-millimeter guns and 1,900 Feldgrau who had been rushed into the key communications center just ahead of the charging American tanks. Thirty Thunderbolts pounded German positions, and American artillery shelled the enemy. Then Clarke launched a full-scale assault, and bitter fighting raged until midnight. At that point the American tankers withdrew with a bloody nose. They had had eleven tanks knocked out. Rennes remained firmly in German hands.

Wood saw that he could not roll his armored columns through Rennes as he had at Avranches. So he left the stubborn defenders to be cleaned out by trailing infantry units, skirted the town, and dashed off toward Vannes and Quiberon, on the Gulf of Morbihan, 65 miles to the southwest.

At 3:00 P.M. General Bradley rolled up to George Patton's CP near Granville. The commander of the 12th Army Group was worried. He had just received information from an "unimpeachable, A-1 source" that Hitler had ordered a major counterattack westward toward Mortain and on to Avranches to cut off Patton's Third Army. Patton didn't inquire about the source, presuming it to be a spy in the German camp. Fearing Bradley would grow cautious because of the report, Patton made light of it. But just to be on the safe side, after Bradley had departed, Patton put in a call to his 90th Infantry Division. "Hurry on toward Avranches [from the north] and take up positions east of there," he ordered.

10

"Let's Talk Big Turkey!"

A SMALL TASK force of 97 officers and men of the U.S. Navy was weaving its way through Avranches and on over the bridge at Pontaubault on the morning of August 2. Commanded by Captain Norman S. Ives, who was in charge of the naval base at Cherbourg, the party was on its way to St.-Malo after hearing that the large port some 35 miles to the west of Pontaubault had fallen to American spearheads. Rolling through a hamlet only a few miles out of Pontaubau.t, Ives and his men were suddenly raked with machine-gun fire. Those not cut down promptly dropped to the ground. The report that St.-Malo had fallen was false.

Captain Ives, Lieutenant Commander Arthur M. Hooper, and four sailors were killed in the ambush; eight were wounded. Only lightly armed, the remainder of the naval group took cover and began returning the German fire. An hour later a roar of engines was heard to the rear of the sailors, and a platoon of tanks of the 6th Armored Division clattered up and opened fire. The German ambushers melted away in the direction of St.-Malo. It was there that a stiff-necked, resolute German commander of the port, Colonel Andreas von Aulock, was feverishly rushing preparations to hold St.-Malo to the last man and the last bullet, as the Führer had ordered.

Colonel von Aulock was disappointed in his designated role as a defender. He would have preferred to be gaining offensive victories for the Third Reich. Yet von Aulock would do his duty. A veteran of

Stalingrad, he had told his commanders as American tanks were barreling toward St.-Malo, "I was placed in command of this fortress. I did not request it. I will execute the orders I have received and, doing my duty as a soldier, I will fight to the last stone."

Von Aulock had always been puzzled by the attitude of the French civilians of St.-Malo. He had treated them fairly and correctly. Yet the natives regarded him as an enemy. When the Allies landed on D-Day he had warned the population, for their own welfare, to flee St.-Malo, which was certain to come under heavy siege. The French ignored the suggestion. Even after Anglo-American bombers pounded the old citadel on July 17 and again on August 1, the citizens stubbornly clung to their homes and to the rubble.

As General Bob Grow's armor was rumbling toward St.-Malo on early August 3, Colonel von Aulock called an urgent meeting of civilian leaders. Look, he said in effect, you're all nice people, but get out of town—immediately—because von Aulock would "rather have you in front of me than behind me." In addition, the German said firmly, he wanted to spare the civilian population avoidable deaths and suffering.

If Colonel von Aulock was so deeply concerned about St.-Malo and its citizens, then why didn't he declare the historic old port an open city and save it from destruction? the town pillars inquired.

Von Aulock replied that he had made such a suggestion to Field Marshal von Kluge and that the German commander in the West, now relegated to Hitler's errand boy in France, had bucked the request on upstairs to the Führer.

"In warfare, there is no such thing as an historic city," Hitler had replied. "You will fight to the last man."

It would be two more days before long lines of St.-Malo citizens, pushing pitiful belongings in carts and waving white flags, reluctantly departed their homes and moved into American positions outside the city.

THIRD ARMY'S EXPLOSION into Brittany was noted that second day of August at the highest levels on both sides. Early in the morning, General Dwight Eisenhower summoned his naval aide, Commander Harry Butcher, into his office. Butcher was greeted by a wide smile. "If Ultra is right, we are to hell-and-gone in Brittany and slicing 'em up in Normandy!" the supreme commander enthused.

At Wolfsschanze, Hitler growled about "that crazy cowboy Patton," who the Führer noted was "galloping along into Brittany with an entire army, not caring about open flanks or risks, as though he owned the entire world!"

EARLY THAT MORNING, August 2, a black Junkers transport plane glided in for a landing at the Strasbourg airport in eastern France. Out hopped forty-nine-year-old General Walther Warlimont, Hitler's emissary, who had flown directly from Wolfsschanze. In his briefcase was a voluminous document that, with favorable weather and a large dose of battlefield luck, would dramatically turn the tide against the surging Americans and alter the entire course of the war. It was the grand design for Operation *Luttich* (Liège) in which a minimum of four panzer divisions would attack westward at Mortain, push on to Avranches and the coast, and trap Patton's Third Army in Brittany. Luttich was Adolf Hitler's brainchild.

At Strasbourg, General Warlimont, bowing to the realities of the situation in France, switched to an armored car that took him to headquarters of OB-West at St.-Germain, outside Paris. Field Marshal von Kluge was at Seventh Army headquarters at Le Mans trying desperately to halt the massive American breakthrough, so Warlimont conferred with Guenther Blumentritt, von Kluge's chief of staff. Tall, amiable Blumentritt listened solemnly and without comment as Warlimont outlined Luttich.

The Führer's order is to reestablish the Avranches-St.-Lô front," Warlimont pointed out. "Our armor will mass on the Mortain hills for the jump-off." Speaking in grim tones, Hitler's courier warned Blumentritt, "Any withdrawal is forbidden. You will keep your eyes riveted ahead on the enemy."

General Blumentritt was stunned by the grandiose proposals in Luttich. Seldom did he raise his voice, but this time he was angry. The panzer operation was totally divorced from the realities of the Normandy and Brittany battlefields.

"We had 1,400 tanks on D-Day and have lost 750," the chief of staff snapped, his face flushed with anger and frustration. "Seventh Army has lost 160,000 killed, wounded, or taken prisoner out of the 450,000 men engaged since the invasion."

Blumentritt paused briefly as Warlimont glared in icy silence.

"You don't know the true situation," von Kluge's subordinate pointed out.

He might just as well have been talking to a stone statue. Warlimont declared, "My orders are to put you on guard against any retreat. You must hold with fanatical determination."

As Warlimont departed to see Field Marshal von Kluge to give him detailed instructions for Luttich, Blumentritt felt as though Hitler had just signed the death warrant for the German armed forces in France.

AT NOON ON August 2, General Bradley dropped into Troy Middleton's VIII Corps CP. He found the normally placid Middleton in a furious state. He was mad at his boss, Patton—plenty mad. The Third Army leader had ordered Middleton's spearheads to dash on south past Rennes and westward toward Brest, "leaving nothing between the extended columns and the main body of the German Seventh Army." Patton had ignored—misinterpreted, the old cavalryman called it—Bradley's specific orders to firm up the base of the Breton peninsula with infantry troops before pushing on deeper into enemy-occupied territory.

"Dammit!" exploded the customarily mild Bradley, "George seems more interested in making headlines with the capture of Brest than in using his head on tactics!"

Bradley's old fears of Patton's "impetuous habits" returned. It looked as though Patton, instead of being a team player, had grabbed the ball, ignored the signals, and launched a broken-field run deep into Brittany, even at the risk of jeopardizing the entire operation in France.

"I don't care if we get Brest tomorrow or ten days later," Bradley snapped. "Once we isolate Brittany we'll get it anyhow. But we can't take a chance on an open flank. That's why I ordered George to block the peninsula neck."

The 12th Army Group commander told Middleton, "Order the 79th [Infantry Division] down to Fougères, and we'll build up there as George was told to do. If the Germans were to hit us with a couple of divisions on the open flank, we'd all look kinda silly."

General Patton, meanwhile, was now in his element, dashing about from one advancing column to the other. When a unit commander would voice concern about his open flanks, Patton would roar as he had before, "To hell with your goddamned flanks! Let the German worry about *his* open flanks!" At other times, the Third Army commander would grin widely, slap a worried officer on the back, and inquire softly, "Now what's the matter with you? Are you getting to be a sissy?"

That afternoon the Third Army commander was jeeping through marching columns of the 90th Infantry Division east of Avranches. Patton scowled. His alert eye did not like what it saw. He knew the 90th had been a problem division since it landed shortly after D-Day, and one commanding general had already been sacked. Patton thought the marching men looked filthy, and their discipline appeared poor. "Halt!" he called to his driver and leaped out of the jeep.

Patton fell in step with the men of the 90th, darting back and forth in the columns, probing this man, that officer. After two miles, he climbed back into his vehicle and growled to aides, "There's nothing wrong with these boys. They're in bad physical shape and poorly led." Before the sun went down, the 90th Division commander of eight weeks, Major General Eugene M. Landrum, who had recaptured the Alaskan island of Attu from the Japanese the previous year, was bounced from his job.

The 90th had repeatedly performed sluggishly, had fallen on its face in several key situations. Patton was hoping the new commander, Brigadier General Raymond S. McLain, a banker in civilian life and a member of the Oklahoma National Guard, could inject the needed spark.

As Patton's tank-tipped columns plunged on deeper into the wide expanses of Brittany, a large clandestine force of domestic guerillas sprang into action—*Les Forces Françaises de l'Interiour* (French Forces of the Interior, or FFI). This irregular paramilitary group was hated and feared by the Germans, and dealt with mercilessly when its fighting men were taken prisoner.

Almost 32,000 Bretons were armed and another 50,000 were supplied with grenades and acted as couriers and guides. These French men and women were from every walk of life—they were school teachers, lawyers, priests, students, mayors, architects, field workers, bankers, laborers, retired army officers, printers, aristocrats, hedge cutters, doctors, nobility, egg packers, business people, trade unionists. They were young and old, rich and poor and somewhere in between. There was one common denominator—they hated the Boche with an intensity unmatched in any other sector of France.

Before D-Day, roving packs of *maquis* (FFI fighters) had been organized into teams by parachuting British and French paratroopers and supplied by nocturnal drops by the Royal Air Force. Now these organized groups were in position, mainly along the two principal roads that ran through the peninsula. They served as flank guards for Patton's flying columns and as spies behind German positions. The maquis allowed American tankers to race on without having to halt to mop up small pockets of Germans or handle prisoners. Many of the latter, terror-stricken on being turned over to the maquis, never reached American POW enclosures. Often their corpses had large bloody blobs where their privates had once been, severed by rusty knives in the hands of French underground fighters imbued with a cold hatred of the Boche over four years of brutal Nazi occupation.

For months the Breton FFI had been ordered to destroy. Now, with General Grow's 6th Armored Division racing for Brest, new orders were received from London: preserve. They were to keep bridges intact in front of Grow's rocketing tankers, clear roads of German mines, and maintain telephonic and other domestic communications. At all costs, the huge stone viaduct outside Morlaix was to be seized from the Germans and held—come what may. If the Germans held onto or destroyed the long structure, Bob Grow's tanks would be halted on the wrong side of a deep gorge.

It was nearly midnight on August 2 when a flight of Royal Air Force planes knifed in over Morlaix and in moments nearly 100 white parachutes blossomed out in the darkness as French paratroopers of the British SAS (Special Air Service, an elite commando force) dropped to earth to seize the crucial viaduct. A short, fierce firefight raged in the night, but in less than an hour the French airborne fighters took control of the span and ripped out German demolition charges.

Alerted to the drop of the 100 paratroopers, leaders of the maquis were ordered to rush to the viaduct in support of the warriors from the sky. Before dawn more than 2,000 heavily armed FFI men had taken up positions in clumps of trees, bushes, and behind other cover on both sides of Morlaix to intercept any German force sent to recapture or blow up the viaduct. With gray streaks of light breaking up the black sky, the maquisards checked their rifles, machine guns, bazookas, and grenades—and waited. They would not have long to wait.

THESE WERE DAYS of heady intoxication at the higher levels of the Allied command. General Joe Collins's breakthrough at St.-Lô, General Troy Middleton's dash down the western coast of the Cotentin Peninsula on the heels of fleeing Germans, and George Patton's bolt into Brittany were the kind of stuff that made bold, blaring headlines in newspapers of the Allied world. Newspaper headlines evolved from a single equation: how many miles were gained and how fast? Almost unnoticed in the media was the continued savage fighting on the left flank (east) of General Hodges's First Army where the stubborn Feldgrau, burrowed into the thick earthen walls of the hedgerows, were inflicting heavy casualties upon the fighting men of Pete Corlett's XIX Corps and Len Gerow's V Corps. There the Germans, their commanders lashed on by Hitler not to give up a foot of ground, fought as though the entire left flank of their Seventh Army had not collapsed at St.-Lô and Avranches.

As the Germans battled tenaciously in front of General Montgomery at Caen, and Corlett and Gerow at Vire, instead of pulling back to reform at a natural barrier as prescribed by the military textbook, an incredible opportunity to destroy the entire German army in northern France began to evolve in Omar Bradley's fertile mind. Bradley would take advantage of Hitler's flaunting of the book and wipe out his Seventh Army and Fifth Panzer Army at Caen.

Bradley's plan was simple in concept: he would encircle two entire field armies. The wide encirclement would be spearheaded by six American armored divisions supported by infantry in trucks and other vehicles. Once Brittany was secure, American armor would strike to the east toward Paris. An entire Allied airborne corps, three divisions of parachutists and glidermen, would land north of Orléans to block the flight of German troops toward the French capital. Bradley's flying columns would swing southeast toward Paris, cross the Seine River, then drive north to Dieppe and the English Channel. This enormous wheeling movement would trap all of Hitler's forces in Normandy.

The 12th Army Group commander's daring plan was not designed just to inflict a massive tactical defeat upon the Germans:

he intended it to end the war. Outlining details to his aides, General Bradley declared in untypical bombast, "Let's talk big turkey. I'm ready to eat meat all the way!"

Omar Bradley's reputation among some as a cautious, methodical infantry plodder was about to go by the boards—in dramatic fashion.

Outside Portsmouth in England, General Dwight Eisenhower had begun to think along the same lines, although his concept was not as enormous in scope as Bradley's grand design. That night of August 2 the supreme commander wrote his boss and mentor, General George Marshall, in Washington suggesting that early plans to send the entire Third Army bolting into Brittany be modified and only a corps be designated to do the job. "This would leave the main forces (Third and First Army) to destroy the enemy to the west of the Seine," Eisenhower declared.

Meanwhile that night, roads down the coast of the Cotentin Peninsula toward the bottleneck at Avranches were loaded with George Patton's vehicles, bumper to bumper for sixty miles. At night the Luftwaffe circled overhead, the distinctive engine throb of its planes described by the Americans as sounding "like a washing machine with one cylinder out of sync." Flares were dropped, always frightening to those on the ground, and bombs fell. A few vehicles were knocked out, but hundreds more raced on to Avranches untouched.

Wandering about American and German lines in the vicinity of Avranches and Brécey were swarms of Wehrmacht deserters who had melted into the darkness, begged or stolen civilian clothes, and now were intent on getting out of the desperate situation into which they had been plunged. These were mainly those conscripted or coerced into the German army: Russians, Alsatians, Poles, Luxembourgers, Austrians, Czechoslovakians.

Over the crucial bridge at Pontaubault scores of German bombers from Luftflotte III (3rd Air Fleet) droned in for the first time, under a full moon. Flares illuminated the landscape as though it were noontime, and scores of American antiaircraft guns positioned around the span with the eleven stone arches barked. Streams of American machine-gun tracers crisscrossed the sky. There were the fluttering sounds of bomb clusters tumbling through space and then the earthshaking kerplunk, kerplunk, kerplunk of each exploding bomb. Here and there the sturdy, massive structure was nicked, but American drivers, perspiring with anxiety, white knuckles gripping steering wheels tightly, pushed accelerators to floorboards and raced on across.

That night General Patton was poring over bits and pieces of data trying to pinpoint the location of his forward spearheads. His columns had been following his instructions to the letter: bypass pockets of resistance, ignore open flanks, drive on ahead at open throttle. A master of innovation, Patton had wheedled the 6th Cavalry Group from Bradley a few days before to gallop about Brittany as the Third Army commander's eyes and ears. Just like the Confederate cavalry of the Civil War, Patton thought. He renamed the unit, commanded by Colonel Edward M. Fickett, the Third Army Information Service; but it promptly was tagged with the monicker, Patton's Household Cavalry.

Fickett, to carry out his communications mission, hurriedly reorganized his command into reconnaissance platoons, each with two officers and twenty-eight men. Each platoon had six armored cars and six jeeps. The troopers had turned into snoopers. It was the mission of each platoon to dash about the Breton peninsula, gather information on assigned areas, and report directly to Third Army— meaning Patton. This second night of August, Georgie Patton was elated over what his Household Cavalry reported: Third Army indeed was "to hell-and-gone in Brittany."

Elated with the speed of his spearheads, Patton strolled out of his operations tent to relax in the night air for a short while before stealing a few hours' sleep in his camouflaged trailer that lay snuggled against a hedgerow. Third Army headquarters was located near the center of the eight-mile-wide Avranches gap because Patton wanted to be close at hand should a problem arise in the funneling of the stream of vehicles through the bottleneck. It was almost midnight. The Luftwaffe put in an appearance, but it had been over almost every night and few at the sprawling complex of tents and vehicles paid any attention. How could the Germans know where Patton's CP was located?

First one green flare was dropped, marking one edge of the target to be bombed, then another green flare some distance away, this one at the other edge. Now Third Army headquarters personnel started to get nervous. The green flares were on either side of the CP. Then came the most frightening of all: the red flare that signified the precise target. It was directly over the CP. Lights in all the tents were rapidly extinguished. There was a scramble in the darkness for shelter next to the earthen walls of hedgerows. It was a particularly nerve-racking affair to young, green officers, most of whom had never been under fire—but were about to be.

Then came the whistling and screaming of bombs and the ground-shaking explosions. Jagged, white-hot shards of steel hissed and sang through the headquarters area. In the midst of the bombing, a courier officer from corps headquarters arrived and began shouting that he had a message for General Patton. The courier was led to an opening in a hedgerow and told, "The general's over there."

He groped through the darkness, illuminated at times by falling bombs and the glare of German flares, and found Patton sitting in a deck chair outside his trailer. Patton was calmly puffing on a long cigar and watching the kaleidoscope of colorful pyrotechnics dancing in the sky. The corps officer, perspiring profusely, nervous, knees feeling jellylike, handed the secret message to the Third Army chief. Patton took it, continuing to gaze upward, and barked, "Those goddamned bastards! Those rotten sons of bitches! We'll get them! We'll get them!"

The bombing halted after an hour. Patton, not foolhardy, knew the Germans had somehow discovered his CP. He ordered that the headquarters be moved south of Avranches after daybreak.

LATE THE NIGHT of the second, General Grow was huddled with his principal commanders and staff. A bold and dashing leader, Grow had suddenly been racked with concern. His slashing spearheads were deep in Indian country, and serious problems were now confronting the progress of the 6th Armored Division. There were no established lines of supply, and thirsty tanks, TDs and trucks were running low on gas. The 79th Infantry Division, scheduled to follow Grow's spearheads to the west, had been ordered by General Bradley to head south, to Fougères. Finally the biggest question of all: what can be expected from the enemy? Earlier that day a group of Germans had ambushed a 6th Armored spearhead near Bree, fought another spearhead west of Antrain, and stoutly defended the road

(above) Adolf Hitler's flying bomb, the V-1. Its impact on London was so severe that pressure was brought on General Eisenhower to postpone Operation Cobra and, instead, attack the V-1 launching sites. *(Imperial War Museum)*

(left) A patrol of American paratroopers, on guard against an ambush, file past dead Germans during the savage hedgerow fighting that preceded Operation Cobra. *(U.S. Army)* (right) American infantrymen take cover in a vine-tangled ditch as a Sherman tank duels with a German strongpoint during the breakout from Normandy. *(U.S. Army)*

(below) Tanks of the Panzer Lehr Division knocked out by massive Allied bombing west of St.-Lô during Cobra breakout. *(U.S. Army)*

(right) American infantrymen take cover in a vine-tangled ditch as a Sherman tank duels with a German strongpoint during the breakout from Normandy. *(U.S. Army)*

(below) Combat engineers of Collins's VII Corps throw up a pontoon bridge to replace a span demolished by the Germans shortly after the Cobra breakout. *(U.S. Army)*

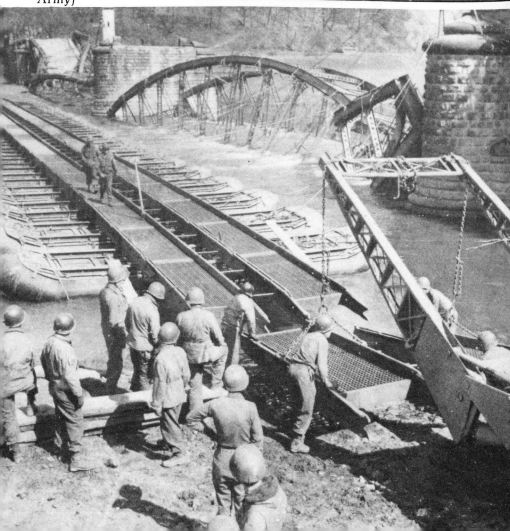

Men of an American armored division pause briefly before resuming the assault after running into a sky blackened by burning German vehicles shortly after Operation Cobra was launched. (*U.S. Army*)

(above) Men of Maj. Gen. Edward Brooks's U.S. 2nd Armored Division outside Saint Gilles soon after the breakout. Brooks's men captured the town after heavy fighting. *(U.S. Army)*

(left) An American infantry team fires a bazooka from behind a thick earthen hedgerow. These earthen barriers bordered each field and served as formidable defenses for the Germans. *(U.S. Army)*

SS General Sepp Dietrich. *(U.S. Army)*

General of Panzer Troops Heinric[h] von Lüttwitz. *(National Archive[s])*

Field Marshal Gunther von Kluge. *(U.S. Army)*

Field Marshal Gerd von Rundste[in] *(U.S. Army)*

(ve) U.S. Lt. General Carl Spaatz helped t the massive air bombardment of the han lines near St.-Lô. (U.S. Army)

(above) Lt. Gen. Lesley McNair, killed by Allied bombs in Normandy during Operation Cobra. (U.S. Army)

w) Maj. Gen. Leonard T. Gerow (after notion to lieutenant general). (U.S. y)

(below) Maj. Gen. Troy Middleton, whose corps broke out of the Normandy hedgerows and raced south to Avranches and then into Brittany. (U.S. Army)

(above) Lt. Gen. George S. Patton, Jr. *(U.S. Army)*

(left) Lt. Gen. Omar Bradley was instrumental in conceiving and directing Operation Cobra. *(U.S. Army)*

(below) Lt. Gen. Walter B. "Beetle" Smith, Eisenhower's chief of staff. *(U.S. Army)*

(left) General Miles Dempsey. *(Imperial War Museum)* (center) General Henry Crerar. *(Imperial War Museum)* (right) Lt. Col. August von der Heydte. *(Imperial War Museum)*

m left) Lt. Col. Carlton Russell, 3rd
red Division. *(Author's collection)*

(bottom right) Maj. Haynes Dugan, 3rd Armored Division. *(Author's collection)*

(left) SS Brigadier General "Panzer" Meyer is congratulated by Adolf Hitler for battle feats in happier times. Meyer's 12th SS Panzer Division ("Hitler Youth") was wiped out in savage fighting as it tried to hold open the escape gap at Falaise. *(National Archives)*

(below) A German Tiger tank. *(National Archives)*

Gen. Jacques Leclerc (with goggles), commander of the French 2nd Armored Division, enters the town of Rambouiller during the operation to wipe out the German forces in northern France. (U.S. Army)

Maj. Gen. Robert Grow, commander of the U.S. 6th Armored Division that spearheaded Patton's dash through Brittany, receives the French Legion of Honor from Gen. Koeltz, French Army. (U.S. Army)

American tanks roll through the badly damaged town of Avranches, the crucial initial objective of a fierce German counterattack. (*U.S. Army*)

Maj. Leonard Dull, who led his battalion into Chambois, confers with Lt. Wladyslaw Klaptocz of the 10th Polish Dragoons, who helped capture the town. *(U.S. Army)*

(above) Wreckage of German armor that tried to stay and fight it out with Americans in Chambois. Capture of the town helped snap shut the trap on two German field armies. *(U.S. Army)*

(below) German soldiers move through ruins of Falaise just before its capture by the Allies. *(U.S. Army)*

Savoring the rout of the German armies in France. From left: Lt. Gen. George S. Patton, Lt. Gen. Omar N. Bradley, and General Bernard L. Montgomery. (U.S. Army)

center of Dinan. Obviously, the drive into Brittany would not be a cakewalk.

Grow's chief of staff recommended caution against "a wild ride through Brittany." He suggested establishing firm bases of supply and keeping the entire division relatively compact for mutual protection.

"Can't do it," General Grow snapped. "We don't have time to go that slow. We've got to get to Brest."

A silence fell over the assembled officers. They cast quick, furtive glances at each other. Brest? This was the first time they had heard that Brest was the objective. Grow had kept to himself until now George Patton's admonition: "Take Brest, Bob." The thought of a single armored division driving 200 miles through enemy territory was exciting, and sobering.

As the conference droned on, a few of the commanders and staff officers fell asleep from exhaustion. All, including Grow, were extremely fatigued. The 6th Armored commander decided he would bolt on for Brest anew on the morrow, but not until noon. That would allow the men a few hours of sleep.

At fifteen minutes before midnight on August 2, a topsecret signal reached Guenther von Kluge. It was signed, Adolf Hitler, Führer:

> Army Group B with all its main armored units will prepare a counteroffensive aiming to break through to Avranches, with the objective of isolating the enemy forces and ensuring their destruction.

11

"The Situation Demands Bold Action"

BACK IN THE States, all eyes were focused on the spectacular drives into Brittany by the Mystery Man of Normandy. Newspaper editorialists were already conjecturing that General George Patton was behind these slashing armored thrusts. By contrast, the First Army under quiet, capable Courtney Hodges appeared to be standing still, even bogged down. Actually, both First and Third Armies were playing equally vital roles in the destruction of the German forces in France. Patton's spearheads were cutting through areas held mostly by a few German defenders, with an occasional fierce battle at a key crossroads, town, or bridge. Hodges's First Army was battling steadily ahead against organized, tenacious, and well-entrenched German units.

On the morning of August 3, General Huebner's Big Red One and its attached Combat Command-A (now called Combat Command-Hickey) of the 3rd Armored Division had been ordered to seize the key road junction of Mortain, some 19 miles east of Avranches in the First Army sector. Led by elements of Combat Command-Hickey, Huebner's men jumped off. The tanks went first, then 1st Infantry Division foot soldiers mopped up. The approach route was a natural ally to the German defenders—broken terrain, narrow, twisting roads, steep-walled valleys.

Hickey's tankers and Huebner's dogfaces overran and destroyed elements of the German 275th Infantry Division, and seized Reffuveille, Le Mesnil-Adelée, Juvigny, and St.-Barthélemy. Hardly pausing, the American task force plunged on toward its primary objective, the now largely deserted and pulverized road center of Mortain.

At 3:15 P.M. Mortain was deathly quiet. The main body of Germans had departed only an hour before. The few French civilians who had remained in Mortain huddled fearfully in damp cellars, anxiously awaiting developments. The previous night they had viewed red flares in the dark sky north and northwest of town, and felt confident that American soldiers were approaching. They waited—and prayed. Ten minutes later the sound of small-arms fire broke out in town. A few German stragglers were killed, several others taken prisoners. At 3:30 P.M. a few trucks carrying American troops poked into town, led by several belching, clanking Sherman tanks.

Liberation was at hand. The French men, women, and children cautiously emerged from their dank places of refuge, broke out into cheers and wild cries, began pelting the Americans with flowers. As the rejoicing accelerated, the peeling of church bells rang out over the rubble. One of those who had remained behind was the mayor. He was aghast. The church bells would reach the ears of the sullen Germans who were in the hills to the east of Mortain! The mayor's fears proved valid. In minutes several German shells screamed into the center of town, sending the frenzied population scurrying for cover. The few brief moments of exultation were over; war had returned to Mortain.

Lieutenant Colonel Wesley Sweat, operations officer of the 3rd Armored Division, took advantage of a brief lull to slip in a hurried shave. He was standing in front of his jeep, razor in hand, outside the CP of Hickey's combat command, which was located in the basement of a doctor's office in Juvigny. Sweat heard a familiar fluttering sound and a sickening thud. A German mortar shell had passed over his shoulder and plowed into the ground some twelve to fifteen feet away—a dud.

The unexploded round was just outside the unflappable Doyle Hickey's door. Hickey came to the opening, puffing on his ever-present pipe, looked at the ominous dud, turned around and went back inside, without comment or change of expression.

Moments later a shaken Colonel Sweat called out with a straight face, "Does anyone have some clean underdrawers they can loan me?"

That afternoon of the third, General Joe Collins met Huebner at a crossroads south of Brécey. Collins pointed on his map to Hill 317, just east of Mortain, which dominated the countryside for miles around. "Ralph," Collins exclaimed, using Huebner's nickname, "be sure to take Hill 317."

"Joe, I've already got it," the Big Red One leader replied with a grin.

It would soon prove to be a fortuitous act.

Meanwhile, that afternoon, General Walther Warlimont was calling on SS General Sepp Dietrich, Commander of I Panzer Corps facing the 21st Army Group outside Caen. Warlimont, Hitler's emissary, was explaining to the squat Dietrich that his armored divisions would be taken away from him to spearhead Operation Luttich, the do-or-die assault to drive westward to Avranches and split Patton's and Hodges's armies.

Dietrich was irate. He protested that if his crack divisions were taken from him, the British would break through to Falaise and possibly on toward Paris. Warlimont explained that infantry divisions from the idle Fifteenth Army along the Pas-de-Calais and one division from Norway were on the way to replace Dietrich's armored divisions. For over a month, I Panzer Corps had denied Caen to Montgomery; since then it had stalled the British just south of that key city. Now Hitler was proposing dismantling that barricade to Allied penetration into the heartland of France. "It's madness, sheer madness," General Dietrich roared to Warlimont. "We shall run into a trap."

Opposition to Operation Luttich by German field commanders in Normandy had been unanimous—von Kluge, Hausser, Eberhard, Dietrich. General Warlimont signaled Adolf Hitler: "Everyone here confident of success." At this stage of the war, the prudent general did not tell the Führer what the Führer did not want to hear.

At Station X, the secret facility at Bletchley Park outside London, Ultra intercepted and deciphered a lengthy message from Field Marshal von Kluge to the Führer in East Prussia. The British decoders were shocked at the tone of the message. Von Kluge had taken brutally frank exception to Operation Luttich: he detailed all the dire consequences that could result from the daring assault. In so doing, the German commander in the West drove yet another nail into his coffin.

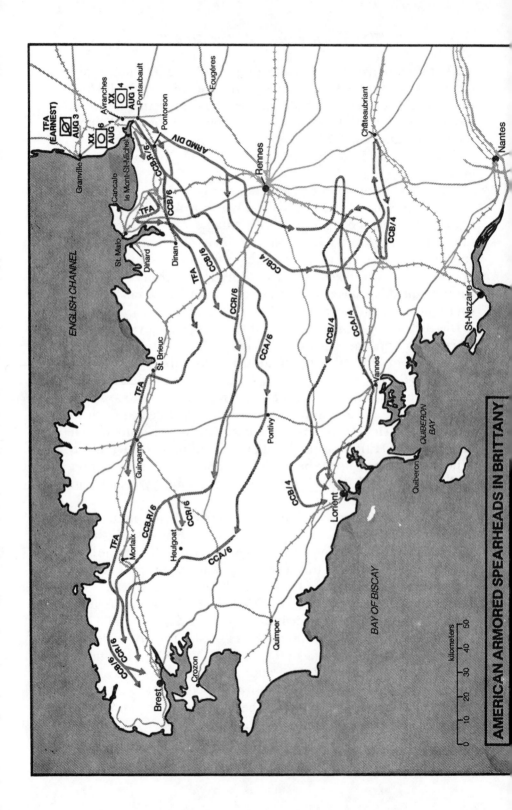

AMERICAN ARMORED SPEARHEADS IN BRITTANY

"Apart from withdrawing the essential defensive armored divisions from Caen," von Kluge declared, "such an attack, if not immediately successful, would lay open the whole attacking force to be cut off in the West."

Hitler replied: "The situation demands bold action. The attack to split American forces must be carried out."

In the meantime, General Patton's armor was plunging on. Despite the efforts of his 6th Cavalry Group, Patton and other commanders were often confused by German troop movements, so rapid had been the American advance. On August 3, Patton received a grim warning of possible trouble from his G-2 officer, Colonel Oscar Koch: a strong column of German armor was advancing fifteen miles southwest of Rennes.

Patton was not unduly concerned. The German force, he told Koch, could at best cut off temporarily some of Third Army's spearheads. But, to be on the safe side, Patton requested Brigadier General Otto P. "Opie" Weyland, leader of the recently activated XIX Tactical Air Command, to dispatch fighter-bombers to pound and halt the German column. Weyland's airmen promptly located the armored force; it was American—tanks of General Wood's 4th Armored Division.

It was shortly after 10:00 A.M. on this August 3 when the 2,000 French maquisards concealed along the main road leading from Rennes to Brest near the key bridge over a deep gorge near Morlaix heard the humming of vehicle motors and the rumble of towed artillery pieces moving toward them. It was a column of nearly 1,000 men of the German 2nd Parachute Division; they had been sent to recapture the bridge from the 100 French SAS paratroopers who had jumped the night before. When the slow-moving column of marching German parachutists and their motor transport had reached a point deep inside the hidden maquisard positions, the underground fighters opened a murderous fire with machine guns, rifles, and rocket launchers from each side of the road.

Several score of German paratroopers, clad in their bowl helmets and camouflaged ponchos, were cut down in moments. Rockets smacked into trucks and trailers towing artillery pieces, setting them ablaze, The sound of gunfire echoed across the green Breton landscape. Surviving German paratroopers scattered into surrounding woods and underbrush where they holed up in tiny groups, pairs, and even individually to escape the ambush into which they had blundered. In the initial burst of violence, more than 30 paratroopers were killed, 21 lay writhing in agony from wounds, some 35 were captured.

Maquisards, with blood in their eyes and vengeance in their hearts, strolled among the wounded Germans, firing bullets into the head of each. The underground fighters split up into groups and set out on what they called "Boches hunts," killing and capturing several more of the dispersed enemy force. Many of the German paratroopers, their effort to recapture the bridge at Morlaix halted by French irregulars, pulled back and reassembled in small groups in surrounding villages that offered some protection against sudden assaults by concealed underground fighters.

The captured German paratroopers were brought together for interrogation by grim-faced maquisards. The FFI men grew red-faced with an even deeper rage on finding French jewelry, money, and other valuables on the men of the 2nd Parachute Division. Sullen and arrogant, the paratroopers refused to believe that the Americans had captured Rennes and were rocketing ahead in Brittany. The Germans were all young, 17 to 20 years of age, and would speak only of their loyalty to Hitler. Each stubborn German prisoner was killed on the spot.

ELSEWHERE IN BRITTANY on August 3, General Bob Grow was observing an attack by his Combat Command A on a bitterly defended crossroads near Mauron when he received an urgent radio message from his corps commander, Troy Middleton: "Do *not* bypass Dinan and St.-Malo. Message follows by courier. Protect your front and concentrate so that we can move on St.-Malo tomorrow."

Grow was stunned. He was already *past* Dinan. This was Wednesday, so how could he reach Brest by Saturday, as ordered by Patton, if he stood in place and waited for Brigadier General Herbert L. Earnest's task force and Major General Robert L. Macon's 83rd Infantry Division to capture St.-Malo?

Grow protested the order by radio. He received no reply. He sent an officer courier to Middleton with his protest. The officer returned late at night. "The answer was no," the courier told General Grow. Sixth Armored's spearheads would be halted in place.

NOWHERE IN FRANCE had American troops seen such wild jubilation, such fierce passion and such bloody retribution as encountered on the morning of August 4 when the last German had been pushed out of Rennes, the capital of Brittany. All hell broke loose as Frenchmen unleashed their pent-up emotions. As American tanks and foot soldiers marched into the city of 80,000, nearly all of the inhabitants were dancing in the streets, singing, crying, and shouting. They threw flowers at passing Shermans. The men in halted jeeps were deluged with hugs and kisses. The strains of the *Marseillaise* filled the air:

> *Allons, enfants de la patrie!*
> *Le jour de gloire est arrivé!*

> (Come, children of the fatherland!
> The day of glory has arrived!)

South of the turmoil, the frenzied citizens could hear the occasional sound of exploding bombs as American fighter-bombers hounded the fleeing Wehrmacht. They paid no attention. Rennes was a physical wreck. Shattered were the post office, the Palais du Commerce, and university buildings. Most of the majestic old cathedral's stained-glass windows were destroyed. It was not American guns and bombers that had created this damage. The departing Germans had planted time bombs that continued to explode periodically throughout the day.

Into the Rennes *mairie* (town hall) marched a group of sullen FFI underground fighters, wearing armbands with the Cross of Lorraine. They carried a motley assortment of French, German, and American weapons and grenades. They were on a mission: vengeance. Cursing and snarling, the FFI grabbed the collaborationist mayor, marched him off with repeated kicks to the buttocks, heavy blows with fists. The mayor, a bleeding carcass when he arrived, was tossed into a jail cell.

A new mayor was promptly selected, by vocal acclamation. Thousands of men, women and children, tears streaming down their faces, thronged the bomb-scarred square to hear him speak from a balcony draped with the tricolor of France and the Stars and Stripes. Emotion clogged the mayor's voice as he gave thanks to the Americans: "Up to now we have been slaves. Today we are Frenchmen!"

The crowd rocked the square and surrounding landscape with their cheers: *Vive la France! Vive l'Amérique! Vive de Gaulle!*

The restoration of government, the speeches, the singing, and the tumult concluded, some among the Frenchmen took to the streets and byways, armed to the hilt and vengeance-minded. Terror would have its day. Patrols of underground fighters corralled 40 terrified men and women in a cellar, among them some of Vichy France's despised *millice* (collaborator police who had done the bidding of their Nazi masters). Most in the cellar were killed by their neighbors. In an alley two French gendarmes pushed a collaborator to his knees, cocked pistols at his head, and forced him repeatedly to salute the tricolor. Nearby, another group dragged along an Italian by the hair, made him kneel and shout *Vive la France!* Then they slugged him on the head with rifle butts, kicked him, and spat on him. But he was lucky. The mob turned its attention to others.

At one corner of the square, 10 or 12 young women were huddled together in fear. They had been branded collaborators, in most cases by anonymous accusers. One by one, each woman had her hair cut, then her head shaved as hundreds of gleeful onlookers jeered and shouted. Then the women were stripped naked, painted with swastikas on breasts and buttocks, and paraded through the streets.

A howling mob descended upon the home of a merchant. He was wealthy, so he *must* have been a collaborator. Windows were smashed, then the house was torched. It burned to the ground as the arsonists cheered. A businessman, denounced by a competitor, was manhandled out of his shop, beaten, and kicked. A buxom young woman, whose husband had been in hiding for months with a German price on his head, was dragged into the street and her clothes were torn off. She had been denounced by a long-thwarted suitor.

Two collaborators were hauled from the refuge of a jail. One was smashed across the face. His nose bled profusely. He began to cry. Then both men were kicked downstairs, stood up against a wall by a group of FFI men brandishing rifles and pistols. A group of American newspaper and magazine photographers were told the pair was to be executed so the photographers could take pictures. One photographer protested that the men should be given a trial. "We've been waiting four years for this—they are traitors!" a snarling Frenchman screamed. There was a volley of gunfire and the two accused men slumped to the ground, their bullet-pierced bodies crumpled like rag dolls. Sickened by the spectacle of instant justice, the photographers walked off, refusing to snap their camera shutters.

AS RENNES WENT berserk that morning of August 4, General Bob Grow of the 6th Armored Division and his staff were feverishly working on plans for action against Dinan as ordered by the corps commander the previous afternoon. A mud-splattered jeep adorned with three stars at front and back drove up to the division CP in a wheat field near Merdrignac. It was just past 11:00 A.M. Unannounced, George Patton leaped from the jeep, a scowl of disapproval etched deeply across his sun-browned face.

Grow was delighted to see his army commander and strode out of his tent to greet him. One look at Patton's face erased the delight. Patton obviously was laboring to control an outburst of anger.

"What in the hell are you doing sitting here on your ass?" Patton exploded in his high-pitched voice to Grow. "I thought I told you to go to Brest!"

Grow tried to explain to an impatient Patton that his advance had been halted.

"On what goddamned authority?" the army commander demanded to know.

"Corps order, sir." Grow had turned pale and had difficulty getting the words out.

Grow's chief of staff, who had been standing nearby, tried to come to the rescue of his besieged boss. He handed Patton the penciled message from General Middleton halting the 6th Armored in place until the fortress port of St.-Malo was captured.

Patton's scowl widened as he read. He stuck the message in his pocket, mumbling something about a "doughboy" (Middleton) trying to run a cavalry operation.

The Third Army leader looked up at Grow and said in a calm voice, "I'll see Middleton about this. Don't take any notice of this order, or any other order telling you to halt, unless it comes from me. Get going and keep going till you get to Brest."

With that, Patton spun on his heel, walked rapidly to his jeep, hopped in and the vehicle sped off down the road, trailing a towering plume of dust.

Hardly had Patton's jeep raced out of sight than an urgent message reached Grow. General Middleton had had a change of heart. He ordered the 6th Armored to continue the dash to Brest. General Grow signaled the reversal in orders to his scattered command at 11:25 A.M., some twenty minutes after George Patton had burst onto the scene: "Division proceeds at once on original mission to Brest. Dinan will not (repeat not) be attacked."

Grow then flashed word to Middleton that he would promptly renew his drive on Brest. But it was late in the afternoon before the 6th Armored, with its hundreds of tanks, armored cars, trucks, jeeps, command cars, wreckers, and other rolling stock could take to the road in a westward direction. Grow was spurred on by hearing a report from *maquisards* that Brest, the crown jewel of Brittany, was virtually undefended and ripe for plucking. But twenty-four valuable hours had been lost.

Unknown to General Grow or other American commanders, even then German coastal garrisons from all over western Brittany were pulling back into Brest where the tough parachute general, Herman Ramcke, would take charge. The backbone of Ramcke's defense would be his own 2nd Parachute Division, zealously dedicated to Adolf Hitler, quite willing to die if need be to carry out the Führer's stern order: "Defend Brest to the last man and the last bullet."

ON THE MORNING of August 5, three regiments of Macon's 83rd Infantry Division were closing in from three sides on the picturesque old port of St.-Malo, some 40 miles, by road, west of Avranches. For three centuries the Norman port served as a lair for pirates who preyed on British shipping. A mile to the west of the ancient walled city, across the Rance River, were the sandy beaches of Dinard, which had been a favorite spot for English tourists in bygone days of peace.

Patton had galloped on past the bastion of St.-Malo in his headlong dash to Brest, but Bradley was fearful of leaving such a significant concentration of Germans to his rear in Brittany, so the 12th Army Group commander ordered that St.-Malo be seized or contained. General Middleton selected Macon's 83rd Division to do the job. Known as the "Thunderbolts" and proudly wearing the word "Ohio" on their shoulder patches, the 83rd had seen its first action on July 4 south of Carentan in the Cotentin Peninsula. Its commanding general had gained wide experience as a regimental leader in North African fighting, but in Normandy he was leading a division for the first time.

St.-Malo bristled with bunkers and guns. For more than two years a thousand civilian workers had poured tons of concrete over steel while building a string of strongpoints on the land side and along the coast facing the sea to the north. The key strongpoints were the Citadel, dug more than fifty feet into a rock ledge on a peninsula between St.-Malo harbor and the port of St.-Servan; the coastal Fort la Varde east of St.-Malo; the casemated bunkers at St.-Ideuc, on the eastern edge of the modern suburb of Parame with its tree-lined streets and fashionable houses, and fortified positions on St.-Joseph Hill, in the southeast outskirts of St.-Malo. Field Marshal von Kluge considered St.-Malo the strongest fortress in France.

Late in the morning of the fifth, American intelligence officers were interrogating Germans captured in the advance to the outskirts of St.-Malo. They learned that Colonel Andreas von Aulock, the commander of Fortress St.-Malo, had his headquarters deep underground in the Citadel, a facility crisscrossed with tunnels. "He's a madman!" a German POW exclaimed, referring to von Aulock. Other Germans said that the St.-Lô commander's wife and children had been killed in Berlin during Allied bombings and that he had "nothing to lose" by defending the port to the last.

Only the day before, Colonel von Aulock, whom American and British newspapers would dub the Madman of St.-Malo, had forced each of his officers to sign a document:

> *It is my duty to hold this position to the last, even if we are encircled and lack food and ammunition. Should I not fulfill my duty, and surrender . . . I shall be courtmartialed upon return to Germany and be punished.*

Von Aulock had told his officers that he would "defend St.-Malo to the last man, even if that last man happens to be me."

Fortress St.-Malo would indeed be a tough nut to crack. American intelligence had placed the number of defenders at between three and six thousand. Actually, the Madman of St.-Malo had more than 12,000 troops burrowed into the casemated strongpoints in and around the port. However, while Grow's 6th Armored spearheads raced on toward Brest, the 83rd Infantry Division laid seige to the ancient port.

Meanwhile that day, Guenther von Kluge renewed his long-distance tiff with Hitler over the Führer's plan for an armored assault to cut off Patton's forces in Brittany by driving to the sea at Avranches. The German commander in the west pulled no punches —he flatly stated that Operation Luttich would end in disaster for his forces. Came back the reply from Wolfsschanze: "Proceed as ordered."

IN LONDON, PRIME Minister Churchill was having the time of his life. For two days he had been on the phone to Station X at Bletchley Park where an official was relaying verbatim the Ultra intercepts of the Hitler/von Kluge feud over Luttich. It was more than just the fact the Allies were obtaining valuable intelligence data that seemed to titillate the impish Churchill. It was the fact that the Prime, as he was known to the Americans, was getting the top secret German signals at almost the precise time they were being read by Hitler and von Kluge.

Meanwhile that day, Combat Command-A, lead by Colonel Bruce Clarke, of the 4th Armored Division, jumped off from Rennes at 2:00 P.M. and sped all the way to Vannes, some 70 miles to the west, roaring into the town seven hours later. The Brittany Peninsula had been severed at its base. A battalion of the FFI had already seized the Vannes airfield, and the FFI men guided Clarke's tanks into the city.

Only the day before, General Middleton had rushed to John Wood's CP to "straighten out" his impetuous 6th Armored commander on future plans. The Professor had been making moves as though he intended to thrust eastward toward Paris instead of to the south and west as planned.

When Middleton drove up to Wood's CP, the Professor exuberantly threw his arms around the corps commander in a spontaneous gesture of welcome.

"What's the matter?" Middleton inquired with a straight face. "Have you lost your division?"

"No!" Wood barked. "It's worse than that. They are winning the war the wrong way!"

Wood's idea of "winning the war" was to dash eastward toward Germany, not westward into the vast expanses of a largely deserted Brittany. It had not yet trickled down to Wood's plateau of command that the Allied high command had been thinking along those precise lines.

AS PATTON'S SPEARHEADS were slicing ahead on the Breton peninsula, General Joe Collins's First Army continued to advance against organized resistance. Colonel Chubby Doan's Task Force X of the 3rd Armored Division was approaching the outskirts of Barentan shortly before dark on August 5. At a small stream in front of the town the Germans had planted mines on the road, and had covered the hasty blockage with several 88-millimeter guns in the overlooking hills.

Here the American forward elements stalled. Lieutenant Colonel Carlton Russell, battalion commander of the 36th Armored Infantry Regiment, moved forward to get the column rolling. He had been under great pressure from upper levels of command to push forward. Always the exhortations had been the same. Keep the German off balance. Reaching the mined area, Russell had a curious thought: there probably is no American farther forward than am I. He was the point of the point.

Colonel Russell began issuing orders to clear the mines when there was a familiar ssswwisshh . . . CRACK! A high-velocity round had hissed in. Then others followed. Explosions rocked the ground around the road and stream. White-hot shell fragments whistled and sang. A jagged piece of metal sliced off part of the muscle of Russell's right arm. Another chunk nearly severed the barrel of his pistol in its holster. A few of Russell's men at the roadblock went down, killed or wounded in the shellfire.

As shells continued to come, Russell crawled into a ditch, where his driver bandaged the gaping, bleeding wound. But the battalion commander refused evacuation until he had notified his boss, Chubby Doan, by radio that he had been painfully wounded and what the situation was at the very point of the VII Corps spearhead. Next Russell summoned his executive officer, Major Dunn, briefed him, and told him to take over command. Only then would Colonel Russell, grown weak from loss of blood, agree to climb into the front seat of an ambulance for the trip to an aid station.

That same evening, a jeep pulled up to the CP of Combat Command-Hickey. Major Richard L. Bradley, commander of the 83rd Armored Reconnaissance Battalion, slowly edged out of the vehicle and began a wobbly walk into the CP building. His muddy olive-drab trousers were saturated with blood. Earlier, an artillery shell fragment had ripped a large chunk of flesh from his buttocks, but he refused to be removed to a medical station until he had made a personal report to General Hickey on the findings of his recon platoons.

IT WAS NEARLY midnight at Hickey's CP when Lieutenant Colonel Wesley Sweat, the 3rd Armored operations officer, Major Haynes Dugan, the division's assistant G-2, and several others were in exhausted sleep in a coal cellar. Suddenly the building was shaken violently. The Luftwaffe was overhead and dropping 500-pound bombs. So great were the nearby blasts that the concrete floor seemed to jump up and bump the now-awakened men in the pitch-black chamber.

After the second bomb exploded, Sweat called out in a stage whisper, "Dugan, are you asleep?" Dugan had been awake since the first bomb exploded and, like the others, had been lying tense and stonelike. Suddenly, Major Dugan broke out in loud guffaws. The thought of his comrade calling out to ask if he were asleep in the midst of ground-shaking blasts struck Dugan as hilarious, despite their peril. Sweat and others in the blackness joined in the gales of laughter that continued unabated for 10 minutes. For the moment, fear had been overcome.

12

The Clock Strikes
Midnight

ON JULY 23, General Omar Bradley had made a solemn promise to war correspondents: give him three hours of good flying weather any forenoon and he would burst out of the Normandy *bocage* like a rocket. Two days later, Bradley got the weather he sought, and the mighty pent-up power of the rocket behind St.-Lô swooshed through a chute carved out by nearly 3,000 aircraft, burst out of Normandy, burned a path to Avranches, and spilled over into Brittany.

But even the most optimistic of the war correspondents, and possibly the American generals, had not anticipated the rocket's carrying power, the astonishing speed it had developed. Bursting again and again, it had shot out spectacular and stunning bolts in all directions. By the morning of August 6, the rocket's red glare had lit up these accomplishments:

- Sweeps that shot across the 100-mile base of Brittany to the Bay of Biscay in four days; a 138-mile thrust westward that reached into the tip of the Breton peninsula. Brittany had been hacked off at the base, then sliced in two from end to end.
- Swift strokes that drove close to all of Brittany's main ports— Brest, St.-Malo, Nantes, Lorient. St.-Nazaire.
- Destruction or near-destruction of 13 German divisions, including 250,000 enemy casualties.

Brest, St.-Nazaire, and Lorient were prizes of particular value. They were the Germans' chief Atlantic U-boat bases. The Battle of the Atlantic might be brought to a speedy end if these three ports could be captured or brought under American artillery fire and fighter-bomber attack.

But the Brittany campaign was the preliminary to the main event, an eastward knifing into the heart of France. To the east of Brittany was open, rolling terrain, interlaced with direct roads to Angers, Le Mans, Tours, Alençon, Paris—and on to the Siegfried Line at the gates of Germany.

To the north the enemy, fighting from positions among the tangled hedgerows, still clung tenaciously to their anchor at Caen and Vire. Only the day before, August 5, elements of Pete Corlett's XIX Corps had jumped off to seize the key road center of Vire, now largely a pulverized mass of rubble. The townspeople of Vire were bitter at the Americans and British since D-Day when waves of heavy bombers flattened the town on the Vire River to prevent the Germans from rushing reinforcements to the landing beaches.

"Don't worry," the Feldgrau had assured those citizens who had not fled, "we'll keep the Americans out of your town!"

Vire, an ancient community of 8,000 inhabitants, was located on hills dominating the Normandy *bocage*. Long a religious and artistic center, Vire had suddenly become an important military objective because of its converging road network.

Tanks of Combat Command-A of Ted Brooks' 2nd Armored Division led the assault against the old town, followed by infantry elements of Major General Charles Gerhardt's 29th Infantry Division, conqueror of the bastion of St.-Lô. Brooks's armored spearhead drove within a mile of Vire, where a company assembled 19 tanks along the hedgerows of two large fields before dashing for an old stone bridge leading into Vire. In minutes, a heavy concentration of German artillery screamed into the assembly area, knocking out 10 tanks. The surviving nine tanks moved onto the road and charged the bridge, but shellfire blew up four more of the iron vehicles and the others pulled back. The assault on Vire had bogged down in a sea of blood and twisted metal.

Deep inside his bunker complex at Le Mans, SS General Paul Hausser was composing an order of the day. Words were hard to find. He must exhort the troops, yet he was convinced Operation

Luttich would result in disaster. "The Führer has ordered a break-through to the coast in order to create a base for a decisive operation against the Allied invasion front," Hausser dictated. He paused and groped for words: "On the successful execution of the operation the Führer has ordered depends the decision of the war itself. . . ."

Hausser urged commanders to grasp the significance of Luttich, then finished off the order of the day: "Only one thing counts now, effort and the determined will to conquer. For Führer, for Herren-volk, for Reich."

Intentionally or otherwise, General Hausser placed the "credit" for Luttich where it belonged—three times in the brief order of the day the commander of Seventh Army laid the plan on the doorstep of Adolf Hitler.

AFTER SEVENTY-TWO HOURS of wrangling between von Kluge's and Hitler's subordinates at Wolfsschanze over O-Tag (D-Day) for Lut-tich, the date and precise time were picked: midnight of August 6. With panzer units rolling toward the hills east of Mortain on the afternoon of the sixth, von Kluge received a call from Hitler himself. The field marshal was shocked by what he heard. For the first time he learned that Hitler had in mind a much more grandiose scheme than merely crashing through Mortain to the coast and seizing Avranches; the Führer planned to launch a massive offensive of several corps to destroy the Allied invaders in Normandy.

"The situation offers a unique opportunity that will never return, to drive into an extremely exposed enemy area and thereby change the picture entirely," the World War I corporal explained to the field marshal. The Führer added that once Patton was cut off in Brittany when German panzers reached Avranches, the U.S. First Army and the British 21st Army Group at Caen would be attacked and "driven into the sea."

On the evening of August 6, the sensitive ear of Ultra at Station X outside London picked up some startling information: the German army in France, thought to be in its death throes, would launch a major assault against Avranches, in only a few hours. Excited tech-nicians at Bletchley Park took down and deciphered the entire plan for Luttich—time, place, and strength of five German panzer di-visions that would lead the assault. These shocking messages were rushed to General Bradley in time for Americans in the path of the attack to be alerted, but too late to shift more units in front of Avranches.

Imperturbable as always, Omar Bradley donned spectacles to study these top secret signals sent out to German commanders over the Wehrmacht's "Enigma" encoding device. He was not unduly concerned. Along with General Collins, whose VII Corps would bear the brunt of the German onslaught, Bradley had anticipated the possibility of an enemy thrust to isolate Patton in Brittany. He was ready. Four of his finest infantry divisions plus strong armored elements barred von Kluge's path to Avranches and the coast.

That same afternoon Leland Hobbs's 30th Infantry Division, the Old Hickories, had relieved the Big Red One in the hills east of Mortain. "Hobbs and his men are bulldogs," General Bradley remarked to his staff. Manton Eddy's battle-tested 9th Infantry Division, veterans of North Africa and Sicily, were nearby. Tubby Barton's 4th Infantry Division, which had assaulted Utah Beach on D-Day and helped seize Cherbourg, was in reserve. Elements of the 3rd Armored Division, which had spearheaded Collins's breakthrough, were in the area, and, by chance, a combat command led by Maurice Rose and belonging to the 2nd Armored Division was rolling southward in the area that the Germans planned to strike at midnight.

Despite his confidence, General Bradley took measures to beef up his defenses east of Avranches, ordering Major General Paul Baade's 35th Infantry Division to move northward from Fougères in Brittany and calling George Patton to halt two of his divisions in the Breton peninsula.

Patton was angered at the order to halt part of his Third Army. He scrawled in his diary: "We got a rumor from a secret source that several panzer divisions will attack Mortain . . . Personally, I think it is a German bluff to cover a withdrawal, but I am stopping the 80th, French 2nd Armored, and 35th . . . just in case something might happen."

In peacetime, Mortain was an unpretentious town of 3,000 residents, some 21 miles east of Avranches, with its time-worn medieval church and a twelfth-century convent. Perched on a large hill overlooking the gorge of the Cance River, Mortain bore great military value. Seven roads radiated from the ancient town. Hitler needed that road hub to catapult his panzers to the sea.

ELSEWHERE IN BRITTANY and Normandy on August 6, as American and German commanders alike were tensely girding for the coming showdown at Mortain, bitter action was raging. General Corlett, leader of XIX Corps, had renewed his assault against Vire with infantry, replacing Ted Brooks's battered tankers in the forefront. As darkness closed in, the final German had been killed or driven from the critical road center.

At Fortress St.-Malo in Brittany, when troops of Bob Macon's 83rd Infantry Division assaulted the city, they were pounded by heavy German guns. American artillery roared in response. One of the first shells struck the spire of the St.-Malo cathedral, toppling the steeple into the street. "A bad omen," frightened French civilians sighed to each other. Later several large fires were burning briskly in St.-Malo. Frenchmen told each other, "The Boche accidentally spilled gasoline while burning secret codes and documents, fires were started but fanatical SS troops would not permit the fire fighters to put out the blazes, and in malice they set more fires."

Americans outside St.-Malo inadvertently added to the woes of citizens trapped inside the fortress. The mayor of St. Servan-sur-Mer had volunteered to point out the location of water valves, and St.-Malo's water supply was cut off to encourage the trapped German garrison under Colonel von Aulock to surrender. Von Aulock's response was to announce that "anyone trying to surrender will be shot."

That night, von Aulock, the veteran of Russia who had vowed to turn St.-Malo into "the Stalingrad of the West," issued an order to take effect immediately: the port would be totally destroyed. For miles around, the countryside shook and jumped as enormous blasts erupted along the shore. Quays, breakwaters, locks, cranes, harbor machinery, port offices—all were blown up. A thick pall of smoke and dust would hover over the entire area for a week as St.-Malo burned.

Early that morning of August 6 in the Caen sector, elements of Lieutenant General Brian G. Horrocks's British XXX Corps were locked in a savage struggle with determined Germans for possession of Mont Pinçon, a 1,200-foot wooded peak that dominated the countryside for miles around. Horrocks had been ordered by his boss, General Miles Dempsey, commander of Second Army, to seize Mont Pinçon "quickly and at once."

Horrocks, husky, capable, and tough, had recently taken over XXX Corps after having been cut down by a German bomb fragment in a night raid on Bizerte, Tunisia, the previous year, a wound that would have killed a lesser man. Horrocks was determined to seize the key elevation as ordered—at once.

The German 276th Division in General Heinz Eberhard's Fifth Panzer Army (as Panzer Group-West was now called) was dug in around the perimeter of the hill, and from its peak could view the English Channel, nearly fifteen miles in the distance. On top of the elevation the Germans had installed a radar station to warn of the approach of Allied aircraft.

The thickly wooded plateau around Mont Pinçon was to have been seized by the British on D-Day + 5. But on this morning of August 6, fifty-six days behind schedule, foot soldiers of the British 43rd Infantry Division were waiting for the order to cross the mine-saturated, narrow Druance River, and assault Mont Pinçon.

The Tommies were in an ugly mood. In their present positions, they had idled in the baking sun for three days. Rations had not arrived; the men were famished. An effort had been made the night before to outflank Mont Pincon from the south, but the troops had been bloodily repulsed at the village of St.-Jean-le-Blanc. Fifty-one Tommies were lost in that attempt.

At 1:40 P.M. the 5th Wiltshires rose from their foxholes and charged forward, only to have their ranks raked by heavy bursts of machine-gun fire. Bullets hissed into and past the Tommies. There were sickening thuds when slugs ripped into men's fragile bodies, and here and there a scream. The Wiltshires, not yet having reached the river, clung to the hot earth, unable to move.

Behind the pinned-down Tommies, there was a mighty roar of powerful engines as Sherman tanks prepared to rush the high hill over a narrow, rickety stone bridge. At 3:05 P.M. a lone engineer corporal slipped up to the span, ripped out German mines, and then a pair of Shermans clanked over the ancient bridge. As artillery fire hammered the Feldgrau on the far side of the Druance, six more Shermans rumbled across. So close to the belching tanks that they could feel the heat from the engine blasting in their faces, some 60 infantrymen ran over the bridge, began climbing the steep, wooded face of Mont Pinçon, and captured a crossroads far up the side of the elevation. The stubborn German defensive line guarding the vital peak had been cracked.

The Wiltshires were ordered to halt in place and secure the crossroads. But a path was discovered that apparently led to the top. The path was narrow and overhanging, dropping steeply on one side, with a sharp precipice on the other. The ascent was sharp, but the Shermans began clawing their way upward. A tank flipped over, another took a direct hit and burst into flame—the remainder climbed on and reached the peak. Mont Pinçon was in British hands—but barely, and only the summit.

Down in the valley, the 4th Wilshires scrambled out of their holes and in single-file order pushed on over the river and up the steep side of Mont Pinçon. The men slipped, staggered, and fell under the weight of their battle paraphernalia. Halfway to the top the Tommies bumped into a force of Germans and a bitter firefight and bayonet clash broke out. The Feldgrau were killed, wounded, or scattered, and the 4th Wilshires climbed on upward. Before reaching the top, darkness had overtaken them.

The men stumbled onward. As the leading elements clambered onto the summit a thick fog had wrapped itself around the hill, and landmarks were invisible. Somehow, the force of Shermans that had reached the top that afternoon was located, and the tankers greeted the 4th Wiltshires with hugs and praises. They had arrived just in time. Around the summit in the fog and darkness, German shouts rang out. Nearby could be heard the scraping of enemy shovels. Most of the British fighting men fell to the ground in exhausted slumber.

Meanwhile, Patton's spearheads raced onward in Brittany. That afternoon Wood's 4th Armored reached the outskirts of the port of Lorient, where part of the German U-boat fleet was berthed. Hitler needed Lorient. His scientists were nearing completion of a revolutionary new type of submarine that could travel underwater as far as Japan, halfway around the globe, without surfacing or refueling. The Professor was concerned. He had reached a blind alley with no further instructions from above. He still cast covetous glances toward the east, to Paris and beyond.

Now he was worried that the 4th Armored, modern warfare's version of the cavalry, designed for quick, slashing attacks and bolts into the rear of the enemy, would become bogged down in a static siege of Lorient. Inside the port, General Wilhelm Fahrmbacher, commander of all German forces in Brittany, had holed up with some 25,000 assorted army, navy and Luftwaffe personnel, and he was furiously preparing defensive positions. Lorient would not be seized quickly or cheaply.

Early in the evening General Wood received a signal from Troy Middleton: "Do not become involved in a fight for Lorient unless enemy attacks. Take a secure position and merely watch developments."

Delighted to learn that his tankers would not have to lay siege to Lorient, Wood now had no place to go. The situation was a cruel blow to his fighting heart. He fired off a signal directly to General Patton, neatly bypassing Troy Middleton's level of command: "Dear George: Have Vannes, will have Lorient this evening. Vannes intact, hope Lorient the same. Trust we can turn around and get headed in the right direction soon."

The 4th Armored leader had reason to skirt corps headquarters and make his appeal to be unleashed eastward directly to Patton. The Third Army commander and Wood held a cavalryman's kinship; infantryman Middleton probably wouldn't understand the need for daring thrusts into and around the enemy. Or at least that was what Wood thought. He could not understand why a powerful mobile force such as his would be allowed to sit idle before Lorient.

As darkness began to pull its ominous cloak over the battlefields of Normandy and Brittany, tension was thick over the separate headquarters of Field Marshal von Kluge, General Hausser, and General Hans Freiherr von Funck. The latter had been named to command the force assigned to breakthrough to Avranches. Von Funck knew it was vital to jump off at midnight, because he wanted to gain at least half the distance to Avranches, 10 to 11 miles, under cover of darkness and before swarms of Allied fighter-bombers pounced on his exposed panzer columns at daylight. His tanks would advance along a ridge between the See and Selune rivers; the two water barriers would provide natural protection against sudden American thrusts into his advancing columns.

It was now only a little more than one hour before the panzers would strike. To achieve surprise there would be no artillery bombardment. Grim-faced Feldgrau plodded along the Norman roads on either side of German tanks, picking their way through the blackness. The 116th Panzer Division, commanded by Lieutenant General Gerhard von Schwerin, was assembling on the northern sector of the assaulting corps, around the village of Périers-en-Beaficel. The mission of Count von Schwerin's division was to smash through to the sea.

The 116th was known as the Greyhound Division, due to the speed and dash with which it moved in 1943 (when it was the 16th Panzer Grenadier Division) to rescue three trapped German divisions on the Russian front. Men of the outfit proudly wore the word "Greyhound" on the side of their caps. Count von Schwerin the previous year had become only the third general in the Wehrmacht to be awarded the Knight's Cross of the Iron Cross with oak leaves and swords. Despite an "unfortunate" blemish on his record—von Schwerin was not a Nazi—Adolf Hitler had praised the count as a "splendid battlefield commander."

Unknown to the Führer at this time, von Schwerin had another "blemish": had the Schwarze Kapelle bomb plot to kill Hitler succeeded, von Schwerin would have been the emissary to approach the Anglo-Americans to negotiate a truce on behalf of the rebellious German generals in the West.

UNDER ROTUND LIEUTENANT General Heinrich Freiherr von Lüttwitz, a monocled Silesian, the 2nd Panzer Division was regrouping for the Avranches assault in the vicinity of Sourdeval. It would thrust forward in two columns, roll through St. Barthelemy and Mesnil-Adelee and dash onward to the sea south of the 116th Panzer Division.*

The 1st SS Panzer Division, once Hitler's personal bodyguard and commanded by SS Brigadeführer Theodor Wisch, was assembling around the hamlets of St.-Clement and La Tournerie. It was to follow the 2nd Panzer Division's breakthrough in the direction of St. Barthelemy and then head for Juvigny-le-Tertre.

Commanded by SS Lieutenant General Heinz Lammerding, the 2nd SS *(Das Reich)* Panzer Division was to form up east of the crucial

---

*Lieutenant General von Lüttwitz would gain wide fame of a sort five months later during the Battle of the Bulge in Belgium when he demanded that the surrounded U.S. 101st Airborne Division at Bastogne surrender and was told by Brigadier General Anthony C. MacAuliffe, "Nuts!"

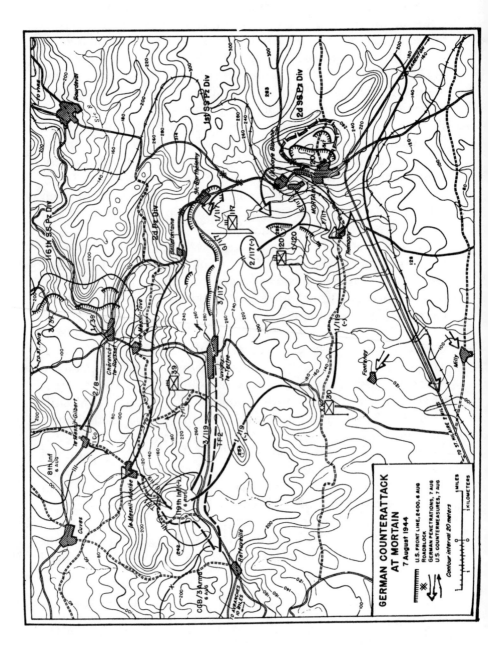

GERMAN COUNTERATTACK
AT MORTAIN
7 August 1944

U.S. FRONT LINE, 2400, 6 AUG
ROADBLOCK
GERMAN PENETRATIONS, 7 AUG
U.S. COUNTERMEASURES, 7 AUG

Contour interval 20 meters

1 MILES

0

0   1 KILOMETERS

Hill 317 east of Mortain, and launch a three-column attack to seize Mortain and Romagny and charge onward to Avranches. Unknown to the Americans at this time, the 2nd SS Panzer Division had innocent blood on its hands. While moving toward Normandy from central France after D-Day, the division reached the village of Oradour-sur-Glane, near Limoges, after having been under constant attack by roving bands of maquisards. Told that explosives had been reported in Oradour-sur-Glane, men of the 2nd SS Panzer locked French males in barns, women and children in a church, and set fire to the village. As the men tried to flee they were machine-gunned, and the church was burned. A total of 245 women, 207 children, and 190 men of the village perished.

At the battle headquarters of General von Funck, the clock was ticking onward: 45 minutes to H-Hour . . . 30 minutes to H-Hour . . . 25 minutes . . . 20 minutes. Von Funck was a worried man. Already snags and difficulties had developed, even prior to jump-off. Heading toward its line of departure, in the darkness the tank regiment of the 1st SS Panzer Division had wandered into a sunken lane over a mile long. Just then an Allied night fighter that had been shot down crashed on top of the leading tank and totally blocked the lane. The panzers had to throw their engines into reverse and, one by one, inch backward out of the depression. The tedious task took hours. It would be daylight before the 1st SS Panzer assault elements were ready to jump off.

General von Lüttwitz's reported his 2nd Panzer Division had not yet received its promised tanks, assault guns, and artillery. On the right, Count von Schwerin's understrength Greyhound Division was having difficulties forming-up in the darkness amid mass confusion.

"Schwerin's messed up the situation!" von Funck howled in a telephone call to his superior, General Hausser. "He'll be delayed by several hours in getting his attack started."

Earlier in the evening, von Funck had demanded that von Schwerin be summarily relieved. "He's not following my instructions," the corps commander complained. Hausser listened, took no action. It was too late to be switching leaders of assault elements.

"We're off to a bad start," the Seventh Army commander told von Funck. "We must hope a good fog tomorrow morning will make up for the time we have lost this evening."

179

At his battle headquarters set up west of Alençon so that he could exercise close supervision of Luttich, von Kluge was made increasingly edgy by the jump-off delay. Radio Calais, a German intelligence agency that snooped on Allied wireless messages, informed the commander in the West that the Anglo-Americans had discovered the shift of massive armored elements from in front of the British at Caen toward Avranches, a report that was not totally accurate. Von Kluge feared his closely packed armor would be bombed out of existence before it could attack.

The field marshal was also disturbed by the presence in his headquarters of the chief of the OKW army staff, General of Infantry Walter Buhle, who had flown in from Wolfsschanze. Hitler was taking no chances that his field commanders, particularly von Kluge, who had been implicated in the July plot, would fail to vigorously execute Operation Luttich. Von Kluge icily received Buhle for what he actually was—a Hitler spy.

13

Hitler Rolls
the Dice

PLATOON SERGEANT WILLIAM Bentley of Tubby Barton's
4th Infantry Division, in VII Corps reserve just north of the See River
and some 18 miles east of Avranches, was picking his way through
the darkness of a large field while checking on the guard posts
established on all four sides of his mortar company's bivouac. The
maps showed the position to be well behind the front lines, but since
Cobra, the entire situation in the Cotentin Peninsula had been in a
state of flux, so security faced in each direction.

Bentley cast a quick glance at his luminous wristwatch. It was
11:25 P.M. This is the way a war ought to be fought, the sergeant was
thinking: the enemy was in disorganized flight, "Lightning Joe"
Collins's spearheads had been moving ahead so rapidly that his
4.2-inch mortar outfit had not fired a round in two days. And now,
on this lovely summer evening in green, lush Normandy a benign
hush had fallen over the landscape. Not a tank engine coughing, not
the muted sound of a distant bomb exploding, not a sharp rifle crack
could be heard.

The twenty-year-old sergeant reached a post manned by Sergeant
Kurt Schroeder, a hulking figure of German ancestry. At age thirty-
nine, Schroeder was an enigma to his comrades. He was one of the
"old guys." How did he, overage for the draft, wind up being drafted
anyhow? And why was he, at thirty-nine, assigned to an outfit where
he would have to undergo the rigors of frontline combat? And,
furthermore, why didn't Schroeder "buck" to get out of his hazard-

ous duties and be reassigned to a paper-shuffling battalion in the rear? There were no answers to these questions, other than the fact that the soft-spoken Schroeder was a first-rate combat man and made no effort to buck his way to a soft and safe assignment.

"Hi, Kurt, what's up?" Bentley greeted the guard.

"Nothing, absolutely nothing. Quiet as a mouse."

The pair heard a faint humming noise in the black sky, but paid little attention. The curious whir of the engine told them that this was a nightly visitor from the Luftwaffe, a pilot whom Americans called Bed-check Charlie. Each night he droned around the forward spearheads, but seldom dropped bombs. Charlie was primarily a snooper.

Bentley and Schroeder promptly did a double take. They couldn't believe their eyes. Not only was Charlie flying much lower than customary on this night, but he had his wing lights and cabin lights glowing.

"What is that crazy son of a bitch doing?" Bentley exclaimed in amazement. The lights would make a perfect target for American ack-ack or Black Widow night fighters.

"Beats the hell out of me!" Schroeder responded, staring fixedly at Charlie.

The lighted Luftwaffe plane flew on a generally south to north route, off to the east from 4th Division bivouac areas. Some distance to the north, Charlie turned around and retraced his route.

"Old Charlie's really gung-ho tonight," the two men of the 87th Mortar Battalion agreed. "The crazy bastard's probably lost and thinks he's flying over Berlin," Sergeant Bentley ventured.

Neither of the dogfaces, nor thousands of other Americans in the darkness on the ground, had any way of knowing the reason for Bed-check Charlie's crazy antics—that he was marking the forward assembly areas for powerful panzer formations that would soon plunge into American lines toward Avranches and the sea.

Several miles to the east, as numerous German armored units struggled to reach jump-off positions, hordes of other ponderous Tigers, sleek Panthers, and squat Mark IVs, their menacing 75- and 88-millimeter guns pointing in the direction of Avranches, were lined up and waiting for the signal to leap forward. They would be plunging into largely unsuspecting Americans who had been cautioned only an hour previously to expect a heavy German assault, but who had heard this cry of "wolf" so many times in the past that, tired and emotionally spent, they paid little attention to it. Besides, how in the hell could the Krauts attack? They'd been running like crazy for days and surrendering, bedraggled and exhausted, in droves.

On crucial Hill 317 just east of Mortain as midnight approached, most members of the 2nd Battalion, 120th Infantry, of Hobbs's 30th Infantry Division, were deep in weary slumber, too exhausted to dig in. Captain Reynold C. Erichson, a company commander, before turning in for a few hours of sleep in the quietude of the 1,030-foot elevation, gave one long last look into the darkness toward the east. Two observers on the hill, lieutenants Robert L. Weiss and Charles A. Barts of the 230th Field Artillery Battalion, groped around in the blackness to locate an OP (observation post) from which they could direct fire after daybreak, in the unlikely chance the Germans would attack the hill.

Nearby, Lieutenant Colonel Sam Hogan, a square-jawed, slow-talking Texan, reminiscent of a young Will Rogers, was making a final check of his Task Force 3 of the 3rd Armored Division before he, too, stole a few winks of badly needed sleep. Hogan, who carried the Lone Star flag of Texas on his jeep and tank, learned that all was quiet. Hogan's force was attached to the 30th Infantry Division in the defense of the key road center of Mortain, but he doubted if his unit would see any action the next day.

At his command post at La Bazoga, west of Mortain, General Leland Hobbs of the Old Hickory Division was satisfied that his defensive position was buttoned up for the night, even though Hobbs's men had taken over the Mortain sector from Huebner's 1st Infantry Division at 8:00 P.M. This had been only four hours before Operation Luttich, unknown to Hobbs, would strike the 30th with great violence. In the meantime, the departing Big Red One was loading onto trucks to drive on Mayenne to the southeast.

At precisely midnight, Tigers, Mark IVs and Panthers of General von Lüttwitz's 2nd Panzer Division began clanking westward. Destination: the sea. Luttich, Hitler's tactical brainchild, had been launched. But only Lüttwitz's right column was moving; his left column had not yet formed-up. Belching flames from rear exhausts into the blackness, the panzers carried infantrymen and engineers of the 304th Panzer Grenadier Regiment. As the armored force plunged ahead through the night, American roadblocks were encountered.

The infantry hopped off the panzers, mopped up the isolated positions, scrambled back onto the iron monsters, and the armored column drove forward again.

Near Tove, Lüttwitz's force ran into a mine field hastily sown in the road, and the leader of the 304th Panzer Grenadier Regiment, Major Hans Schneider-Kostalsky, was killed. Engineers rapidly cleared the mines, working with great difficulty in the darkness, and the column swept onward to le Mesnil-Tove. An American antitank gun began pouring fire into the German force, holding up the column for nearly a half-hour until an 88-millimeter shot blew up the American gun and killed its crew.

Onward charged Lüttwitz's right-hand column. It was within three miles of its objective, an advance halfway to the coast above Avranches. But now faint streaks of gray began to splinter the black sky as dawn drew near. Furtive glances upward told the concern in each German's heart—daylight would surely bring swarms of Allied fighter-bombers. Yet their leaders had assured the Feldgrau that the long-absent Luftwaffe had promised an umbrella of three-hundred fighter planes, which would sweep the feared Jabos from the skies.

Lüttwitz's left column did not jump off until dawn, six hours late, but the gods of war were with it. A thick ground fog cloaked the force from Allied fighter-bombers. The column pushed on through Bellefontaine; then at St. Barthélemy it ran into stubborn resistance. Grenadiers scrambled off the panzers, formed a skirmish line, and wiped out the defenders, seizing more than 100 prisoners. Again the left column pushed forward but soon bogged down when it ran into Lieutenant Colonel Sam Hogan's 3rd Armored Division tankers. Hogan's men were assaulted repeatedly, but refused to budge.

Both columns of the 2nd Panzer Division had now ground to a halt. But General von Funck committed his ace in the hole, the 1st SS Panzer Division, Hitler's former bodyguard. The 1st SS Panzer, whose mission in Luttich was to race through a hole created by Lüttwitz's division and seize Avranches, found no hole there. American defenders, taken by surprise even though they had been warned of an impending assault, quickly rallied and resisted savagely.

On the right (north) flank of the German attack, a fiasco developed. Count von Schwerin's Greyhounds never broke out of the starting gate. The count, one of the German army's most decorated generals, had lost hope for victory. He simply withheld the attack orders from his subordinates. That afternoon. von Schwerin was sacked by Hausser and von Funck and replaced by von Funck's chief of staff, Colonel Walter Reinhard. Finally the Greyhounds jumped off—and promptly ran into fierce antitank fire. The division was stopped cold.

On the left (south) flank, General Lammerding's 2nd SS Panzer Division, fresh from savage battles in Normandy and the massacre of hundreds of villagers at Oradour-sur-Glane, had jumped off on schedule, precisely at the stroke of midnight. With infantry perched piggyback on tanks, Lammerding's troops quickly overran Mortain, destroyed antitank positions of the U.S. 30th Infantry Division, and stormed the high ground to the west of Mortain. In the now battered ancient town of Mortain, the onrushing 2nd SS Panzer captured the commander and his entire staff of the 2nd Battalion, 120th Infantry of the 30th Division at the battalion CP in the Hotel de la Croix-Blanche. The battalion was dug in east of town on dominating Hill 317.

As the morning progressed and the ground haze started to dissipate, Lammerding's SS grenadiers and tankers were ready to make a final dash directly into Avranches from the southeast. Standing in the path of the 2nd SS Panzer was the battalion of Old Hickories on Hill 317. Although surrounded, the American battalion refused to budge. After learning that the battalion commander had been captured in Mortain, Captain Reynold Erichson took over command on the hill.

The sprawling hill was the southern spur of wooded highland, convulsed and broken terrain around Sourdeval called *la Suisse normande* (Norman Switzerland) by peacetime tourists. Near the juncture of the old provinces of Normandy, Brittany, and Maine, Hill 317 gave a panoramic view of the landscape. Domfront, sixteen miles to the east, and the Bay of St.-Michel, twenty miles to the west, were visible on clear days. But more vital in the present situation was the view of the roads down in the valley over which the 2nd SS Panzer's tanks, grenadiers, and supply trucks would have to travel to continue the attack to seize Avranches.

Hill 317 was an abcess in the German side. It would have to be surgically removed, at once.

The heavy weight of the coordinated German assault was not quickly grasped by American defenders, despite early enemy successes. General Hobbs at 30th Division headquarters made no report to corps until 3:15 A.M., when enemy panzers had already punched through Mortain and penetrated four miles into Old Hickory territory. Hobbs's operations officer reported that he was "not yet greatly concerned" by developments. Ninety minutes later he called General Joe Collins's headquarters and vowed that the German penetration would be "cleaned up" after daylight.

Collins's staff passed on these reports to General Hodges at First Army with the observation that the massive German offensive was only an effort by "uncoordinated units attempting to escape." It was not until dawn that American commanders at the higher levels became aware of a stark reality: the enemy penetration at Mortain threatened to carry through to Avranches and split Patton's and Hodges's armies.

Shortly after daybreak, swarms of Allied fighter-bombers were hovering over airfields in the Paris region where the promised three hundred Luftwaffe fighter planes were taking off to provide "ceaseless sorties" over the Mortain battle. In the clear blue skies above the French capital, scores of dogfights broke out. Not a single Luftwaffe aircraft reached the Mortain area.

But aircraft did appear over the German fighting men locked in mortal combat far below: hundreds of Thunderbolts, Mustangs, Lightnings and ten squadrons of rocket-firing British Typhoons. Circling overhead like angry hawks while they picked out the choicest of the panorama of German targets, the Allied warplanes peeled off one by one and pounced on von Lüttwitz's 2nd Panzer Division at Le Coudray, halfway to Avranches, and Lammerding's 2nd SS Panzer Division that had knifed four miles behind 30th Infantry Division lines.

Each Allied fighter-bomber dropped its pair of 500-pound wing bombs. Pulling out of their steep dives, the warplanes returned to sweep over roads and fields at treetop level, firing heavy fusillades from their machine guns. Grenadiers, caught in the open along the roads, fled to the fields where they dropped and lay stone still and helpless as torrents of bullets riddled them and the ground around them. In desperation, crews of stalled Tigers, Panthers, and Mark IVs ducked inside their vehicles and slammed shut the hatches.

After American warplanes had raked the enemy columns, the first squadron of Typhoons, led by Royal Air Force Wing Commander Charles Green, arrived overhead. They dived on the stalled columns of the 1st SS, 2nd and 2nd SS Panzer divisions. The eerie swishing noise made when the Typhoon rockets were released added to the terror felt by helpless tankers, grenadiers, and engineers caught in the rain of explosives. With uncanny precision, the rockets crashed into German tanks, sending long plumes of black smoke gushing upward. For three hours, the Allied fighter-bombers pounded the enemy on the roads to Avranches and the sea.

Dust-covered, frightened, weary, the Feldgrau cursed the absent Luftwaffe. "Where in the hell are our three hundred airplanes?" bitter Germans shouted to each other during brief pauses in the deluge of bullets and bombs. "If the bastards aren't coming out for *this*, what in the hell *are* they waiting for?"

As the day wore on, the vast expanse of landscape on the approaches to Avranches was dotted with the smoking and blackened hulks of German armored vehicles. Sprawled grotesquely along the roads and in the green fields of summer were the lifeless bodies of hundreds of Feldgrau. The devastation wreaked by the Allied warplanes had been enormous: 81 panzers had been knocked out, 54 were damaged and 26 were abandoned. Hundreds of destroyed trucks, armored cars, Volkswagens, supply wagons, artillery pieces, and antitank guns were scattered about the lanes, farms, villages and roads.

At his battle headquarters west of Alençon, Field Marshal von Kluge had been intently digesting the flow of reports from German spearheads. All of the reports were depressing and rife with looming disaster for Luttich. Frontline leaders were urgently seeking permission to pull back from the rain of steel and explosives. Von Kluge knew that any faint hope for success had vanished and prepared to give the order to withdraw from the slaughter. Then came an urgent signal from the Führer:

"I command the attack to be prosecuted daringly and recklessly to the sea, regardless of the risk. [You are to] remove forces from Eberbach [at Caen] and commit them to Avranches attack in order to bring about the collapse of the enemy's Normandy front. . . . The greatest daring, determination, and imagination must give wings to all echelons of command. Each and every man must believe in victory. Cleaning up in rear areas and in Brittany can wait until later."

If von Kluge could see a glimmer of hope for Luttich, it had to be at Mortain. There Lammerding's 2nd SS Panzer Division spearheads had penetrated four miles in fierce fighting with elements of the U.S. 30th Infantry and 3rd Armored Divisions, and the 17th SS Panzer Grenadier Division had moved forward in order to wipe out the stubborn Old Hickory battalion dug in on dominating Hill 317. Soon the pent-up fury and frustration of the Germans would be unleashed against the beleaguered Americans on that elevation.

Undaunted by their desperate situation, surrounded far from the main body of the 30th Division, Captain Erichson and his Old Hickories were equally determined to hang onto Hill 317, come what may.

Late that afternoon, General Bradley summoned top commanders to a conference at his CP in an apple orchard near the village of Colombières, 15 miles northeast of St.-Lô. As General Collins reached Bradley's tent, he found George Patton already there. The two men had not seen each other in three years.

"You know, Collins," Patton exclaimed exuberantly in his high-pitched voice, "you and I seem to be the only sons of bitches around here who are enjoying this goddamned war!" Then pausing thoughtfully, Patton added, "But I've got to do something spectacular to get out of the goddamned doghouse!"

However, Supreme Commander Eisenhower was not yet ready to remove his impetuous "bad boy" from the doghouse—at least, not publicly. That afternoon of August 7, two months after D-Day, Eisenhower moved his headquarters to France. His office was in an enormous tent surrounded by tall earthen hedgerows. Patton's columns were running wild in Brittany and soon would swing eastward to get in behind two German armies in Normandy. Yet the public in the States was left in the dark on Patton's role in the Allied scheme of things.

On this day of the move to France, Commander Harry Butcher, Eisenhower's debonair aide, pleaded with his boss to release Patton's name to the world, if for no other reason than to prove that Eisenhower had been right all along in keeping Patton on the team when others were screaming for the Third Army commander's scalp.

Eisenhower grimly shook his head. "Why should I tell the enemy?" he replied.

AS GERMAN SECRET messages decoded by Ultra poured into General Bradley's CP, the 12th Army Group commander by the night of August 7 became convinced that the German attack was not "just a bluff to cover a withdrawal," as Patton had concluded, but rather was a full-blooded effort to crash through to the sea at Avranches and cut off Third Army in Brittany. Bradley was now faced with his most critical decision of the war to date.

Twelve American divisions had poured through the narrow north-south corridor running through Avranches. Should Bradley call back some of those divisions to help repulse Hitler's threat at Avranches, thereby slowing or halting Patton's momentum in Brittany, or would Joe Collins's corps of First Army be able to blunt the massive German assault so that Patton's twelve divisions could continue their forward surge?

Bradley could be cautious, halt Patton's spearheads, and bring some of Third Army's divisions back to Avranches to deal with the German breakthrough effort, or he could play the role of a daring riverboat gambler with an enormous pot of gold on the table. He chose the latter course of action, betting that Joe Collins and his fighting men could halt the German attack on Avranches without outside help.

Bradley had chosen the "riverboat gambler" strategy because he was struck by the fantastic opportunity presented to the Allies by Hitler's desperate offensive—the chance to trap two entire German armies in Normandy. And within a matter of days.

Turning to an aide, Bradley declared, "Hitler's action at Mortain is the greatest tactical blunder I've heard of. Probably won't happen again in a thousand years!"

While Operation Luttich was beating its head against Joe Collins's veteran corps in an effort to reach Avranches, Bradley was prepared to turn George Patton's spearheads eastward to knife in behind Hausser's Seventh Army and Eberhard's Fifth Panzer Army. On reaching Le Mans, Patton's flying columns would alter their eastward course and head to the north, toward Argentan, to form the southern jaw of a gigantic trap. Meanwhile, Montgomery's 21st Army Group, attacking southward from the Caen region, would advance to Falaise, forming the northern jaw of the trap. Patton's and Montgomery's converging forces would then link up in the vicinity of Argentan-Falaise, pocketing the bulk of the German Seventh and Fifth Panzer Armies.

Bradley was elated over the possibility for an enormous German disaster on a scale that would surpass Hitler's catastrophe at Stalingrad the year before. But success for the huge deathtrap would require the cooperation of the Führer. The Germans would have to continue attacking at Avranches with the bulk of their armor in Normandy in order to give Patton two or three days to slice in behind the two enemy armies.

Shortly before midnight, twenty-four hours after Luttich had kicked off, General Bradley was checking late reports from the front. Joe Collins, though heavily engaged, seemed to be holding. Conditions were right for the Allied trap to be sprung. An exuberant Omar Bradley turned in for a few hours sleep. In the morning he would reveal to General Eisenhower his plan for inflicting a Stalingrad in France upon the Germans.

MEANWHILE, OLD CAVALRYMAN Patton never halted or slowed his rampaging spearheads, even when the German thrust erupted to his rear at Mortain and threatened to cut off and isolate his entire Third Army. Repeatedly he had to remind himself of another of his favorite maxims: "Never take counsel of your fears." The previous day, August 6, a bedraggled American air corps pilot, Lieutenant Colonel Howard G. Coffey, and an officer in the FFI had been brought to Patton's trailer by intelligence officers. They had electrifying information.

Colonel Coffey had been shot down three weeks previously near Angers, more than 100 miles southeast of Avranches, a city on the Lôire River that Patton had had his eye on ever since the Cobra breakthrough. The pilot had been snatched from under the noses of German search parties by the maquis and hidden in Angers. Later slipping out of town, the FFI officer drove Coffey to the vicinity of Avranches, taking three days to cover the distance.

"We drove over back roads," the young colonel told Patton, "but didn't see any large formed bodies of Germans. Only German signal detachments taking up wire and moving east."

Patton puffed on his cigar. His eyes flashed with excitement. "How about the bridge at Angers?" he eagerly inquired.

"Still intact, sir," Coffey responded. The FFI man nodded in agreement.

Georgie Patton's mind was made up in light of the information from the air corps colonel. It was just as he had thought. German forces east of Brittany were minimal or nonexistent.

"I'm moving on Angers without consulting General Bradley," Patton told key aides. "I'm sure he would consider the operation too risky." He paused briefly, puffed on his cigar, then reflected, "It *is* slightly risky—but so is war."

Patton now hurriedly contacted Major General Wade Hampton Haislip, namesake of one of General Robert E. Lee's dashing cavalry leaders in the Civil War, and told him to head his four divisions to the east, toward Mayenne, Laval, and Le Mans. The fifty-five-year-old Haislip gulped hard. His flanks would be wide open. But he had been seized by Patton fever, and at noon on August 6 exhorted his commanders, "Push all personnel to the limit of human endurance."

Perhaps emulating his flamboyant Third Army leader, Haislip added, "Your actions during the next few days might be decisive for the entire campaign in western Europe."

Wade Haislip, a firmly packed native of Virginia, was the corps commander closest to George Patton. But it had not always been that way. A West Point graduate of 1912, Haislip had seen heavy combat in the First World War, and later spent nineteen years in various service schools and in desk jobs. He had commanded the 85th Infantry Division since 1942, but Patton was leary of him when Haislip was given command of XV Corps by General Eisenhower. Patton was leary of almost any noncavalryman, until proven wrong.

Haislip had been "sitting around the War Department in swivel chairs for so long he's muscle-bound in the ass," Patton had exclaimed. The XV Corps commander had won his spurs with George Patton in the only possible manner, by asserting himself on the battlefield as an audacious leader.

Patton's drive for Angers, which had become his pet project, actually had opened on the morning of August 5 when a task force of General Raymond McLain's rejuvenated 90th Infantry Division climbed into trucks, tanks, and half-tracks at St.-Hilaire-du-Harcourt, seven miles southwest of Mortain. Under Brigadier General

William G. Weaver, assistant commander of the 90th Division, the mission of the task force was a simple one: dash thirty-one miles southeast to Mayenne, cross the steep-banked, seventy-five-yard-wide Mayenne River, then push on forty-eight miles deeper toward Le Mans.

If Weaver's force met pockets of resistance, it was to go around them. "Don't stop for any goddamned reason!" Patton had barked.

French underground groups, armed, eager and with the scent of German blood in their nostrils, numbered some 2,500 men in the vicinity of Laval and Mayenne. The maquisards were to harass any German forces discovered along Task Force Weaver's path. But no American commander knew where the FFI bands were or how to contact them.

It would be a new kind of warfare for the men of the 90th Division, who had been involved for weeks in bloody hedgerow fighting and minimal advances in Normandy. They would be introduced to the tactics of Jeb Stuart whose cavalry raids struck terror in the hearts of Union soldiers nearly ninety years before.

General Weaver's force of infantry, engineers, and tanks roared out of St.-Hilaire on the mad dash to the southeast. The advance was as wide as the width of a truck or tank. There were no flank guards, scouts, or reconnaissance units. No resistance was encountered on the first leg of the dash, and just west of Mayenne the infantry dismounted from the trucks. Weaver sent one battalion across country to hit the town from the northeast. The rest of his infantry moved at a rapid pace by foot south of the town about a mile. On the way, a force of Germans spotted the attackers and quickly pulled back into Mayenne.

Alongside the bank of the deep Mayenne River were two old wooden skiffs. Only one had oars, but the Americans knocked down a farmer's fence and used the slats to man the second skiff. Weaver's infantrymen started paddling across the stream, tense and expecting at any moment to be raked by machine-gun fire from concealed positions. They reached the far bank unmolested. Not a shot had been fired. In a shack ten Germans, totally lacking in fighting spirit, were rousted out with hands in the air.

Meanwhile, the battalion sent to attack the town from the northeast, commanded by Lieutenant Colonel John Hamilton, slipped into Mayenne through side streets while the Germans were shooting madly into a hill to the rear of the Americans. Reaching a point about one hundred yards from the Mayenne bridge, Colonel Hamilton ordered his men to open fire, and a Wild West shoot-out erupted from riflemen and Tommy-gunners. Hamilton wanted to pin down the Germans while his men rushed the bridge, before the enemy could blow it up.

Shooting from the hip while they ran wasn't very accurate, but the heavy fire drove the German defenders from the bridge and the Americans rushed in to rip out eight explosive charges that had been attached to the span. Along with the bridge, Hamilton's men seized 152 prisoners. Most expressed shock at suddenly finding Americans assaulting Mayenne, which they thought was some 30 miles behind the "front."

Darkness had started to gather as Colonel George H. Barth, leading one of the 90th Infantry Division spearheads, set up his CP in an old saloon on the edge of Mayenne.

Soon Barth's men around the saloon heard the hum of vehicle motors, and two camouflaged trucks ground to a halt in front of the CP. Out hopped forty-five Germans, laughing and chatting, who headed into the saloon, presumably to quench their parched throats. They never reached the door. A swarm of Americans leaped out of the darkness, weapons at-the-ready. Shouts rang out: "Hands up, you bastards!" The startled Germans, who thought Mayenne was still in friendly hands, had just driven into town. They were added to General Weaver's bag of prisoners. Before the night was out, six more enemy vehicles drove up to the saloon, with similar results.

"This must have been a hell of a popular spot for the Krauts," an American beamed.

With the arrival of dawn, Weaver's task force split into two columns. Objective: the city of Le Mans, headquarters of General Paul Hausser's Seventh Army. Colonel Barth's column headed southeast on a secondary road toward Monteseure and the other force of equal size was directly under General Weaver. The latter column shoved off along a main highway.

Weaver's force promptly ran into stiff resistance, but Barth's column captured Monteseure and St.-Suzanne. At 7:00 P.M., with only a platoon of infantry and a platoon of antitank guns with him, Barth learned that the Germans had moved back into Monteseure. His column had been cut off except for lieutenant Colonel Hamilton's force, which had pushed on to the northeast. "It looks like we might have stuck our necks out too far," Colonel Barth mused calmly. He radioed an urgent call for help to Colonel Hamilton's battalion, then some distance away. But could Hamilton arrive in time? Could he find tiny St.-Suzanne over strange roads in the gathering dusk?

Barth deployed his little force in the village. On all sides, the Americans could hear the rumble of trucks loaded with heavily armed grenadiers. Soon the men in St.-Suzanne were virtually surrounded, as the Germans left their trucks, quickly formed-up, and were closing in. Shouted German commands could be heard, even though the attackers were not yet visible.

Colonel Barth, cradling a tommy gun, had a curious thought: "Now I know how General Custer must have felt when he made his last stand at the Little Big Horn!"

Then an ominous sound sent chills surging through the besieged American band—the roar of tank motors, the grinding of steel treads. This was the end, the men thought. Panzers were about to crash into St.-Suzanne, and there was not an American tank in the village. Barth and his men stared intently toward the sound of the tank motors. They blinked in amazement as the first of Lieutenant Colonel Hamilton's ten tanks, infantrymen riding piggyback on each one, swung around a corner in a cloud of dust, and clanked on into the village. Barth and his tiny band cheered uproariously and literally danced with joy.

BY NOW THE Germans had entered St.-Suzanne, and American tanks, riflemen, and machine gunners went into action. For nearly an hour, until darkness had cloaked the village, a house-to-house fight raged until all Germans were killed, captured, or sent fleeing into the night. But the Feldgrau were not ready to give up the savage little battle.

An hour later about one hundred Americans were idling about the St.-Suzanne square when the blackness was suddenly pierced with a ssswwiisshh-CRACK! A shell had exploded in the square. A hundred Americans instinctively dropped to the cobblestones. The Germans had moved a gun into range and were pumping flat-trajectory shells into the village. A few Shermans returned the fire, and soon the enemy gun fell silent.

Some distance to the southeast of General Weaver's 90th Infantry Division task force, the sky glowed with pink shimmerings over Le Mans. With the Americans fast approaching, the Germans were pulling out. It was near chaos in the town. All night there had been an unending eruption of fires, explosions, and destruction. German engineers had blown up six bridges over the River Sarthe. Only one span was left standing, the Gambetta Bridge. Antitank guns and artillery pieces dashed to and fro throughout the night; German commanders didn't know from which direction the town would be attacked by the oncoming Americans.

When the Americans did arrive, they would need that one bridge to race on into Le Mans. But the Germans had wired the span and would blow it up in the faces of the Ami tanks when they arrived. A platoon had been assigned to defend the key bridge, but for some reason during the night a German sergeant ordered that bridge force to withdraw, and they scrambled to the rear. Several Le Mans civilians, seeing the Gambetta Bridge defenders flee, rushed to the span and cut the wires leading to the explosive charges. Shots rang out from across the river, and two civilians went down. But the bridge had been saved.

IT WAS 11:50 P.M. on the night of August 7 as an orderly officer emerged from a building on the Rue de Chanzy in Le Mans. Since July 1942 the structure had been the headquarters of the German Seventh Army, whose mission had been to repel an Allied landing in Normandy or Brittany. Close on the heels of the officer was Paul Hausser, the sixty-three-year-old SS general. Each man was wearing a cap, ankle-length coat, and knee-high boots. The streets were deserted. The night was black. Here and there in the city isolated fires burned themselves out. Except for blown bridges, Le Mans had few scars of war.

The departure of an army commander would normally have been an occasion for much pomp and circumstance. But now there were no bugles, no banners, no heel-clicking and deference by honor guards.

Hausser paused briefly, looked up and down the dark street. Then he walked to an armored car waiting by the curb. There were no distinguishing marks on the vehicle, no indication that a lofty Obergruppenführer was aboard.

Alone except for an orderly, a defeated German commander slinked out of town like a thief in the night as American spearheads bore down on Le Mans.

14

Canadians Strike
for Falaise

IT WAS NEARING midnight on August 7 as men of the untested German 89th Infantry "Horseshoe" Division lay anxiously in their foxholes along the Caen-Falaise plateau. An ominous hush cloaked the front lines and no-man's-land. These grenadiers had undergone an extensive change in recent days. They had been enjoying a relatively easy life training in Norway. Suddenly and without prior warning on August 2, they had been hustled to the ships, trucked rapidly across Holland and Belgium, then into France, and on to the front lines. There they replaced the 1st SS Panzer Division, which had been pulled out of the line on the night of August 4 and dispatched through the Allied fighter-bomber gauntlet to Mortain to spearhead the drive to seize Avranches.

Three days previously trucks crammed with grim-faced men of the 89th Division moved up the road from Falaise toward the front. The green Feldgrau gaped at the battered villages and at wrecks of panzers and other vehicles caught on the road and blasted by Allied fighter-bombers. Few had ever seen a Jabo, except those high in the sky escorting heavy bombers over the Reich. But they had heard tales through the Wehrmacht grapevine, frightening tales that reached all the way to Norway. Tales told of the carnage that resulted when marching troops, tanks, and truck convoys were pounced on by hordes of Allied fighter-bombers.

Now, as August 7 drew to a close, the men of the 89th had been in the static front lines for only forty-eight hours, but to them it seemed like a lifetime. They were seized with foreboding. Over there about a mile, the Canadians were clearly up to something, and it didn't take an old stubble-hopper to know that. The worst part was the waiting. Even these untried soldiers knew they were about to be hit with an enormous blow.

Suddenly the nervous waiting was over. Off in the distance could be heard an ominous sound—the hum of powerful aircraft engines, hundreds of them. Fear gripped the hearts of the men of the 89th. The noise in the sky grew louder, then turned into a mighty roar. Burrowing through the black air were 1,020 Halifax and Lancaster heavy bombers of the Royal Air Force, each craft's bay bulging with explosives.

The sharp knives inside each Feldgrau's stomach took a quick twist as overhead green and red flares burst through the darkness—target-marking shells from Canadian artillery. The brilliant, colored flares were directly over the heads of the men of the 89th. Moments later came the rustling sound of falling bombs. Then the earth-rocking explosions. Clouds of smoke, dust, and flame geysered upward. German soldiers were shredded, their limp bodies tossed about like dolls. The blood-letting up and down the line was enormous as the RAF heavies did their work for more than an hour. Then the last Halifax turned for home, its engine noise fading into the darkness.

A brief ghostly silence fell over the pock-marked terrain. A solemn hush. Soon the stillness was shattered. Along a narrow six-mile sector between the villages of St.-Martin and Soliers, out of concealment in sunken lanes, smashed hamlets, lush green fields, and tangled hedgerows, a thousand Canadian and British tanks and other vehicles edged forward into no-man's-land, into an enormous cloud of dust and smoke left from the bombing. Soon pandemonium reigned as tank drivers and foot soldiers alike were blinded and disoriented by the thick pall and blackness of night. Chaos erupted.

At 11:45 P.M., fifteen minutes after assault elements of the Canadian 2nd Infantry Division and the 51st Highland Division jumped off, jagged streaks of light and a thunderous roar erupted over the heights to the rear of the attackers as 360 Canadian and British artillery pieces opened fire. In seconds the tortured landscape only 200 yards ahead of leading Cromwell tanks burst into sheets of flame as thousands of shells exploded. Then 360 more big guns joined in the creeping bombardment. The impact area was advanced 200 yards every few minutes as tanks and infantry edged forward.

Adding to the ghostlike scene, nineteen British searchlights to the rear flooded the landscape with brilliant fingers of illumination, starkly silhouetting the advancing Tommies, Cromwell tanks, and low-slung Bren gun-carriers.

Often a foot soldier could not see his nearby comrades. When he did glimpse a shadowy form he didn't know if it was friend or foe. So he fired at it. Streams of tracer bullets crisscrossed the landscape in grotesque geometric patterns. Cromwell drivers, blinded by obscuring dust, lost sight of other tanks. One Canadian Cromwell fired its gun at another Cromwell. Then a British tank opened up against a friendly tank. The latter returned the fire. There were crunching, grating noises as British and Canadian tanks crashed into each other. Officers hopped out of armored vehicles, and shouts rang out in the smog as they yelled instructions to confused columns.

Now many Canadian and British tanks suddenly burst into flames, having been struck by shells from German panzers that were dug in hull down, and by shells from more than ninety 88-millimeter guns. The high-velocity weapons in the antitank screen belonged to the 12th SS Panzer Division, known as the *Hitlerjugend* (Hitler Youth), most of whose members were teenagers fanatically loyal to the Führer. The 12th SS Panzer was serving as a backup to the green 89th Division and the veteran 272nd Division.

Despite the pandemonium and the intense German fire, the attackers pushed onward and by dawn had overrun several villages. Fleeing in front of them were panic-stricken men of the 89th and 272nd, many of whom had tossed away weapons and helmets. Under the hurricane of steel and explosives, the two German divisions had disintegrated, their members dead, wounded, captured, or racing to the rear.

Standing on the side of a road and watching the panicky Feldgrau hot-footing it away from the advancing Canadians and British was thirty-three-year-old *Brigadeführer* (SS Brigadier General) Kurt Meyer, a blond, handsome officer who commanded the 12th SS Panzer Division. Meyer was the youngest of German generals. He had gained the monicker Panzer Meyer on the eastern front because of the daring armored slashes he led into Russian lines. Hitler had personally decorated him for Meyer's "courageous service to the Fatherland and to the Führer."

Seeing the fleeing grenadiers of two other divisions racing past him, Panzer Meyer was struck with the realization that if this all-out assault by elements of Montgomery's 21st Army Group was not halted, the road to Falaise and beyond would be wide open. Meyer knew that it was up to his teenagers of the 12th SS Panzer to halt the Canadian and British tide, but he had only 48 tanks left out of 214 after several weeks of heavy fighting in the Caen area.

Realizing he had to do something to halt the headlong flight, General Meyer calmly lit a cigar and moved out into the center of the road. He shouted and cursed at the disorganized rabble streaming past him to the rear, threatened and cajoled. "Do you intend to leave me alone to fight the British?" Meyer yelled. Some fleeing soldiers halted, turned, and went back. Others, confused and frightened, milled about in circles. Many ran even harder, away from the sound of the guns.

The full-scale attack was code-named Operation Totalize and was spearheaded by the Canadian II Corps commanded by Lieutenant General Guy G. Simonds. In picking Simonds to lead off Totalize, Lieutenant General Henry D. G. Crerar, commander of the Canadian First Army, had a bold and capable soldier at the helm. Simonds had won his battle spurs in Sicily the previous year. He was ambitious and ruthless, could not tolerate minds he felt were less forceful and keen than his own, yet held the respect of those who served under him.

General Simonds approached a battle as a scientist would a major experiment, always seeking innovative methods for achieving success. It was Simonds who had proposed the unprecedented technique for kicking off Totalize, the employment of heavy bombers at night to pound the enemy just in front of his assault troops.

General Crerar, buoyed by the success of the Americans' Cobra to the west, had high hopes for Totalize. Only the night before Simonds's assault troops jumped off, the Canadian First Army leader told his senior officers, "We have reached what very much appears to be the decisive period of this five-year war." He predicted that a resounding victory in Normandy would "result in a crushing conviction to Germans that general defeat of their armies on all fronts had become an inescapable fact. A quick termination of the war will follow."

AT DAWN ON August 8, Panzer Meyer, his trim SS uniform covered with dust, stood on a knoll at a forward position and surveyed the scene to his front through binoculars. He was chilled by what he saw: Canadian and British tanks were jammed along the Caen-Falaise road for as far as he could see. Meyer turned to an aide and gasped, *"Mein Gott!* What if they move in on us now?"

All the young general had to oppose this mighty armored force were 48 tanks and two badly hurt battle groups of his 12th SS Panzer Division. Meyer was deeply puzzled. Why had this powerful enemy armored formation not plunged on forward into the disintegrating German lines? Why was it sitting idle? He had no way of knowing the true reason for this curious Allied inaction: in their first major offensive, the inexperienced Canadian commanders were cautious and unsure of themselves, fearful of plunging headlong into disaster from a powerful German antitank screen of 88-millimeter guns as had befallen many other attacks by the 21st Army Group in the Caen sector since D-Day. With the gate to Falaise ajar, the Canadians hesitated.

Kurt Meyer knew that there was only one hope to keep the entire German front from cracking wide open—attack. "We will jump off at 12:30 P.M.," he ordered.

While General Meyer rapidly prepared a do-or-die counterthrust into a far superior enemy force, heady intoxication was rampant in 21st Army Group upper echelons over the apparent success of Totalize. A staff officer scrawled in the log of the Canadian First Army: "If this is a success, the war is over!" Major General Francis "Freddie" de Guingand, Bernard Montgomery's amiable chief of staff, told a hastily called press conference that morning, "The war should be over in three weeks." Seated alongside, Canadian General Crerar nodded in agreement.

THAT MORNING AT Wolfsschanze, Adolf Hitler was ranting violently over failure of Operation Luttich to break through to Avranches. The target of his wrath: Field Marshal von Kluge. Turning to General Walther Warlimont, Hitler exploded, "The first effort failed because Kluge did not have the courage to wait until all preparations were completed. He attacked too soon. He did that intentionally to show that my orders could not be carried out."

The Führer was not about to call off Luttich after the battering his assault troops had taken the previous day. He ordered a new attack to be launched against Avranches on August 11, this one to strike with six panzer divisions, two more than on the first day. The *Schwerpunkt* (point of maximum effort) would be farther south than before. Hitler also needed a scapegoat for the failure of the initial attack, so he sacked General von Funck and replaced him with Heinz Eberhard, leader of the Fifth Panzer Army, which had been holding on desperately against the British and Canadians in the Caen sector.

Nearly one thousand miles west of Wolfsschanze that morning, Leland Hobbs's 30th Infantry Division and attached units at Mortain were fighting for their lives, locked in close combat with the 2nd SS Panzer Division. The massive German assault had chopped up the Old Hickories into disorganized and isolated bands. Communications throughout the division had virtually vanished. Wires were cut by the Germans or shot out by shells. Infiltrating SS troops and raiding parties cut down messengers and assaulted command posts. The 30th Division had lost more than 600 men, many tanks, and much equipment the previous day, but after absorbing the initial shock of the enemy assault, generally held on to key terrain features. The corporation had dissolved, but small groups of Old Hickories went into business for themselves.

The beleaguered General Hobbs was alternately jubilant and pessimistic. "We are holding and getting in better shape all the time," he told General Joe Collins. "It was hairy for a while ... [but] we're doing everything in God's power to hold." Later he called the corps commander and observed that "our positions might be untenable." Collins cut him off in mid-sentence. "Stop talking about untenable!" he snapped at Hobbs.

At midmorning, the 30th Division operations officer, red-eyed after fifty hours without sleep, called a regimental commander. "What does the situation look like down there?" he asked, hoping to erase any tinge of undue concern from his voice. "Looks like hell!" came the response. "We [Americans and Germans] are just mingled in one big mess. Our CP is getting all kinds of fire, tanks within five hundred yards of us!"

On a hilltop south of Mortain, Lieutenant Joe Herrick and his platoon of the 3rd Armored Division were manning a roadblock. A hasty surface minefield had been thrown across the road, covered by a 57-millimeter antitank gun, with riflemen and machine gunners dug in on either side of the block. Even before Herrick and his men were open for business, the first customer came along.

A German on a motorcycle, obviously aware that he was dashing through contested territory and subject to ambush, had the throttle wide open and was speeding toward Herrick's roadblock. At the last moment the motorcyclist spotted the mines and went into a series of swerves that brought him through without touching a mine. The concealed Americans inwardly admired his dexterity, but it was of no help to the German. A BAR stuttered, and the bullets flung him off the bike. The enemy messenger's corpse was dragged off into some bushes, his bike wheeled away to the platoon's stable of mobile loot.

An hour later an unsuspecting German ammunition truck came lumbering down the road. It plowed into the minefield. One mine went off, setting the vehicle ablaze. Then a shell from the 57-millimeter gun struck the truck. There was an enormous roar that shook the ground violently. The vehicle went high in a blinding sheet of flame, rockets, shells, and bazooka ammunition screaming and whining through the air for thousands of feet. Hedges on each side of the road were flattened for a hundred yards. Pieces of the truck landed as far as two hundred yards away. A huge, black-rimmed crater had been gouged out of the roadbed where once the truck had been.

After the pyrotechnics died down, Herrick and his men inspected the minefield and found all of them detonated. From then on, they would have to rely on the 57-millimeter and machine guns. The gun could halt a truck or jeep but its shells would bounce off a German tank.

Shortly afterward the next customer rolled down the road toward Herrick's concealed platoon—an armored car. One shot from the 57-millimeter gun blew it apart. There was a chorus of feminine screams. Herrick's men were stumped by this unexpected occurrence. Closer inspection of the defunct vehicle disclosed a red cross painted on each side, but not visible from the front. "The gals must have been Kraut nurses or WACs or maybe some French broads going along for the ride," Lieutenant Herrick mused.

The bearded, grimy, weary, and hungry members of the platoon returned to their ambush positions. There they would hang on for four more days.

That morning all over Germany civilians eagerly switched on Radio Berlin. The day before they had been regaled with accounts of Adolf Hitler's master stroke to seize Avranches and split two American armies. At Cologne, Hamburg, Munich, Essen, Berlin, Nuremburg and Aachen, at war factories in Schweinfurt and Regensburg, at modest farmhouses in the Black Forest, at neat white cottages tucked away in the Bavarian Alps, at tiny villages and crossroads stores, the population glued ears to the wireless sets. Now they would hear of their armed forces' glorious entry into Avranches. They were disappointed. No mention was made of Avranches. Instead this alarming report was beamed over the airways on Radio Berlin:

"The six tank divisions of General Bradley's mechanized forces are fanning out in a southwesterly, southerly, and southeasterly direction, each of them maneuvering separately."

At his battle headquarters west of Alençon, a harassed and depressed Guenther von Kluge was on the telephone to General Heinz Eberhard, whose Fifth Panzer Army had been struck a massive blow during the night in the all-out effort by 21st Army Group to break through to Falaise. Von Kluge was deeply alarmed.

"We didn't expect this to come so soon," he told Eberhard, "but I can imagine that it was a surprise to you [also]."

"No," Eberhard responded, "I have always awaited it and looked toward the morrow with a heavy heart."

AS DEPRESSION SWEPT through the German high command in France, across the lines General Omar Bradley could hardly restrain an outward display of elation on that morning of August 8. France was drenched with sunshine, and so were the soaring spirits of Allied commanders, despite the touch-and-go situation around Mortain. Reason for the unbridled jubilation: Hitler was sticking his neck deeper and deeper into the Anglo-American noose.

Bradley remarked to his aide, Major Chester B. Hansen, "Chet, either the German is crazy or he doesn't know what's going on. I think he's too smart to do what he is doing. Surely the professional generals must know the jig is up."

That same morning, Bradley hopped into his staff car and went searching for his boss, Dwight Eisenhower, who was touring the battle areas in Normandy in his olive-drab Packard Clipper with his attractive aide and confidante, Kay Summersby, at the wheel. Eisenhower was located near Coutances. Bradley got into the Packard and over a roadside meal of K rations sketched his proposal for trapping both German armies in Normandy: "Courtney Hodges's First Army, mainly Joe Collins's VII Corps, would halt and throw back the all-out German effort to crash through at Mortain to Avranches. George Patton's Third Army, less one corps fighting in Brittany, would wheel to the north from the vicinity of Le Mans and link up with the Canadians and British coming down from the north around Falaise and Argentan. Inside this gigantic steel noose would be the German Seventh and Fifth Panzer armies—if all proceeded according to plan.

Eisenhower, his face flushed with enthusiasm, took in each detail. He had been thinking along the same lines for several days, as had other Allied generals.

Bradley took the Supreme Commander to his maple-paneled trailer at 12th Army Group headquarters where the two generals hauled out maps and probed the proposed entrapment plan at greater length. Then Eisenhower gave his approval on the spot.

The two American commanders put in an urgent phone call to General Bernard Montgomery at his headquarters near Creullet. "Hitler's staking his life on the attack at Mortain," Bradley told the Allied ground commander. "If we can only drive in force to the east while the enemy is attacking at Mortain, we could turn north. . . . We've been given an exceptional opportunity for closing our pincers behind von Kluge."

There was a brief silence on the other end of the line as Montgomery contemplated the proposal. It was, after all, a complete revision of Overlord planning that had called for the American and British armies to advance abreast to the Seine River, from neatly drawn phase line to phase line, a methodical type of warfare. Despite his reputation for military rigidity, Montgomery proved flexible in this instance. He agreed that the prospect for an enormous victory was great and gave his approval.

A boundary line was drawn through Argentan, south of Falaise, where Americans attacking northward and the British pushing southward would link up, snapping shut the trap. Montgomery was confident that the Canadians would rapidly seize Falaise long before Patton's spearheads drove up from the vicinity of Le Mans.

After Eisenhower departed 12th Army Group headquarters, Bradley went to a cupboard in his trailer and took out two bottles of Coca-Cola, reserved for some auspicious occasion. He opened them, handed one to his chief of staff, Major General Leven C. Allen, and remarked in his low-key style, "Lev, this decision will cost the German an army and will bring us France."

Bradley promptly drew up orders for fashioning the gigantic steel noose. Now crafty Allied deception artists went to work to bamboozle Hitler. The Führer was to be baited, through devious stratagems, to continue his all-out thrust for Avranches long enough for Bradley and Montgomery to snap the trap shut on Hitler's armies in Normandy. The Hitler-baiting deception plan was code-named Tactical Operation B.

The thrust of the deception plan was to convey in a subtle manner to the Führer that American forces were weak in front of Mortain, that one more full-scale assault by German panzers would carry through to the sea and cut off twelve American divisions to the south. The British Special Plans Branch was assigned the responsibility for implementing Tactical Operation B.

A script for enemy consumption was hurriedly drawn up. It indicated that the 4th and 6th Armored divisions in Brittany were in big trouble—short of tanks, infantry, and supplies—that their supply lines were being constantly attacked, and that they were having trouble capturing the Breton ports (this last was true). The growing American army was having difficulty supplying its forces over the Normandy beaches, and the seizure of the Brittany ports was vital, the script continued. So Patton's divisions were to be hurried into the Breton peninsula to seize Brest, St.-Malo, and St.-Nazaire. Bradley, therefore, was stripping his Mortain defenses to rush troops into Brittany for an even more vital function.

Allied double-agents at Avranches, Cherbourg, and in England, who had been German spies captured by the Americans and British and given the choice of sending false data to their German masters in Berlin or being stood up against a wall and shot, were furnished the script. With Allied overseers at their elbow, the high-grade intelligence bonanza was radioed to Berlin in code previously supplied by German controllers.

AT ABOUT 9 A.M. on August 8, a mud-splattered jeep draped in white sheets and flying a flag of truce was edging toward German-held Brest at the western tip of the Brittany Peninsula. In the vehicle were Major Ernest W. Mitchell, intelligence officer of Bob Grow's 6th Armored Division, and Master Sergeant Alex Castle. The 6th Armored had advanced in three columns to the outskirts of the major port the evening before. Major Mitchell was carrying a surrender ultimatum from General Grow to the commander of the Brest garrison.

Reaching a German outpost, the Americans were blindfolded, driven into Brest, and when the blindfolds were removed Mitchell and Castle found themselves seated at a long conference table. Across from them were several German officers. An enemy officer raised his arm in the Nazi salute and called out, "Heil, Hitler!" Major Mitchell, taken by surprise, hesitated briefly, then gave the standard American army salute.

Mitchell handed the surrender document to the senior German officer, who denied being able to read English. Sergeant Castle translated the paper by voice:

> The United States Army, Naval and Air Force troops are in position to destroy the garrison of Brest. This memorandum constitutes an opportunity for you to surrender in the face of these overwhelming forces . . . and avoid the unnecessary sacrifice of lives. . . .

Major Mitchell and Castle labored to keep straight faces. They did not want to give away the fact that the ultimatum was a gigantic bluff, that only forward elements of the 6th Armored Division were outside Brest.

The senior German officer declared he could not surrender. Mitchell inquired if he knew what that meant, and the enemy commander replied that he did. The German "heiled"; Major Mitchell saluted, left the room, and returned to American lines. He reported to an eagerly awaiting Bob Grow that the surrender bluff had failed.

There was no alternative now: General Grow hurriedly called for air support for the following day to wipe out heavy guns, oil tanks, strongpoints, and troop concentrations. He would attack Brest in the morning.

Meanwhile that morning and afternoon, General Grow received a flow of alarming reports from his rear elements closing up to Brest. Stray German vehicles and tiny convoys were "coming out of nowhere" and crashing into these 6th Armored units from behind. Who were they? Where were they coming from? Sporadic but violent fire fights erupted far to the rear of Grow's forward elements.

That afternoon an outpost of the 212th Armored Field Artillery Battalion spotted a vehicle racing toward it from the rear and trailing a plume of dust. As it got closer, the artillerymen could see it was a German command car carrying several officers. The Americans leaped out into the road, weapons at-the-ready, and halted the vehicle. Out climbed Lieutenant General Karl Spang, commander of the 266th Infantry Division, and several of his staff. Spang wore a startled look; he was not aware Americans were in western Brittany.

The German general's division had been engaged in the fighting around St.-Malo but had been ordered to join the garrison at Brest. Spang had preceded his troops to locate facilities for them. It was vehicles from his 266th Division that had been bumping into 6th Armored Division rear elements all day.

General Grow now cancelled plans to assault Brest in the morning and turned around some of his units to deal with the 266th Division threat from his rear. Several columns were to move northeast toward Plouvien in order to destroy previously unsuspected elements of the enemy division, who were approaching in route march formation.

Grow was in a tight situation. An apparently strong German garrison faced him in Brest and could sally forth at any time, and to his rear the 266th Division was marching steadily toward him. There was danger that Grow's CP Might be overrun, so a number of soldiers were stationed next to the electric code machines. If need be, they would destroy the secret devices with thermite grenades.

Until the previous day when 6th Armored Division tanks clanked and roared down the main street on the way to Brest, Plouvien was just another of the quaint, peaceful villages that dotted the Breton peninsula—a set pattern of small, tidy houses, large untidy barns and barnyards, a few shops, a church at the crossroads. Even the names—Plouescat, Plougonven, Ploudaniel—bore the patina of time. *Plou* is the ancient Celtic prefix for parish. The citizens were poor, neighborly, and deeply religious.

Plouvien had been left behind in the wake of American tank columns bearing down on Brest, ten miles away. But the unexpected arrival of the men from across the Atlantic Ocean set off a celebration, and the houses and streets were decked out with the French tricolor and a smattering of tiny American flags. It was an occasion to rejoice.

But then a contingent of some 1,500 Germans approached the village, sending fear through Plouvien's 2,300 citizens. Flag-decked Plouvien infuriated the German commander. He sent shells screaming into the streets. The Plouviennois had to leave their dead and wounded behind and flee, panic-stricken, to cellars as explosions rocked the tiny town. German troops entered the village and looted wine shops and shell-torn houses in search of more alcoholic beverages. They were sullen and nasty when they entered Plouvien, then became drunk and rampaged out of control. A group of Germans went to the opening of a bomb shelter, called on the men to come out. There was a burst of machine-gun fire as each emerged—the parish priest, farmers, and townspeople were cut down, twenty-three in all.

Shortly afterward, elements of the 6th Armored Division reached Plouvien, caught the Germans in the town by surprise, and trapped them as they tried to flee in horse-drawn wagons and motor vehicles. Of the 1,500 Germans who had marched into Plouvien, only 71 emerged unscathed, as prisoners of war.

That night General George Patton returned to his trailer quarters after a long and exhausting day of touring his widespread spearheads. Yet he took a few minutes to write wife Beatrice back in Boston, closing with: "The war may end in ten days."

The Bugles
Fall
Silent

15

"No Truce with Those Bastards!"

COLONEL GEORGE BARTH in St.-Suzanne, northwest of Le Mans, was stealing a few winks of sleep early on the morning of August 8 when he received a radio message from his task force boss, Brigadier General William Weaver. "Get on the road," the assistant commander of the 90th Infantry Division told Barth, "and head out for Le Mans." The men of Task Force Weaver were weary. They had ridden, marched, and fought almost continuously since jumping off in a Jeb Stuart-like raid deep into German-held territory two days previously. But by 10:00 A.M. Barth's column was rumbling southeast toward Le Mans.

There were periodic brushes at German roadblocks, but Barth's men pushed on and reached the small town of Chau Fleur Notre Dame. Just as the first American Sherman clanked up to the main crossroads there, a long German column of 88-millimeter guns roared out of Le Mans directly toward the advancing force. It appeared that the enemy column was unaware of the presence of Americans, so the Shermans took cover alongside the road. When the first German vehicle had almost reached the crossroads, several Shermans opened fire. The leading truck caught fire and veered crazily before crashing astride the road, blocking the remainder of the twenty-five German vehicles.

Unable to move forward, the enemy column ground to a halt. American tanks moved out of their concealment and in a short fight picked off each enemy vehicle, setting most of them ablaze.

Weaver's column meanwhile was advancing to the right of Barth, driving Germans and their vehicles in front of it. A massive German traffic jam developed, and soon American fighter-bombers appeared overhead. For nearly an hour the Thunderbolts and Mustangs pounded the stalled enemy tanks and trucks. Huge clouds of black smoke rose over the hunting grounds. Barth's men alone rounded up two hundred and fifty prisoners.

With both Weaver's and Barth's columns several miles west of Le Mans, the 90th Division commander, General McLain, halted the advance, brought up more of his units, and prepared to assault the city. But the 90th was destined to lose the race to Le Mans. At 5:00 P.M. that day a column of the 315th Infantry Regiment of the 79th Division, with Lieutenant Colonel John A. McAleer in the lead, dashed over the Gambetta Bridge and into the city. They were immediately deluged by thousands of frenzied, wildly cheering natives who were shouting at the top of their voices. Only a short time before the American entry, two Frenchmen clutching a tricolor had scrambled apelike up the tower of the St.-Julien Cathedral and planted the national flag. They were fired on by a few Germans but reached the top unscathed.

The 5th Armored Division, commanded by Major General Lunsford E. Oliver, had been playing the role of fireman in the speedy 75-mile advance to Le Mans by Wade Haislip's XV Corps. Haislip had ordered the 5th Armored to advance to the rear of Major General Ira T. Wyche's 79th Infantry Division and took the unusual step of authorizing Oliver's tankers to use any roads they desired in the corps sector, providing the infantry divisions were not interfered with. If the infantry ran into heavy opposition, Haislip declared, Luns Oliver's "firemen" were to dash to the trouble spot, pass through the infantry, and stamp out the "fire."

On the night of August 7-8, the 5th Armored reached and crossed the Sarthe River south of Le Mans, crushed sporadic opposition and bypassed Le Mans. Oliver's tankers swung in a wide arc and moved around the eastern outskirts of the city. By midnight of the eighth, the three assaulting divisions had blocked all exits from Le Mans.

General Haislip now awaited orders. "Don't be surprised," George Patton had told him, "if instead of going on east you turn north toward Alençon." Haislip knew what that meant. His corps would be the lower jaw of the gigantic trap being set for Field Marshal von Kluge's armies in Normandy.

214

At this juncture, Allied intelligence officers at every level were hard put to keep track of Patton's racing spearheads. Third Army was attacking toward every point on the compass: westward to Brest, north toward St.-Malo, east toward Le Mans, and south in the direction of Angers. Anglo-American intelligence was only slightly less confused than were their opposite numbers among the Germans, so speedy had been the American advance since Cobra was launched on July 25.

So rapid was the dash eastward that American pilots encountered great difficulty in identifying targets. Often German columns were withdrawing eastward *behind* Patton's spearheads advancing in the same direction. On one occasion, a flight of American fighter-bombers detected three columns heading eastward almost abreast on parallel roads only a mile or two apart. Circling high overhead to inspect the three columns, the flight ignored the outer two columns, which were American, and pounced on the one in the center, which was German. The center force had one telltale identification marking it as German—horse-drawn vehicles were interspersed in the convoy.

A safeguard against bombing of American columns by "friendly" aircraft was the use of large panels of red and yellow fluorescent material that were attached to vehicles. Always the wily battlefield fighters, the Germans started displaying identical red and yellow panels on their tanks and other vehicles. This was countered by the Allies issuing the "color of the day." Each twenty-four hours, ground and air forces would be told which color, red or yellow, would be used that day. That meant that the Germans had to guess.

It was about 7:00 A.M. when Colonel Brenton Wallace, a liaison officer at Third Army headquarters, and several others were heading for breakfast in a small wood where Patton's forward CP had been set up. Overhead an airplane could be heard circling, but few paid any attention to it. Moments later there was the chatter of a machine gun and the whistle of a diving airplane. Bullets zipped through the woods. Wallace and the others ducked behind trees, leaped for ditches. Crouching there, they peered through branches heavy with the morning's dew and saw that it was an American fighter-bomber. Probably one captured by the Germans and used for sneak hit-and-run raids, Colonel Wallace and the others agreed.

Again they set out for the huge mess tent. Again the sound of an aircraft overhead, then the hiss of .50-caliber bullets cutting through the tree branches. Once more Wallace and his comrades dashed for cover. It was the same American aircraft. Now ack-ack guns fired, the crews being certain that a Luftwaffe pilot was at the controls, even though the fighter-bomber was marked with the white star of the U.S. Air Corps. A shell hit the aircraft and it crashed.

Colonel Wallace and others hopped into jeeps and went searching for the crash site. Soon they found the wreckage. Inside was the mangled body of a very young American pilot.

THE LOT OF a Patton liaison officer such as Colonel Wallace during this period of spectacular advances by tank-tipped spearheads was one fraught with peril. Day and night the information had to keep flowing in to the Third Army commander. This would mean that a liaison officer would climb into a jeep with a driver and dash off through "Indian country" as the Americans called it in search of flying columns that had plunged twenty to thirty miles ahead. It meant running a gauntlet through marauding bands of Germans who had closed in again once the American armor had passed. Night rides were especially eerie. If the lone jeep didn't stumble into Germans, it stood in danger of coming under fire from trigger-happy American sentinels.

One liaison officer and his driver plunged off the end of a blown bridge on a pitch-black night, crashed into rocks and water thirty feet below. They suffered numerous broken bones, but survived. Another liaison officer and his driver in search of a spearhead simply vanished. Some days later their graves would be found side by side in a patch of woods.

Speed was the essential ingredient in these jeep rides into "liberated" territory and in pursuit of spearheads whose positions and routes of advance were not always known. Tommy guns were carried constantly at the alert. Eyes strained for any subtle hint of looming peril. Officer and driver relaxed slightly when passing open fields, but nearing a wooded area the accelerator was pushed to the floorboard and the jeep would race through at 60 miles per hour or more. "We took off like scared jackrabbits," Colonel Wallace would tell comrades later.

AT NOON ON August 8, far north of Le Mans, youthful General Kurt Meyer was hurriedly making last-minute preparations for the counterattack his two battle groups of the 12th SS Panzer Division would launch against the hesitating Canadians. Meyer knew that his assault could result in total disaster—he was sending forty-eight tanks against nearly six hundred Canadian and British tanks. But the gamble had to be taken, or the Canadians would break through the series of German strongpoints that served as a front and then race to Falaise and beyond for a possible linkup with American forces to the south.

In the meantime that morning, General Guy Simonds, leader of the Canadian II Corps, enthused by the three-mile penetration in the first hours of Operation Totalize and envisioning another Cobra-type breakout, got ready to shoot the works. He committed the Canadian 4th Armored Division and the Polish 1st Armored Division, neither of which had tasted battle. These two fresh formations were to pass through the Canadian 2nd and British 51st Highland divisions and set out for Falaise.

But the Germans struck first. Precisely at 12:30 P.M. Meyer's panzers rumbled forward, followed by grenadiers of the 12th SS Panzer. In the forefront as was his wont, General Meyer peered through binoculars at the horde of Canadian tanks drawn up on either side of the Falaise-Caen road as though on maneuvers. One battle group with eight 62-ton Tigers and fourteen 45-ton Panthers would strike on the left toward Cintheaux, and the other Kampf-gruppe on the right with twenty Tigers would attack along the road leading to St.-Aignan-de-Cramesnil.

Meyer's panzers had moved forward but a short distance when there was a mighty roar in the sky, which told of the approach of 492 Flying Fortresses of the U.S. Eighth Air Force. The target of the heavies was the tortured six-mile-wide strip of terrain already struck by Totalize. General Jimmy Doolittle's Flying Fortresses were to administer the coup de grace to the battered German positions facing the Canadians and the British, and blast open the road to Falaise.

Minutes later hundreds of bombs plastered into power the villages that dotted the Falaise plateau, likely hiding spots for German tanks. Kurt Meyer's panzers and grenadiers had been in these villages only an hour before, but having pushed forward they escaped the bombardment.

The Poles of General Waldimar Maczek's 1st Armored Division

were not as fortunate. Bombs rained down on the green fighting men, killing 24 and wounding 131.

As Doolittle's heavies plastered the terrain behind the Germans, tanks of the 12th SS Panzer Division's left-hand column crashed into Cintheaux and seized the town from the Canadians, who had also been struck by errant American bombs. Meyer's right-hand battle group ran into the Polish 2nd Armored Regiment and a fierce tank battle erupted. The Poles, despite being inexperienced and disorganized when "friendly" bombs fell on them, destroyed six of the twenty Tigers in the column. In turn, twenty-six Polish Shermans were knocked out, nine of them blazing at the base of a hill, victims of a single 88-millimeter gun.

Panzer Meyer's counterattack was halted, but it had achieved its purpose at heavy cost. In the evening, the Canadians and Poles dug in. General Montgomery's breakthrough effort had been thwarted, eleven miles short of its objective, Falaise, a tannery and textile center of four thousand citizens, where William the Conqueror was born.

As a lull settled over the Falaise-Caen road and each side drew back to lick its grievous wounds, Major Peter Simonds, brother of the commander of the Canadian II Corps, was walking along a stretch of captured road in his capacity as supervisor of a telephone line-laying operation. His eyes spotted a German hanging over a wire fence. Drawing closer, the younger Simonds saw that it was but half a man. In the nearby road was the top half of the body, helmet still strapped on securely, arms stretched rigidly skyward. As he brushed on past the upper portion of the German torso he noted the collar insignia—89. A member of the green division that only a few days before had been training in Norway.

Farther along the road, the blackened, burned-out hulks of a Canadian Sherman and German Tiger sat like mute sentinels. The gun of each tank was pointed at the other. The iron vehicles were less than seventy yards apart. Apparently a point-blank shoot-out had taken place, and German and Canadian gunners had fired at precisely the same moment. Hanging out the open turret of the Sherman was a charred object, burned to a crisp. It had been a human being.

SEVERAL HUNDRED MILES to the east, in Ploetzensee Jail in Berlin on this same night of August 8, a German cameraman was nervously checking his equipment. He had been ordered to record on film the events soon to take place there for later viewing by the Führer. The first of the Schwarze Kapelle conspirators were to be hanged, and Hitler wanted to savor every second of the agonizing deaths of ringleaders of the July plot to murder him.

One by one the doomed men, ordered to be executed while naked, to strip them of their last shred of human dignity, entered the death chamber—General Erwin Witzleben (who was to have commanded the armed forces on Hitler's demise), General Helmuth Stieff, General Erich Fellgiebel, Colonel Georg Hansen, among others. Each conspirator mounted the gallows and a heavy rope was placed around his neck, he was lifted, and the other end of the rope was looped around a large hook—and he was allowed to swing. Each lingered in agony for a long period, face bulging and purple as he slowly strangled to death. Hitler had ordered that the victims were not to be accorded a quick, merciful death.

Word of the first mass hangings of Schwarze Kapelle leaders reached German commanders in France and cast an even deeper pall of gloom and despair over battle headquarters. And the executions served a purpose: generals were dramatically reminded of the fate awaiting those who crossed the Führer.

AT DAWN ON August 9, the Lost Battalion of Leland Hobbs's 30th Infantry Division was still stubbornly holding out on the wooded slopes and summit of crucial Hill 317, just east of Mortain. For two days and nights the Old Hickories had been cut off, pounded relentlessly by German artillery, assaulted repeatedly by elements of the 17th Panzer Grenadier Division, which had been rushed forward to rapidly remove this abcess from German lines of communication in the drive for Avranches.

From the heights of the ear-shaped elevation, artillery forward observers lieutenants Charles Barts and Robert Weiss of the 230th Field Artillery Battalion had been directing devastating shell-fire on German tanks and troop concentrations in the valleys on all sides of the hill. The isolated Old Hickories had many wounded, and were short on food, medical supplies, and other needed items. That morning General Hobbs sent two light planes over the embattled peak to drop supplies by parachute, but they had to turn back when greeted by a murderous stream of German ack-ack fire.

Meanwhile, Lieutenant Colonel Lewis D. Vieman, commander of the 230th, conceived a novel idea for resupplying the beleaguered men on the hill. Using smoke-shell cases customarily utilized for sending propaganda leaflets into enemy positions, Vieman's gunners fired crucially needed bandages, morphine, and other supplies to the men of the Lost Battalion. It was impossible to shoot in blood plasma, which was vitally needed on the hill, but the unexpected arrival by artillery shell of other medical supplies provided an enormous boost to the morale of the surrounded Old Hickories.

That morning Captain Reynold Erichson, who had taken command of the battalion on Hill 317, radioed General Hobbs: "Not too worried about the situation as long as [friendly] artillery fire continues."

Still the Lost Battalion, pounded day and night, seemed doomed.

The men on the hill were thirsty. Their drinking water had been exhausted the night before, and the only well on the elevation was in the sights of concealed German marksmen. Food was low. A garden with cabbages and a small potato field had been located and diligently raided. That source of sustenance was depleted. Men devoured green apples. An officer who had eaten nothing but one K-ration and apples for ninety-two hours exclaimed, "I feel like I've got a belly full of razor blades!"

Old Hickory wounded, scores of them, were made as comfortable as possible, bedded on piles of leaves with folded olive-drab blankets for pillows in ditches and ravines, hovered over by battalion medics, like mother hens tending their brood. One medic brought out two bottles of cognac that he had previously "liberated" and was harboring for some future undetermined celebration. But not a soldier asked for a pull from the bottle. Instead the cognac helped light fires so that hot potato soup could be made for the more seriously wounded. All the while the midsummer sun beat down with unmerciful intensity.

Only the night before, the Germans had proposed a truce to allow each side to evacuate wounded from shell-swept Hill 317. Hearing of the enemy proposal, an Old Hickory whose leg had been blown off two days previously and whose stump was developing gangrene, called out weakly, "I don't want any truce with those bastards!"

That evening the German drumfire on the hill suddenly ceased. At 6:20 P.M. an outpost of Company E called out. "There's a couple of Krauts coming up the hill waving a white sheet or some goddamned thing!"

Into the line of American foxholes stalked a shiny-booted SS officer and his aide. Lieutenant Ralph A. Kerley, a tall, gaunt, phlegmatic Texan who commanded E Company, came out to meet the German emissaries. Kerley's black-bearded face and mud-splattered, torn clothing were in sharp contrast to the clean-shaven and immaculately garbed Germans.

"I demand that you honorably surrender to the German government," the officer of the 2nd SS Panzer Division declared. "You are surrounded."

Lieutenant Kerley eyed the man icily. "Your commander, Lieutenant Colonel Hardaway, is our prisoner," the German continued in flawless English. "Your position is desperate."

Now the SS officer grew more persuasive, concluding from Kerley's silence that the American was on the verge of capitulation. "You'll be well treated," he stressed. "But on the other hand, if you don't surrender by eight o'clock tonight you [and your men] will be totally destroyed!"

"Go to hell!" Lieutenant Kerley raged. "My men will fight until their last bullet has been fired and every one of our bayonets is sticking in a Kraut belly!"

The German officer stiffened. His face flushed. He turned on his heel and, with his aide trotting along behind, picked his way back down the hill.

A half-hour later, German big guns were plastering the height. Several panzers, supported by grenadiers armed with Schmeisser machine pistols, sprayed American positions, paying particular attention to Lieutenant Kerley's E Company sector. The savage assault took its toll, but the Germans were driven back down the hill. The Lost Battalion continued to bar Hitler's route to Avranches and the sea.

16

"A Most Unwelcome Mission"

COLONEL DORRANCE S. Roysdon was red-eyed from lack of sleep, and near exhaustion. A heavy stubble of beard covered his lower face. He and his men of Task Force 1 of the 3rd Armored Division had been locked for three days and two nights in a death struggle with elements of General von Lüttwitz's surging 2nd Panzer Division in the vicinity of Le Mesnil-Adelée and Le Mesnil-Tove, some three miles northwest of Mortain. For sixty hours Roysdon's armored force had been shelled and assaulted repeatedly by low-slung, ponderous Tigers and by determined grenadiers. The shelling was particularly bad, the worst Roysdon and his men had been under in Normandy. Big stuff. Approaching shells sounded like a freight train rushing through a tunnel.

At 11:45 A.M. on August 9, large-caliber guns began to plaster Colonel Roysdon's CP. A shell struck a half-track belonging to Lieutenant Colonel Rosewell King—blew it up in a cloud of smoke and flame. An effort was made to move Roysdon's command half-track, with its essential communications equipment. A shell hit the tracked vehicle, wounding an officer. The thin-skinned half-track resembled a sieve, riddled with fragments. One metal chunk pierced the radio. A tree burst, exploded over Roysdon's tank, another round landed by the front sprocket. Roysdon and a few of his staff were underneath the tank at the time. The shelling continued for four hours.

A short distance away, near Juvigny-le-Tertre, Colonel William

223

W. "Jug" Cornog, Jr., the stalwart leader of the 3rd Armored's Task Force 2, had convened a commanders' conference in a small outbuilding near a large farmhouse that had been demolished by shellfire. Cornog was a big, husky man, huge. He worried constantly that his formation wasn't moving fast enough, and it had been his habit to be up front to keep things going. Now the last officer had arrived. All were standing except one, who was lying on the floor next to the wall.

Colonel Cornog had just started to speak when they heard the sound of a shell rushing toward the building, and then a mighty explosion. The rickety farm building was cloaked in a cloud of dust and black smoke. A direct hit had killed Cornog and Lieutenant Colonel Vincent E. Cockfair, a battalion commander. All who had been standing were killed or seriously wounded. Lieutenant Walter May, the mortar platoon leader who had been lounging on the floor, escaped unscathed.

Technical Sergeant Norman Kruse had been in the hut. But he had been sent on a mission and had stepped outside the old structure only seconds before the shell screamed in.

A short time before one projectile wiped out the command group of Cornog's task force, Staff Sergeant George D. McLemore and his squad were bunched up in a sunken road behind the hut. Captain James B. Nixon, the company commander, came along on his way to Cornog's conference. "Don't bunch up there," Nixon called to McLemore and his men. "One shell will get you all." Nixon then went inside the hut, and minutes later was one of those killed—by one shell.

Sergeant McLemore and his squad moved into a wheat field on the forward slope of the hill on which the hut was located. Almost immediately the dispersed squad was pounded by artillery and heavy rockets. The shelling continued relentlessly. "The Krauts somewhere are looking right down on us," McLemore thought. Nervous men lit cigarettes. The smoke brought down a torrent of shells. Smoking ceased. They lay there the rest of the day, concealed only partly by the golden growth of grain. Thirst consumed them. One man volunteered to take five canteens and crawl back to a stream a short distance to the rear. There was the rotting corpse of a German soldier face down in the water. Nearby in the stream was a dead cow lying on its back, body bloated and legs sticking up in the air. But it was the only water available, so the soldier filled the five canteens. As he arduously crawled back through the wheat field, he thought it best not to inform his comrades of the human and animal cadavers in the stream. McLemore and his men, throats parched, eagerly gulped down the water.

Later that day, as the fighting raged, Sergeant McLemore learned that all officers in his company had been killed or seriously wounded and evacuated. McLemore, a squad leader, by seniority and rank became company commander.

As McLemore and his men were being pounded by rockets in the wheat field that day, some 30 miles to the west, across the blue Bay of St.-Michel, Bob Macon's 83rd Infantry Division had run into a buzzsaw while trying to capture Fortress St.-Malo. For four days and nights the 83rd had been assaulting the port city from three sides. They encountered belts of barbed wire, thickly sown minefields, rows of steel gates, antitank ditches, and machine gunners in concrete bunkers. Mortar and artillery fire from inside the ancient walled city rained down on the attackers.

INSIDE THE GERMAN defenses, fifty feet underground in the granite of the Citadel, Colonel Andreas von Aulock, a survivor of Stalingrad, curtly dismissed an American officer carrying a surrender ultimatum from General Macon. A French woman who had been the mistress of von Aulock was sent into St.-Malo by the Americans with a plea for "honorable capitulation to avoid senseless killing." She too was summarily rebuffed.

Medical supplies for German wounded went in under a flag of truce. A captured chaplain relayed an ultimatum. Aulock's reply: "Capitulation to an American is not compatible with the honor of a German soldier." The Madman of St.-Malo, the Allied news media called him. A hero of the Fatherland, was the German view.

ON AUGUST 9, General Heinz Eberhard, who for seven weeks had held back British attempts to break through from Caen toward Paris, was on the phone to Field Marshal von Kluge. "I consider this attack [on Avranches] to be a desperate throw. I find this a most unwelcome mission."

Eberhard, whom Hitler had picked to replace General von Funck for the second all-out effort to break through at Mortain, had grown leary of his new mission. Was he being set up as the scapegoat if the attack should fail?

Other factors in the renewal of Operation Luttich gnawed at Eberhard. He had been ordered to turn over his Fifth Panzer Army to an SS general, Sepp Dietrich, the former Nazi beer-hall brawler and Hitler bodyguard. "Dietrich is totally unqualified for the job," Eberhard had anguished to aides.

General Eberhard was furious to learn that his Luttich force would be placed under the orders of another SS general, Paul Hausser of Seventh Army, and he was amazed that Hausser would be entrusted to command a crucial assault the SS leader had already termed hopeless.

Eberhard promptly began launching protests to von Kluge. "What am I supposed to do with [only] 77 Mark IVs and 47 Panthers?" he shouted at the field marshal.

Eberhard held out for postponing the renewed assault until August 20. "I can attack only at night due to Allied air supremacy," he declared, "and for that I need a full moon. The next full moon to give me light won't occur until the twentieth." Otherwise, Eberhard stressed to von Kluge, "the Typhoons will blast me as they did vor Funck."

The request to postpone the attack to August 20 was promptly relayed to the Führer at Wolfsschanze. Came back the prompt reply: "You will attack on the eleventh as planned."

While General Eberhard was wrangling with von Kluge that morning of August 9, on the other side of the lines Omar Bradley paid a visit to George Patton's command post at St.-James, near Laval. He had exciting news for the Third Army commander. Instead of continuing the dash eastward, Patton was to turn Wade Haislip's XV Corps directly northward from Le Mans for an eventual linkup with Montgomery's British and Canadian forces driving down from south of Caen. Argentan, 14 miles south of Falaise, was designated as the stop-line for Patton in order to avoid a possible disastrous collision with Montgomery's advancing troops.

George Patton, audacious by nature and through military design, was disappointed. He wanted to drive even farther south and east before turning north. That night he would write a confidant: "We are attempting to encircle the Germans doughboy fashion, rather than cavalry fashion." He wanted a much larger net cast to "haul in more fish."

When an enthused Omar Bradley took leave of Patton, hopped into his staff car, and sped off to meet General Eisenhower in the Cotentin Peninsula, the Third Army commander retired to his quarters, took out his pad of yellow lined paper, and began putting down his attack order to Wade Haislip. As was his custom, Patton phrased his wording with thinly veiled subtleties. For the record, there would be the mission as outlined by higher headquarters. Carefully inserted would be catch phrases, which his corps commanders had learned to isolate, permitting great latitude of action should an opportunity arise to inflict telling blows against the enemy.

"You will advance along the axis Le Mans-Alençon-Sees with the purpose of initially securing the line Sees-Carrouges, *prepared for further advance* utilizing the 5th Armored Division, the 79th and 90th Infantry divisions, and the 2nd French Armored Division, which is hereby attached to your corps," Patton's order to Haislip read.

The catch phrase was "prepared for further advance." Who could ever fault a general for cautioning his commanders to be ready for pushing ahead?

Actually, General Patton had little confidence that the Canadians and British would reach the boundary at Argentan that Bradley and Montgomery had negotiated the previous day. If the British stalled in front of Falaise, and they were now stalled, Patton intended to snap the trap shut himself. Wade Haislip grasped the full meaning of the Pattonese "prepare for further advance." In the attack northward from Le Mans on the morrow, Haislip knew that Patton did not want him to halt his corps at Alençon, twenty-five miles distant, but to push on to Argentan, another twelve miles generally to the north, then on some fourteen miles to Falaise where, hopefully, the British would be met.

About sixty miles north of Le Mans where Haislip's XV Corps was preparing to jump off the following morning, at 6:45 A.M., the British Columbia Regiment of Guy Simond's Canadian II Corps set off to seize the dominating heights north of Falaise. Visibility was poor due to the haze. Hill 195, the primary objective, looked to tank drivers precisely like Hill 140 a short distance away.

227

It was the baptism of fire for the British Columbia Regiment, but hopes were high. Major General Alan Kitching, commander of the Canadian 4th Armoured Division, intended to capture Falaise that day.

Led by Lieutenant Colonel D. G. Worthington, tanks of the assaulting regiment moved forward parallel to Route Nationale 158, the main Caen-Falaise road. On either side of the advance fierce fighting raged, but Worthington's men soon found themselves atop their objective, Hill 195. Or was it? They had met virtually no resistance, and the path to Falaise appeared open.

Back at the 4th Armoured Division CP, eyebrows were raised at the relative ease with which Worthington had pushed up the slopes of Hill 195 and taken possession of the summit. Intelligence had reported that General Kurt Meyer's 12th SS Panzer Division was entrenched on that key elevation. The Canadian tanks had lost their way. They were not on their objective, but on Hill 140.

From his position on another small peak, Panzer Meyer watched through his binoculars as the Canadian tanks milled about the summit of Hill 140. By happenstance, a force of Meyer's panzers was on one side of Worthington's hill and more of Meyer's tanks were on the other side. The SS general gave the order to attack.

Soon massive Tigers were crawling up the east slope of Hill 140 and Panthers up the west slope. Edging into range, the panzers opened fire against the Canadian tanks. It was over in only thirty minutes. Ten of Worthington's Shermans had been set ablaze.

A beleaguered Colonel Worthington, caught in a trap in his first battle action, hurriedly put in a call for fire support. He gave what he thought were his position coordinates—those of Hill 195. Soon Canadian shells were falling around the front and sides of Hill 195, but no one was on it. The heavy barrage lasted for fifteen minutes.

Now Worthington's radios had gone silent. Tanks of the Governor General's Foot Guards were hurriedly dispatched to Hill 195 to learn what had happened to Worthington's regiment. On the way to the elevation, the Foot Guards had fourteen tanks knocked out, but eventually reached the hill and found it vacant.

On Hill 140, mistaken for the true objective, Worthington's Canadians were under heavy attack from all sides—and from above. Kurt Meyer's panzers were pouring shells onto the summit, British Typhoons mistook the Canadian Shermans for panzers and raked them with rockets and bombs, and Polish artillery, also under the impression that the force on Hill 140 was German, pounded Worthington's men.

Twelve hours after the British Columbia Regiment had jumped off in its initial attack with the hope of being in Falaise by dusk, the unit had been virtually wiped out. Forty-seven Shermans were mere wrecks on Hill 140. One hundred twelve officers and men had been killed, scores of others wounded, and thirty-four were missing and presumed captured. Only eight tanks rumbled down the back slope to the early-morning line of departure.

Once again the door to Falaise had been slammed shut by circumstances—and General Kurt Meyer's Hitler Youths.

SHORTLY AFTER DAWN on August 10, Wade Haislip's tanks and infantry roared northward in trucks out of the Le Mans region. Destination: Alençon, the key road center where the Rennes-Paris and Bordeaux-Rouen highways cross. Befitting a cavalryman, Patton ordered his corps commander to "lead with your tanks." Luns Oliver's 5th Armored Division and the newly arrived French 2nd Armored Division would spearhead the advance, side by side, followed by the 79th and 90th Infantry divisions to mop up bypassed pockets of resistance. Also new on the scene, the 80th Infantry Division, untested in battle and commanded by Major General Horace L. McBride, would protect the corps's rear.

Privately, General Omar Bradley was concerned about the quality of the troops in Haislip's corps. He wished that they had more battle experience. The two armored divisions leading the attack were the least experienced of their type. Bradley was particularly worried about the French 2nd Armored Division and its commander, Major General Jacques Philippe Leclerc. That was the nom de querre of Philippe François Marie de Hautecloque.

Leclerc was a bold fighting man who had seen much action in North Africa. But . . . he was notoriously erratic and undisciplined. Bradley was convinced that Leclerc's only goal was the early liberation of Paris and that he would not take kindly to the order to halt Haislip's eastward drive to head due north for Alençon.

Oliver's and Leclerc's armored divisions drove ahead abreast like a two-horse tandem. They ran into only sporadic opposition from rag-tag German units—a few short, sharp tank clashes, some artillery fire, several roadblocks. But they pushed on for 15 miles, halfway to Alençon.

Stretched across the XV Corps zone of advance was the Forêt de Perseigne, a thick woods where General Haislip feared the Germans might conceal strong forces to pounce on his columns. His concerns were heightened when spearheads encountered tanks and concentrated artillery fire on the approaches to the ten-mile-wide forest. Nearing the densely wooded area, a column of 5th Armored trucks was suddenly raked by machine-gun fire at a roadblock. Drivers slammed on brakes and leaped for the ditches beside the road. Private Charles P. McGuire of the 47th Armored Infantry Regiment, driving the lead truck, saw the source of the trouble—a dug-in German crew some 50 yards to the front. Clutching his Garand rifle, McGuire started slithering forward in the ditch, unnoticed by the enemy gunners who continued to fire into the convoy of stalled trucks.

When less than twenty-five yards away from the German automatic weapon, McGuire leaped to his feet and started pumping bullets into the startled enemy crew. He killed them all, the final one slumping over the barrel. McGuire returned to his truck, started the motor, and led the column forward once again. Minutes later there was a sharp crack and an 88-millimeter shell tore into the truck. Charlie McGuire was killed instantly.

Now General Haislip called for dropping oil incendiary bombs on the forest to burn and smoke out Germans. A flight of Thunderbolts arrived and drenched the woods. But the enemy had pulled back before the fighter-bombers did their work.

Meanwhile at his headquarters at St.-James, George Patton was impatient for news of Haislip's progress. As usual, he was puffing on a long cigar and pacing about like a caged tiger. A reporter moved up to him and inquired, "General, can the Germans stop you before you close the trap?" Patton glared at the man. "Hell, no, the Boche can't stop me!" he shouted. "The only thing that can stop me are those goddamned phase lines!"

In Wade Haislip's three-division push northward to Alençon, the unpredictable French General Leclerc was giving the corps commander fits. Haislip felt as though Leclerc was fighting his own private war. When Haislip assigned the French 2nd Armored certain roads for its zone of advance, Leclerc used those roads or intruded upon those of the adjoining division as he saw fit. Most American commanders believed that the French armored leader was obsessed with reaching Paris at the earliest possible time. And the way to do that, it would seem to the Frenchman, was to race ahead at full throttle, the neighbors' roads be damned.

At a crossroads, an American military policeman directing traffic complained bitterly to his lieutenant. "Those goddamned Frog drivers are crazy as hell!" the harassed MP exploded. "One convoy of French trucks came barreling through the intersection at forty-five miles an hour. One truck kept going straight ahead, one whipped off to the left, and another charged off to the right. All I saw were clouds of dust in all three directions!"

Whatever he may have lacked in military discipline, Jacques Leclerc was Patton's kind of soldier. Bold, audacious, fearless—and he hated the Boche. The Third Army commander loved France and anything French. He beamed widely when he received a message from Haislip that Leclerc's fighting men were "killing Germans with gusto and efficiency." When Haislip was livid over Leclerc's "hogging" the roads and stymying the 5th Armored's attack, Patton said soothingly, "Hell, Wade, don't get so upset. He's only a baby."

THAT NIGHT OF August 10, Field Marshal Guenther von Kluge was staring the haunting specter of stark military reality directly in the face. What he had feared since Cobra shook loose American armored columns from the Normandy bocage on July 25 and Adolf Hitler shunned the advice of his skilled professionals to pull back to the Seine River, was in its final act. The gigantic trap around von Kluge's two armies was in the process of being snapped shut. And there was little he could do about it.

The field marshal placed a call to General Jodl, Hitler's confidant at Wolfsschanze. "I suggest that we temporarily withdraw the Eberbach panzer group from Mortain and use it to halt the American attack northward toward Alençon," he stated. Aware that Hitler already suspected his loyalty after the July 20 bomb attempt, von Kluge quickly added, "All the generals under my command think that we should withdraw."

There was a silence from the other end of the line. This would mean abandoning the assault against Avranches that was scheduled to be launched the next day. Hitler had put all his chips on driving to the sea and splitting the rampaging Third Army from First Army. Finally Jodl said that he would pass the suggestion on to the Führer.

Predictably, Hitler was furious. He felt that von Kluge had already botched Operation Luttich by not following his orders to the letter. Now the commander in the West was proposing that Avranches be abandoned.

In less than two hours, Hitler's reply was received. He bombarded von Kluge with questions: Why can't the attack to Avranches be launched before August 20? What does General von Funck think about a new thrust there? What forces will be used to recapture Le Mans? When will the 11th Panzer Division arrive from southern France?

Meanwhile that day, Beaver Thompson, the correspondent for the *Chicago Tribune,* was at Courtney Hodges's First Army headquarters south of St.-Lô filing a story. Thompson had made two combat jumps with paratroopers in North Africa and the assault landing at bloody Omaha Beach on D-Day. He was accustomed to covering stories from the front lines and to violence and armed Germans. Not so all of his colleagues and military staff personnel at First Army headquarters, a complex of tents and trailers around an ornate château.

At about noon there was the roar of airplane engines, and scores of heads popped out of tents, trailers, and the château to view a dogfight raging high in the blue sky between a Thunderbolt and a black German fighter plane. The Luftwaffe aircraft began smoking, a figure was seen to bail out, and a parachute blossomed. The German pilot was coming down directly into woods only one hundred yards away.

Bedlam erupted as headquarters officers, soldiers, and correspondents scrambled for their weapons. Now they were going to finally see "action." Waving pistols and rifles and screaming like banshees, some thirty of them dashed like jackrabbits across a field to the woods where the Luftwaffe pilot had landed. Moments later, Beaver Thompson, watching from outside his tent, saw the German, hands over head, emerge from the cluster of trees. Surrounding him were thirty Americans, looks of triumph on their faces, weapons leveled at the hapless lone captive.

Thompson shook his head and returned to writing his story on frontline action that he had viewed that morning.

17

Hitler's World
of Fantasy

WHILE GENERAL PATTON'S free-wheeling flying columns were charging northward from Le Mans to trigger shut the steel trap on von Kluge's two Normandy armies, furious fighting was continuing to rage along the First Army front at Mortain. Early in the morning of August 11, elements of General Matt Eddy's 9th Infantry Division were slugging their way toward Pérriers-en-Beaufice, some five miles northwest of Mortain. On the previous day, Eddy's men had received a bloody nose and were stopped cold in an effort to seize the key town and its dominating heights.

Out in front with assaulting infantrymen was Lieutenant Irving Tepper, a diminutive officer who had been with the 9th Infantry Division since the invasion of North Africa in November 1942. Tepper, disheveled, bearded, and weary, was a typical dogface except for one significant factor—he was a chaplain, a frontline chaplain. He had been offered a cushy job at corps headquarters, but had summarily rejected it to remain up-front with "my boys." He had become a legend in the 9th Division. Men of all faiths had come to Chaplain Tepper for advice and spiritual sustinance.

Now in the assault toward Pérriers-en-Beaufice, Tepper's battalion of the 60th Infantry Regiment came under heavy shellfire. Chaplain Tepper was cut down, his body pierced by 22 pieces of shrapnel. Two days later, the little man with the huge heart would die. A mournful rifleman would mutter the highest praise a dogface could give: "Chaplain Tepper was always up-front."

Even as life was trickling from the body of the rabbi that morning, his comrades in the 9th Division, raked by withering machine-gun fire and pounded by artillery and mortars, fought their way forward and seized Pérriers-en-Beaufice and the key heights around it. Chaplain Tepper was in a coma at an aide station. He would never know of his comrades's feat of arms.

All along General Collins's VII Corps sector in the vicinity of Mortain, American troops were no longer on the defensive, but were edging slowly forward against fierce resistance. The Germans were desperately trying to hang onto the ground they had seized in Operation Luttich in order to have a springboard for the renewal of the offensive to seize Avranches. In recent days south of Mortain, Paul Baade's 35th Infantry Division had been inching ahead under heavy fire and relentless German counterattacks in an effort to cut the road leading from Mortain to Barenton, six miles south. Elements of Baade's division reached the road, but it had taken four days and more than six hundred casualties to get there. As a result of the 35th Division pressure, the Germans withdrew from positions southwest of Mortain and pulled back from Romagny.

Ted Brooks's 2nd Armored Division had been attacking northeast from Barenton toward Ger, punching a tank-tipped spear into the flank and rear of enemy forces trying to break through to Avranches. The penetration by Brooks's tankers and a small task force of the 3rd Armored Division hampered enemy troop movements and communications.

Northwest of Mortain, a combined force of the 119th Infantry of Hobbs's Old Hickories and Colonel Boudinot's Combat Command-B of the 3rd Armored Division drove the 2nd Panzer Division out of the road junction of Le Mesnil-Tove, and elements of the 30th Division ejected the enemy from the town of Mortain.

The five days of fighting around Mortain had been as bitter and bloody as any in the war. But by late afternoon of August 11, Joe Collins and his fighting men had not only halted Hitler's all-out plunge for Avranches but had regained lost territory.

American losses were heavy. Hobbs's 30th Infantry Division, which had been struck by the main blow, had suffered two thousand casualties in less than six days, and Eddy's 9th Infantry Division had lost more than one thousand men. Barton's 4th Infantry Division had over six hundred killed.

Back of Hodges's First Army front, bodies of young Americans, shrouded in white-gray mattress covers were stretched out in long rows. Burial details were hard-pressed to keep up with their work. An urgent order was placed in England to rush additional mattress covers to Normandy. As each corpse, stiff and cold, was lowered into the ground, a wooden cross or Star of David was placed at the head of the grave, and the soldier's dog tag was nailed to the marker.

But in the six days of vicious fighting, German forces had been severely hurt. A regiment of von Lüttwitz's 2nd Panzer Division had been wiped out around Le Mesnil-Tove. The 1st SS Panzer Division had lost nearly three-fourths of its Tigers, Panthers, and Mark IVs. The 2nd SS Panzer Division, which had captured Mortain and penetrated four miles into and behind 30th Infantry Division lines in the early hours of Luttich, had been cut to pieces by accurate American artillery fire. Allied fighter-bombers had caused enormous devastation.

As Collins's corps pushed forward, the Lost Battalion was rescued from embattled Hill 317 where for six days and nights it had held off everything the Germans could throw at it and had scorned an enemy surrender demand. But the epic battalion action had taken a terrible toll. Of the eight-nine hundred Americans—the Bulldogs of Mortain—who had been on the dominating hill, fewer than three hundred, many of them wounded, all weak and suffering from lack of food, answered roll call.

That morning of August 11 in Bletchley Park outside London, Group Captain F. W. Winterbotham and his Ultra associates at Station X eagerly watched for Hitler's response to von Kluge's urgent suggestion of the night before that Eberhard's panzers be pulled back to the east from Mortain to strike at Patton's column surging northward from Le Mans. Von Kluge's request amounted to abandoning Luttich. Winterbotham heard nothing. It was a good omen. At this crucial moment in the West, when all the chips were on the table, the German high command in France was paralyzed by lack of orders from Wolfsschanze.

At his sprawling complex of bunkers and headquarters buildings in East Prussia, Hitler was ignorant of the true situation in France. He wallowed in self-delusion, convinced that it was not his strategic planning that was at fault in the fighting in the West, but rather the incompetence of his generals and their failure to carry out his instructions to the letter. Since his miraculous escape from Count von Stauffenberg's bomb on July 20, the Fuhrer distrusted nearly all of his high-ranking military men.

From his vantage point one thousand miles from the cauldron in France and surrounded by protective subordinates, Hitler refused to recognize the smothering Anglo-American air power that precluded his commanders from making large-scale troop movements by day. Neither did he take into account the extreme exhaustion of the Feldgrau, who had been fighting almost continuously since D-Day, more than nine weeks before. He ignored the battered state of German equipment and rolling stock as well as the shortage of supplies and ammunition. And he failed to accept the great mobility of Anglo-American tanks and mechanized infantry.

Hitler was furious that his forces were being cut to pieces by Americans. He held the American fighting man in particular disdain, referring to him repeatedly as "an effeminate ribbon clerk." On his enormous battle map at Wolfsschanze, German divisions were indicated by tiny flags; HItler shuffled them about as a chess master would move his pawns. But the flags did not indicate that the strength of most of his divisions had been severely reduced, and that many were mere skeletons.

As Hitler was calling the shots in France, often down to battalion level, it was impossible for his commanders there to take immediate actions. By the time information or his battle leaders' recommendations reached the Führer, were digested by him, and discussed with his confidants, and by the time his instructions reached the front, as long as twenty-four hours had elapsed. Then it was too late for von Kluge, or Hausser, or Eberhard, or Dietrich to act, for the entire battlefield picture had changed.

Yet there was nothing that could be done. Any hesitancy to implement the Führer's detailed instructions could mean the immediate dismissal of a top commander, or even his execution for disloyalty or defeatism. Some fellow generals in France pleaded with Obergruppenführer Dietrich to intercede in person with Hitler and tell him the truth. Dietrich, who was as close to the Führer as anyone, having fought side by side with him in the early days of Nazism, shirked from the task.

"If I want to get shot, that's a good way to do it!" the squat, pug-nosed Dietrich responded.

Weeks before, Sepp Dietrich had told Field Marshal Erwin Rommel that Adolf Hitler was "a madman." But it was too late to do anything about it. Dietrich and other German commanders in France would have to fight on to the end, come what may.

EARLY ON THE morning of August 11, an exuberant General Patton fastened on his ivory-handled revolvers, clamped his lacquered helmet with its three gleaming, oversized stars onto his head, and set out to chase his spearheads in the direction of Alençon. He turned to his chief of staff, Major General Hugh Gaffey, and exclaimed "Well, Gaffey, to coin a phrase, this is it!" He was convinced that Hitler's armies in Normandy would be trapped within days, possibly hours.

Then to his aide Lieutenant Colonel Charles Codman, he said, "Be sure to bring along a bag of Bronze Stars for Leclerc's sons of bitches."

In his customary whirling-dervish style, Patton called on Wade Haislip at XV Corps headquarters; he also visited the 5th armored, 79th Infantry, and 90th Infantry divisions, then started roaring about a countryside full of scattered bands of Germans in search of General Leclerc. He never found the French leader who himself was shuttling about to his various spearheads.

For several days Patton had voiced to Bradley and to his own aides a healthy doubt about Montgomery's ability to close the gap at Falaise-Argentan. Now, on August 11, the Third Army commander was convinced that he had been right. At this point, with one of history's great victories in the offing, the trapping of two entire enemy field armies, Patton was unconcerned about phase lines, boundaries, or the niceties of inter-Allied protocol and harmony. He had no intention of sitting idle and allowing the quarry to flee the trap. George Patton would take matters into his own hands.

While calling on Haislip of XV Corps that morning, Patton had bellowed, "Wade, pay no attention to Monty's goddamned boundaries. Be prepared to push on past even Falaise if necessary. I'll give you the word." The gap between Haislip's spearheads and the stalled Canadians to the north had been reduced to twenty-two miles.

At his headquarters in the vicinity of Caen, General Bernard Montgomery that morning also gave indications of concern over the closing of the trap. He called General Crerar, leader of the Canadian

First Army, and urged him to push on. "It is vital that it [the capture of Falaise] be done quickly." Montgomery ordered Crerar to continue past Falaise and link up with the Americans at Argentan, the east-west boundary between the British and Patton's forces.

Inside what was rapidly developing into a gigantic pocket, a beleaguered Guenther von Kluge was holding a desperate conference with his top commanders, generals Paul Hausser of Seventh Army, Sepp Dietrich of Fifth Panzer Army, and Heinz Eberhard of the Luttich armored force. The morning-long conference was saturated with gloom. None of the battle leaders had anything except depressing news to report from all sectors. At noon von Kluge put in a call to General Jodl at Wolfsschanze:

> "The offensive in the direction of Avranches is no longer possible. The enemy is all out to encircle the army group. He has fresh troops. The thrust to the sea will be a bitter long-drawn-out battle. The panzers are outnumbered."

Once again, the wily von Kluge was careful not to give the impression that this morbid view of the battle situation in France was his alone. He knew that the Gestapo was still probing his possible implication in the July 20 Schwarze Kapelle plot, and that the Führer was especially suspicious of him.

"In the opinion of Obergruppenführer Hausser and General Eberhard, [with] which I entirely agree, the consequences [of continuing Luttich] will be hard to swallow," von Kluge declared. He had projected these "defeatist" views as coming from two staunch Nazis, Hausser and Eberhard, and he, von Kluge, was endorsing their opinions.

After a moment's silence, General Jodl inquired, "Am I to inform the Führer that you have definitely abandoned a breakthrough at Avranches?" Again, words uttered to "cover" Jodl. Hitler's confidant was now on record as pinpointing the commander who wanted to abandon the Führer's strategic plan for victory in France: that man was Gunther von Kluge. It was von Kluge, not Jodl, who wanted to abandon Luttich.

That night, the 5th Armored and the French 2nd Armored divisions were approaching Alençon, the primary objective of XV

Corps. Corps commander, Haislip, again examining the wording in Patton's directive to "be prepared for further advance," established a new objective—Argentan. There he would link up with the Canadians coming down from the north and shut the trap on von Kluge's armies.

Whatever the personal consequences, Field Marshal von Kluge signaled his battle commanders: *Seventh Army will withdraw from the Mortain salient tonight*. Two corps fighting in the Mortain sector were to regroup north of Alençon, fifty miles east of Mortain, and prepare to attack Haislip's XV Corps, which was driving north to spring the trap. It was an order to retreat fifty miles. But since Hitler had ordered him not to give up a foot of ground in Normandy, von Kluge cloaked his order in a subtlety: he called the maneuver the Alençon Plan.

South of Alençon that night, Jacques Leclerc, clutching his cane in the front seat of his jeep, was waiting patiently for his aide to unravel a minor mystery: just where were they. In the blackness his lost driver had taken a wrong turn. Moments later an automobile came racing down the road toward the Leclerc jeep. "Boche!" someone called out. The general's aide leaped from the jeep, aimed his pistol, and fired. The bullet killed the German driver, causing the car to veer crazily and grind to a halt. Several officers emerged with hands in the air.

The captured Germans were searched and a valuable discovery made—German plans for the coming day in front of Leclerc's 2nd Armored Division.

Based on this captured information, General Leclerc ordered one of his task forces to jump off immediately in two columns. They were ordered to rendezvous in Sees. Leclerc was not inhibited by the fact that Sees was in the zone of advance of Oliver's 5th Armored Division.

Shortly after 10:00 P.M. tanks, armored cars, and trucks crammed with infantry of the 5th Armored rumbled into the town square of Sees. Frenzied natives by the hundreds descended on the halted American column, waving tiny tricolors and cheering the new arrivals. Less than two hours later, at about midnight, Jacques Leclerc's task force rolled into town. Now scores of tanks and nearly two hundred vehicles, in addition to large numbers of American and

French infantry, were jammed into and around the square. Chaos had erupted over the sudden arrival of Leclerc's column in an American objective.

A heated argument erupted among American and French commanders about the roads to be used by the 5th Armored and the French 2nd Armored as townsfolk mingled among the fighting men of two Allied nations. A massive traffic jam had developed.

Red-faced with anger and frustration, the chief of staff of the 5th Armored shouted at the French task force leader, "You have no right to be here! Sees is in our zone of advance! We need this road to get to Argentan!"

The French commander shrugged his shoulders. "We're only passing through," he replied, ignoring the fact that his force was blocking the forward movement of the entire 5th Armored Division.

Presently a mud-splattered jeep carrying the tricolor of France carefully edged into the swirling mass of humanity and scores of tanks, jeeps, and trucks jammed into the square. Out hopped General Leclerc, his customary goggles strapped around his high-beamed officer's hat, who promptly joined in the vigorous debate with 5th Armored officers. Leclerc never could figure out these crazy Americans. Why were they so excited over who would use which roads? The French general's cold blue eyes flashed with anger as the argument grew more acrimonious. Much like George Patton, Leclerc could summon up a fierce scowl when the occasion demanded it, one that often frightened others as well as his own men.

Eventually a gentlemen's agreement was negotiated to untangle the traffic mess and allow both Oliver's and Leclerc's spearheads to continue the advance. The French general issued immediate orders for one of his task forces to get on the road. Objective: Alençon.

At 3:00 A.M. the night air was pierced by the sudden revving of engines as tanks, trucks, and other vehicles of the French 2nd Armored Division began crawling northward out of Sees. It was pitch black. The Frenchmen in the column were tense, for they were moving into territory believed held by the Germans and at any moment they might hear the shriek of shells fired point-blank out of the darkness. It was an ideal situation for enemy ambushes.

In the leading jeep, driven by a captain, was a young French underground fighter who had volunteered to guide the column into

Alençon. As daylight was fast approaching, the jeep reached the Neuf bridge at the southern outskirts of town. There the French column paused . . . and listened. There was not a sound from the houses and buildings on the far side of the stream. Most citizens were asleep, for the Germans had posted a 2:00-6:00 A.M. curfew that kept normal early risers in bed longer. Why was it so quiet? Had the Germans fled? Or were they in concealed machine-gun nests and 88-millimeter-gun positions in the darkness along the far bank?

The maquisard and the French captain dismounted, carefully edged onto the bridge, and searched for explosives. When they found none they waved the tanks onward. The tracked vehicles slowly crept over the span, and spread out to cover all of the town's exits. By now it was daylight, and a few citizens appeared on the streets. They rubbed their eyes in amazement. The Germans had vanished in the night. In their place were strange tanks manned by soldiers in strange uniforms. Shouts of glee erupted. Other citizens poured into the streets.

"Vive les Americains!" rang out over and over.

Leclerc's dust-covered men replied to these tumultuous greetings in French.

"Vive les Canadians!" came the new cry.

The liberators pointed to the Cross of Lorraine on their vehicles and tunics. The tumult turned to bedlam as word spread that France's very own were in Alençon. In minutes Calvados was flowing freely. For the moment the war was forgotten as Leclerc's grimy fighting men and newly liberated civilians rejoiced.

Meanwhile, after the elements of the French 2nd Armored Division had cleared out of Sees and other roads in the 5th Armored Division zone of advance, Luns Oliver sent his tankers plunging forward. They bypassed Alençon to the east and prepared to race on to the boundary line at Argentan.

At the same time that the men, women, and children of Alençon were erupting in wild jubilation, some fifty miles westward bedraggled survivors of the rescued Lost Battalion were filing down shell-pocked Hill 317 east of Mortain. Grim-faced, bone-weary, and hungry after existing for days on raw apples, radishes, and potatoes, they were headed for a brief respite from the horrors of war.

There was no sign of heady triumph etched into these tired,

hollow-eyed, unshaven, and once-youthful faces. They had had a job to do, and they did it. Too much had been seen. Too much had been endured. Too many close friends had been cut down in the prime of their lives.

As the surviving three hundred picked their way along, unseeing eyes focused in that fixed stare that is reserved for those who have come face to face with the haunting specter of death and mutilation. They passed scores of rotting corpses of Feldgrau sprawled about the slopes. Here and there was the blackened remains of a Tiger or Panther struck by American artillery directed from the top of the elevation.

Marching at the head of the surviving three hundred was the young commander of the Lost Battalion, Captain Reynold Erichson, who had suddenly been shouldered with enormous responsibility when the battalion commander was seized in Mortain. Then there were the stalwart company commanders, Captain Delmont K. Byrn of the heavy weapons company, and lieutenants Ronal E. Woody, Jr., Joseph C. Reaser, and Ralph Kerley.

In the valley, the phlegmatic Texan Kerley was approached by a colonel from another Old Hickory regiment who had heard that Kerley had rejected an SS officer's surrender ultimatum by telling the Nazi to "go to hell!"

Said the American colonel, "Ralph, you had a hell of a nerve to tell the Krauts that!"

Replied Lieutenant Kerley in a matter of fact tone, "They had a hell of a nerve to put a proposition like that up to me."

18

"The Encirclement Is Imminent!"

ON THE MORNING of August 12, General Guy Simonds's Canadians, so crucial to the trap being forged for the Germans, were still bogged down twelve miles north of Falaise. The mood around Omar Bradley's 12th Army Group headquarters was ugly. Wrote one of Bradley's aides in the daily log: "The British [Canadian] effort appears to have bogged itself in timidity and succumbed to the legendary [General] Montgomery vice of over-caution."

General Bradley himself had another deep concern in his mind on this beautiful summer day. Ultra intercepts had informed him that strong panzer formations had been pulled back from the Mortain sector overnight and were moving eastward, presumably to smash into the side of Wade Haislip's columns racing northward toward Argentan. The bitter death struggle around Mortain had ended, so that afternoon General Bradley put in a call to Joe Collins, whose VII Corps had met and thrown back Hitler's full-scale assault to reach Avranches.

"Joe, I want you to go all-out to the northeast, toward Argentan, and insert your corps between Haislip and the bulk of the Germans withdrawing from Mortain," Bradley directed.

With typical alacrity, Collins had his entire VII Corps on the road that night. In the vanguard were Huebner's Big Red One, Eddy's 9th Infantry Division, and the 3rd Armored Division, which had received a new commander on August 7. He was Brigadier General Maurice Rose, a product of the Colorado National Guard, who had

243

led a combat command in Brooks's 2nd Armored Division in the Cobra breakout. Tubby Barton's 4th Infantry Division would be in reserve. The four divisions would head southwest for Mayenne that night, then drive northeast toward the Argentan region shortly after dawn.

Knowing that Collins's corps was racing for the southern jaw of the trap in support of Haislip's strung-out divisions brought a measure of relief to Bradley. He considered VII Corps, the victor of Mortain, conqueror of Fortress Cherbourg, and assaulter of Utah Beach on D-Day, the finest in his command. Haislip's corps of Third Army and Collins's corps of First Army would hold the southern jaw and, Bradley hoped, join up soon with Montgomery's forces coming down from the north.

AT 7:30 A.M. on August 12, directives went out to army commands from St.-Germain, headquarters of Commander in Chief, West. The orders were signed by Guenther von Kluge, who had been little more than a figurehead for some time. From far-off East Prussia, Hitler was still calling the shots. The directives were simple in tone: General Eberhard's panzer force at Mortain "will restore the situation at Alençon, will destroy the enemy there, then will return to Mortain to launch the all-out assault to seize Avranches." It was an order totally divorced from battlefield reality. Eberhard's panzer group, already battered from five days of bitter fighting in Operation Luttich, would be able to muster only twenty-nine tanks for the 2nd Panzer Division, fifteen for the 116th Panzer, and thirty for the 1st SS Panzer.

Eberhard had established his headquarters in a village eight miles southeast of Argentan. The assault ordered by Hitler to "restore the situation" at Alençon never got off the drawing board. Eberhard's headquarters itself was being heavily shelled, and Allied fighter-bombers had set fire to scores of vehicles there, which were blazing ominously on all sides. The panzer general expected American tanks and infantry to burst into his headquarters at any moment. Gunfire was heard all around. Late that evening, Fuhrer orders or not, Eberhard pulled out of his CP. He would be of little use to the Third Reich as an American prisoner, or dead. Left behind to halt the powerful American and French spearheads was a noncombat company of German bakers.

Now an ominous word was being whispered through the ranks of the Feldgrau, and in dark, deserted corners of high-level German headquarters in France. The word was heard over and over. The word was *Kessel* (pocket). From the disheveled teenage machine-gunner up through the lofty office of Commander in Chief, West, the Germans in Normandy knew that they were on the verge of being trapped.

On that afternoon of August 12, the great German flight to escape the closing prongs of the Allied trap got underway. First there was only a trickle of vehicles edging through Argentan, headed eastward —mainly ambulances and assorted conveyances carrying the seriously wounded. They lay in the vehicles unknowingly, tunics saturated with blood, crimson-stained white bandages wound around heads. Complexions of the dying and the greviously mutilated were sallow. Then a tank or two joined the flight, and soon armored cars and trucks entered the stream moving eastward out of the forming Kessel.

Grenadiers stared hollow-eyed as they trudged through town, many without weapons or helmets. Battered automobiles, some with windows shattered, others without doors, all loaded with once-proud members of the German Wehrmacht and Waffen SS. Bicycles. Carts. Horse-drawn wagons. Anything to escape the Allied hurricane of steel and explosives. All heading eastward.

A barely audible murmur escaped the ranks of the fleeing rabble as gunfire erupted south of Argentan. The shooting marked the approach of General Oliver's 5th Armored Division, which had halted on the southern outskirts to await further orders.

At 11:30 P.M. Oliver's boss, Wade Haislip, put in a call to General Patton at Third Army headquarters near Laval. The aggressive Haislip, who remembered Patton's order to "be prepared to advance further northward," remarked to Patton that the 5th Armored was about to seize Argentan and that he had no mission beyond that. However, he added pointedly, should Patton so desire, he was prepared to attack toward Falaise with the 5th Armored and French 2nd Armored divisions.

Without consulting Bradley, Patton ordered Haislip to continue his attack *beyond* the boundary, or stop-line, and "push on slowly in the direction of Falaise," and when he reached there to "continue to push on slowly until contact [is made with] our Allies."

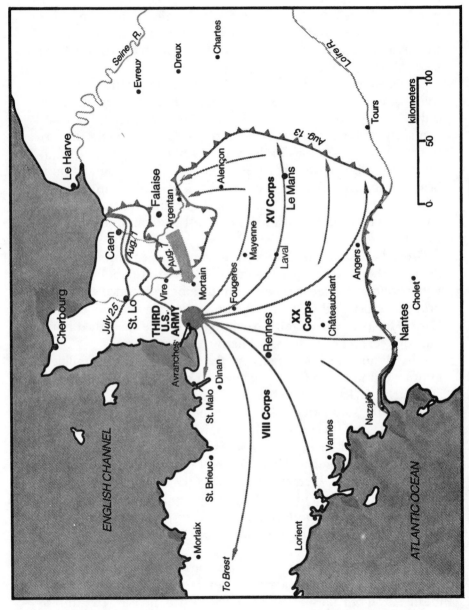

The Great Allied Trap Takes Shape

AT HIS HEADQUARTERS at Creullet Manor that night, Bernard Montgomery was discussing the situation with his worried chief of staff, General Freddie de Guingand. "Every hour that passes empties the sack we want to close," de Guingand observed gloomily.

"Completing the encirclement won't be easy," Montgomery responded. "The German knows his life depends on this corridor [between Falaise and Argentan]."

Meanwhile, George Patton and his entire Third Army were still fighting under a strict news blackout. Only the American homefront was kept in the dark. Radio Berlin for days had been reporting of Patton's involvement. On the morning of August 13, the *Washington Star* brought the issue out into the open. Quoting from a German news agency account, an editorial observed that it was past time to give the Third Army and its commander credit for battlefield achievements. The blackout remained in effect.

George Patton's colorful personality, flamboyant dress, and his aggressive armored attacks presented a problem for Supreme Commander Eisenhower. Patton, outgoing, eager for publicity, sought the limelight. On the other hand, Omar Bradley and Courtney Hodges, both reserved and indifferent to personal public recognition, tended to be overlooked by the press.

"Our problem is," a SHAEF public relations officer confided to a newsman, "that when we take the wraps off Patton the media is going to make it look as though he won the war single-handedly and that Bradley and Hodges were along just for the ride."

ON THE MORNING of the thirteenth, a platoon of 5th Armored Division tanks edged into the crossroads at le-Bourg-Saint-Leonard, a village that was significant because the east-west road running through its center led to the Seine and provided a German escape route. Scores of jubilant villagers emerged from houses and deluged the "liberators" with hugs, kisses, and Calvados. Bourg-Saint-Leonard was actually in no-man's-land.

Into the midst of the celebrating crowd pedaled a German on a bicycle, unaware that Americans were in the village. Suddenly he halted. His jaw dropped. He spun around and started pedaling furiously back out of town as the Americans raised weapons to fire. At that moment a solemn funeral procession edged across the square on its way to the church, The 5th Armored tankers held up until the procession had passed, then opened fire on the hapless fleeing German. He made his getaway under a hail of bullets.

That morning, General Fritz Bayerlein was clinging to the bottom of a slit trench next to his farmhouse headquarters a few miles northwest of Argentan. Bayerlein's once-elite Panzer Lehr Division had been virtually wiped out in the July 25 massive sky bombardment that launched Cobra and in ensuing action during the American breakout from the *bocage* country of Normandy. At Hitler's East Prussia headquarters, Bayerlein's little band of survivors was carried on maps as a kampfgruppe, a designation totally divorced from reality.

Now General Bayerlein and a few aides in the slit trench were under heavy attack by Jabos. His nearby farmhouse had been hit and was blazing fiercely. Horse-drawn vehicles had been shot up and littered the roads. The planes swept up and down the narrow roads, strafing and bombing. One fighter-bomber zipping in on a strafing run at thirty feet banked as it passed over Bayerlein in his trench. The German general could see the pilot's face. Pilot and panzer leader locked eyes. The American airman appeared to be laughing as he whisked on past, as if to say, "Stay right there, you bastard! I'll be back in a minute to take care of you!"

The fighter-bomber turned, headed back toward Bayerlein's slit trench with machine guns blazing. Bullets hissed past the general and his aides, and thudded into the dirt around them. Then two terrific explosions showered the Germans with dirt, pieces of wood, and leaves—the Jabo had dropped its bombs. Bayerlein and a few others clawed their way out of the debris. All were wounded. Under the fresh mounds of dirt several dead Germans were buried.

At about the same time General Bayerlein was being blasted from the sky, General Wade Haislip was on the phone to George Patton. Haislip was furious. The unpredictable French General Leclerc was continuing to give the corps commander fits. In the push toward Argentan the previous afternoon, Haislip had ordered Leclerc to bypass the Forêt d'Ecouves, an extensive, thickly wooded area standing like a natural barricade in front of Argentan. The French armored leader ignored the order. He sent his columns around the forest on both sides and three other columns dashing directly through the woods. Although Leclerc's own advance was accelerated, the procedure blocked the roads for Oliver's 5th Armored Division, delaying the latter's attack for six hours.

As a result of hundreds of Leclerc's vehicles clogging roads assigned to the 5th Armored, the French 2nd Armored arrived first at the outskirts of Argentan. Inside the villagers were decked out in their Sunday best, ready to attend mass, for this thirteenth day of August was a Sunday. Word quickly spread that "American liberators" were just outside the town, and the excited population hurriedly unfurled the French flag from the balcony of the town hall and two more tricolors from the tower of St.-Germain church.

The joy would be short-lived. There were only a handful of Germans in Argentan that morning, but by evening the enemy would move back into town and man strategic points with Tigers and Panthers and machine-gun posts. Soon shells were screaming into town, American shells, flattening houses, knocking roofs off buildings, punching holes in walls. The citizens of Argentan took to their cellars and prayed.

At headquarters of Fifth Panzer Army, the teleprinter was clacking early that morning. General Sepp Dietrich was sending a desperate warning to Army Group B headquarters at La Roche-Guyon, nestled in a scenic setting in a great bend of the Seine River north of Paris. Only a few days before, Dietrich had declared that "a good way to get myself shot" would be to tell Adolf Hitler the truth about the situation in France. Now Dietrich was risking that ultimate possibility.

"If the front held by the [Fifth] Panzer Army and the Seventh Army is not withdrawn immediately and if every effort is not made to move these forces toward the east and out of the threatened encirclement, the army group will have to write-off both armies," General Dietrich declared. "Within a very short time resupplying the troops with ammunition and fuel will no longer be possible. Therefore, immediate measures are necessary to move to the east before such movement is definitely too late. It will soon be possible for the enemy to fire into the pocket with artillery from all sides."

Dietrich, in his grimly realistic warning, had voiced the views of each German general in France acquainted with the battle situation. The pocket had been squeezed to an area some thirty miles long and fifteen broad. Only a narrow gap remained between Argentan and a few miles north of Falaise through which German supplies and reinforcements could be brought in, or through which the Germans could escape. Inside the pocket, mass confusion reigned. American intelligence could no longer keep track of the German order of battle, neither could German intelligence.

Only seven generally east-west roads were still available to the Wehrmacht between the two jaws of the Allied trap. Most of these were narrow dirt roads. All were in artillery range of Canadians on the north and Americans on the south, and a choice target for swarms of Anglo-American fighter-bombers.

Early in the morning of August 13, General Omar Bradley was livid with rage. He had just received word that Patton had disregarded his stern instructions and had sent Wade Haislip's patrols on past the stop-line at Argentan. Several of Haislip's patrols during the early morning hours had pushed on past the boundary for eight miles, to within six miles of pulverized Falaise.

Much of Bradley's anger came from deep concern over the situation at Argentan-Falaise. His intelligence officer, Brigadier General Edwin L. Sibert, had solemnly advised the 12th Army Group chief that elements of nineteen German divisions, presumably fully organized and equipped, had begun a mad rush for the narrow exit from the pocket. Bradley feared that Haislip's corps would be stretched too thin and unable to hold back the onrushing German tide about to smash through the escape corridor from the west. Actually, the remnants of Seventh and Fifth Panzer armies, numbering some one hundred thousand men, were milling about in confusion and in most cases heading eastward on their own without direction or orders from higher headquarters.

Bradley and Patton had a sharp exchange over the telephone that morning. The Third Army commander was unrepentant over his flagrant violation of orders.

"Let me go on to Falaise and we'll drive the British back into the sea for another Dunkirk!" Patton exploded in his high-pitched voice.

"Nothing doing," Bradley replied. "You're not to go beyond Argentan. Just stop where you are and build up on that shoulder. Sibert tells me the German is beginning to pull out. You'd better button up and get ready for him."

Haislip's patrols north of Argentan were called back.

For two hours George Patton stewed in his headquarters at St.-James near Laval. One of the great opportunities of the war was rapidly slipping through timid Allied fingers, he was convinced. Patton put in a call to Bradley's headquarters near Coutances, and General Leven Allen, 12th Army Group chief of staff, took the call. He said that Bradley was at Shellburst, Eisenhower's headquarters near Tournieres.

"Listen, Lev," an excited and agitated Patton pleaded, "try to find Brad for me and ask him to reconsider his order. And get in touch with Monty about the boundary. He may agree to let us go through."

While Patton was fretting, Brigadier General A. Franklin Kibler, Bradley's operations officer, placed an urgent call to Montgomery's headquarters. He got the 21st Army Group chief of staff on the line. Kibler pleaded with Freddie du Guingand to seek permission from his boss, Montgomery, for Patton to drive on north past Argentan.

"I am sorry, Kibler," de Guingand replied, "but we can't grant that permission." Kibler knew that de Guingand, like any competent chief of staff, was merely fronting for his boss, that Montgomery had anticipated such a request from the Americans and had already given his answer. That answer was No.

General Allen was able to locate Bradley at Shellburst a short time later and told him of Patton's frantic appeal for reconsideration of the "stop" order. Bradley discussed the crucial question with Eisenhower and urgently advised that Patton's request to push on to Falaise be rejected. The supreme commander concurred. Bradley called General Allen: "Tell George the answer is negative."

After Allen broke the bad news to Patton, the Third Army commander turned to his chief of staff, Hugh Gaffey. He was bitter. "The question why [Haislip's] corps halted on the east-west line through Argentan is certain to become of historical importance," Patton declared. "I want a goddamned stenographic record of this conversation with General Allen included in the history of the Third Army."

A disillusioned Patton scribbled into his diary: "This corps [Haislip's] could easily advance to Falaise and completely close the gap. . . . I am sure that this halt is a great mistake, as I am certain that the British will not close on Falaise."

Patton was not the only target of the normally placid Omar

Bradley's ire. He was mad at Bernard Montgomery, also—boiling mad. Bradley felt that the Americans had done their part in the master plan to trap Hitler's armies in Normandy, including reining in George Patton to keep him from plunging onto Falaise. The lower jaw had been set in place. But, to Bradley, the methodical and often inexplicable Montgomery was less than aggressive in closing the upper jaw. Why, Bradley mused, had Montgomery turned over to the untested Canadians and Poles the crucial mission of closing the gap? Why, he wondered, did not the British commander reinforce his assault with battle-tested British armor and Tommies when he saw that the inexperienced Canadians and Poles were faltering?

Omar Bradley's ire was increased when he and Eisenhower had lunch that day with Montgomery at 21st Army Group CP. Montgomery chose that occasion, when the trapping of the entire German force in Normandy hung in the balance, to unveil a scheme he had developed for an advance toward Germany in which Bradley's army group would play second fiddle to Montgomery's forces. Montgomery could not have picked a worse time to spring his scheme on the two American generals. Eisenhower and Bradley were dismayed.

They would have been more dismayed had they known the true German situation in the pocket. Bits of signals intercepted by Ultra and other intelligence information indicated that large numbers of Germans had already escaped from the trap through the Argentan-Falaise Gap. They had been moving through the escape corridor, hounded each step of the way by Allied fighter-bombers, but these refugees from the pocket were mainly wounded soldiers and non-combat troops. Most of von Kluge's fighting formations were still inside the pocket, and it would be two more days before the German commander in the West gave the formal order to withdraw.

Had the gap been closed then, on August 13, nearly all the combat elements of the German Seventh and Fifth Panzer armies would have been in the sack and, as General Dietrich had declared that morning, unable to receive ammunition, fuel, and supplies.

That same day across the English Channel, paratroopers and glidermen of the newly formed Allied First Airborne Army had been moved to airfields in England and were standing by, if needed. Commanded by U.S. Air Corps Lieutenant General Lewis Brereton, the airborne army consisted of the U.S. 82nd and 101st Airborne divisions, the Red Devils of the British 1st and 6th Airborne divisions, and the Polish parachute brigade. General Bradley wanted the glider and parachute outfits to be held in readiness in the event he would want them to close the Argentan-Falaise gap by landing on the seven roads leading out of the Kessel.

Inside the pocket at nightfall, a haggard Guenther von Kluge returned to his headquarters after an exhausting period of dashing from one threatened spot to another. He had been shelled and even machine-gunned. Some fifteen times he had leaped from his still-moving Horch and into roadside ditches to escape Jabo attacks. He was trying desperately to re-form a front, to bring some sort of order out of chaos.

At 8:00 P.M. von Kluge sent a signal to Jodl at Hitler's headquarters in East Prussia: "The enemy is trying strongly to complete the encirclement of Fifth Panzer and Seventh army. In reality, the encirclement is imminent."

19

A Fateful
Decision

"ON TO PARIS!"

The joyful cry rang through the tank-tipped columns of Maurice Rose's 3rd Armored Division as they rolled out of Mayenne on August 13 and set a course for the Argentan region. Rose's division was fresh from the cauldron at Mortain, where the tankers and infantrymen had struggled for five days with Hitler's SS divisions trying desperately to break through to Avranches. Now Rose's men were involved in a new kind of war, one much more to their liking. Instead of being greeted by high-velocity German guns, the men of the 3rd Armored were pelted with flowers, deluged with hugs and kisses, and inundated with Calvados by cheering French citizens who lined the route of advance.

"On to Paris!"

Leading the almost festive drive toward the lower jaw of the great Allied trap was Rose's Combat Command-A, led by the imperturbable, pipe-smoking Brigadier General Doyle Hickey. His tankers set out in two parallel columns, Task Force X under Colonel Chubby Doan on the south and Task Force Y commanded by Lieutenant Colonel Walter B. Richardson on the north. The 3rd Armored was an element of Joe Collins's VII Corps, which had been ordered by Bradley to rush to the Argentan area to shore up defenses there in expectation of a massive German stampede to break out of the pocket.

Rose's men basked in the sunshine along the route, gulped proffered Calvados and cognac, and accepted the adulation of the frenzied masses. Overhead flights of Thunderbolts and Mustangs, fusillages twinkling in the rays of the hot summer sun, moved gracefully through the clear blue skies, on the lookout for any ambitious Luftwaffe aircraft that might try to pounce on Rose's lengthy columns.

As the 3rd Armored tanks and trucks crammed with so-called armored infantrymen ("Our only 'armor' is the buttons on our shirt," a dogface would explain) rolled on mile after mile without a single shot being fired, it did indeed appear to the dust-covered men that they would push on to the French capital unopposed. But at Couptrain and Javron there were the sharp cracks of 88-millimeter guns. Men scrambled out of trucks and took cover, tankers buttoned up, smiles vanished. The resistance was isolated and quickly wiped out. "Only a few gung-ho Krauts," the men told each other. "Nothing to worry about. The Heinies are on the run."

Late in the afternoon, war in all its stark reality returned to the men of the 3rd Armored. As they approached the key crossroads town of Carrouges, eight miles southwest of Argentan, the tankers and truckborne foot soldiers ran into a strong force of German Tigers and Panthers. Within minutes the panzers and Hickey's Shermans were engaged in a fierce shoot-out. Artillery joined in the battle, and American fighter-bombers swooped down to blast the enemy positions. Soon a thick pall of greasy smoke clung to the town. Roads were littered with the burned-out hulks of panzers and Shermans. Lifeless forms dotted the roadsides and fields—olive-drab-clad dogfaces and Germans in gray-green uniforms. The carefree ride to Paris for the men of the 3rd Armored ground to a halt.

The stench of death filled nostrils. As darkness approached flames licked at scores of Carroughes houses and buildings. Overhead in the blackness, JU-88 bombers droned, cast out flares that illuminated the landscape and dropped clusters of bombs on Rose's men. Near Carrouges, Colonel Richardson of Task Force Y was glued to his radio in a farmhouse serving as his temporary CP. Heavy curtains at the windows shielded the light of the kerosene lamp on the kitchen table. Richardson, a Texan from Beaumont, was tuned to the tank of Staff Sergeant Lafayette G. Pool for a play-by-play account of the savage nighttime fight raging on all sides. On the side of Pool's Sherman was its name—"In the Mood."

Pool, a lanky former Golden Gloves boxing champion and also a Texan, was heard to say over his radio, "I ain't got the heart to kill the bastards. . . ." He apparently had a quick change of heart. There was the angry rattle of his .30-caliber machine guns over the airwaves, followed by the sergeant's triumphant call to his crew: "Watch them bastards run! Give it to 'em, Close!" Close was one of Pool's crew.

Outside Carrouges, Captain Cyril Anderson radioed his leading tank commander, Staff Sergeant George Carver: "Keep moving toward Ranes until something heavy hits you!" Carver's Sherman revved its engine and, followed by other tanks of Task Force X, edged forward in the blackness on the road to Ranes. There were frequent clashes with 88-millimeter guns, but the task force pushed on ahead. As dawn drew near, Colonel Doan's Task Force X coiled up in fields outside Ranes and established security posts facing each direction. The armored spearhead was isolated.

AUGUST 14 DAWNED bright. In the stalled north jaw of the vast Allied trap, the Canadian II Corps was a beehive of activity. Its commander, General Guy Simonds, was preparing to launch Operation Tractable and had massed a formidable array of tanks, infantry, and artillery. Simonds would strike on a narrow front with his concentrated force in order to provide maximum thrust for reaching his objective, the high ground outside Falaise.

For seven days Simonds and his Canadians had been entrusted by General Montgomery with the crucial task of reaching Argentan and triggering the trap. For seven days the inexperienced Canadians had either made short advances or bogged down entirely. Tractable would be the third all-out effort to break through and link up with Patton's and Hodges's men in the vicinity of Argentan.

Barring a breakthrough to Falaise was the narrow Laison River, behind which General Kurt Meyer's teenagers of the 12th SS Panzer Division were deeply entrenched with a large number of 88-millimeter guns. It was these high-velocity weapons that twice before had played havoc with British and Canadian efforts to crash through to the south. Alongside Meyer's men were remnants of the 85th Division.

As time neared for Simonds's Canadians to jump off for Falaise, a large flight of medium bombers of the British 2nd Tactical Air Force appeared overhead in the clear blue sky. Bomb-bay doors opened and hundreds of missiles began tumbling earthward. All along the slope leading down to the Laison River a crescendo of explosives erupted as Kurt Meyer's grenadiers hugged the bottom of foxholes and panzer crews huddled in their buttoned-up vehicles. For nearly a half-hour the mediums blasted the positions of the 12th SS Panzer Division; then hundreds of heavy bombers winged in and dropped thousands of bombs up and down the Laison River where the Canadians hoped to break through. The sky bombardment took a heavy toll among the Hitlerjugend.

Not all the bombs fell on the German side of the Laison. Another "friendly" bombing tragedy had occurred. Royal Air Force bombardiers, accustomed to night operations, were apparently dazzled by the bright sunlight. They dropped many of their bombs on the Canadians, killing more than one hundred of them and wounding three hundred and fifty.

Despite the disruption in Canadian ranks caused by the errant bombs, at 11:35 A.M. Simonds's Churchill and Sherman tanks rolled forward. The Churchills were equipped with flamethrowers to burn enemy grenadiers out of their foxholes. On the right the Canadian 3rd Infantry Division pushed forward on foot and in armored personnel carriers known as Kangaroos. To the left, tanks of the Canadian 4th Armoured Division clanked across fields of tall, golden wheat. The bombing had left a cloud of smoke and dust drifting across no-man's-land along the gentle-flowing Laison, partially masking the attacking force from Meyer's sharp-eyed gunners. But even as the man-made smoke screen provided concealment for the advancing Canadians, it also disrupted their attack.

Brigadier E. L. Booth of the 4th Armoured Brigade was in his Churchill at the head of a column of tanks approaching the Laison River. A shell crashed into his vehicle, killing Booth. His force stalled at the water's edge. Up and down the stream German gunners poured deadly fire into Canadian tanks as though the SS men had known in advance where the attackers would try to cross the Laison. Soon there were burning Churchills and Shermans dotting the landscape on the north side of the river. Operation Tractable had failed.

Indeed the Germans had known in advance the crossing sites and had congregated their 88-millimeter guns at those points. The previous night a Canadian officer had inadvertently stumbled into a 12th SS Panzer outpost and was captured. A search revealed detailed plans for Operation Tractable.

That afternoon, at the time the Canadians were being smashed by waiting gunners of the Hitlerjugend, General Bernard Montgomery was dictating a letter to a British cabinet member in London. "These are great days," the commander of Allied ground forces in France enthused. "This week may well see great events. We have the great bulk of the German forces partially surrounded. Some will, of course, escape."

In the southern jaw of the closing trap, some twenty-five miles south of Simonds's Canadians stalled along the Laison River, Brigadier General Doyle Hickey's task forces X and Y jumped off shortly after dawn to attack northward and seize Ranes. Chubby Doan's Task Force X promptly ran into a buzzsaw. It was hit by savage attacks by elements of the 1st SS Panzer and 9th SS Panzer divisions. Doan's stalled column was pounded by artillery; bands of German foot soldiers infiltrated Doan's positions and bitter hand-to-hand fighting broke out. American staff officers, cooks, clerks, and truck drivers joined in the battle. The SS troops were fighting desperately to hold open the narrow escape corridor between Falaise and Argentan.

As fighting raged all around him, General Hickey found his CP located only one field behind his leading tank elements. Undaunted, he puffed on his ever-present pipe and calmly issued orders. Machine-gun fire whistled past the command half-track in which he was seated, and snipers fired an occasional round in his direction. Mortar and artillery shells crashed around the general. Overhead, swarms of Thunderbolts and Lightnings circled gracefully before pouncing on nearby panzers and German gun positions.

A Thunderbolt diving to bomb enemy tanks only 100 yards in front of leading American elements dropped a bomb short, killing one 3rd Armored Division man and wounding several others. Another errant American bomb fell in General Hickey's field, its fragments injuring several GIs. Hickey looked up from his map and glanced at the smoking bomb crater, saw that the wounded were being tended to, and went back to his work without missing a draw on his pipe.

All day the fighting continued. As night pulled its cloak over the battlefield, Hickey's combat command was isolated. Men wounded during the fight were stretched out in the darkness around makeshift aid stations. Combat medics and surgeons worked ceaselessly, but many of the 3rd Armored wounded died because they could not be evacuated through German forces for urgently needed treatment.

Unknown at the time to General Maurice Rose or any of his commanders in the 3rd Armored Division, the advancing tankers and infantry had run head-on into General Heinz Eberhard's attack eastward through Ranes to seize the town of Sees and "restore the situation at Alençon," as Hitler had ordered.

While Hickey's combat command was fighting for survival, the 3rd Armored's Combat Command-B under Colonel Truman Boudinot had swung a left hook toward Ranes. CC-B ran into stubborn resistance, but moved steadily forward. Boudinot's men knocked out 16 panzers and captured more than 1,000 prisoners, most dazed, disheveled, hungry, and exhausted. These prisoners were the same men who had been pounded by Allied fighter-bombers and artillery at Mortain for five days and nights, then hustled fifty miles eastward and ordered to attack once more to hold open the gap.

Although General Eberhard's attacking force battled with customary ferocity, German units involved had been chopped to pieces in Operation Luttich at Mortain. When the 9th Panzer Division launched its assault against Ranes that morning and collided head-on with Rose's 3rd Armored, it was a division in name only, consisting of two hundred and sixty men, twelve tanks, and a few artillery pieces. The 1st SS Panzer Division could muster only three hundred and fifty-two men, eight self-propelled assault guns, and 14 Mark IV and seven Mark V tanks. The 2nd Panzer Division, which had difficulties in jumping off on time in Operation Luttich, was in the best shape of any of Eberhard's forces. But it had been whittled down to one-quarter strength and had 2,230 men, five self-propelled guns, and nine Mark IV, and three Mark V tanks.

While the Canadians in the north and the Americans and French in the south fought desperately to close the escape gap that day, Field Marshal von Kluge received a message from Hitler at Army Group-B headquarters at La Roche-Guyon:

> "The present situation in the rear of the army group [at the southern jaw of the Allied trap] is the result of the failure of the first attack on Avranches."

The Führer stressed that Eberhard's panzer force had been committed too far north (against the southern jaw) at Ranes. Hitler wanted Eberhard to attack farther south and "destroy the U.S. XV Corps."

It was a preposterous order. Von Kluge read it without change of expression. He had grown accustomed to receiving from the Führer orders that were totally divorced from battlefield reality. Hitler was now proposing that a group of virtually burned out panzer divisions, totaling fewer than three thousand exhausted men and a handful of tanks and artillery pieces and under continuous fighter-bomber attack, assault and destroy a powerful American corps of some seventy thousand men and six hundred and fifty tanks.

"The man is mad!" von Kluge muttered in resignation, flipping Hitler's message onto his desk.

Elsewhere, Allied forces around the perimeter were compressing the trapped Germans into a shrinking pocket. East of Mortain Brooks's 2nd Armored and Hobbs's 30th Infantry divisions attacked eastward from the vicinity of Ger and seized Domfront, which had been a key German supply center for the assault to capture Avranches. Domfront was defended by an ad hoc battalion of stragglers, supply personnel, guardhouse detainees, and men with minor wounds. Many were roaring drunk when the Americans burst into the town.

Confusion around the gigantic pocket was not limited to the German side. General Horace McBride's green 80th Infantry Division had been ordered to attack northward in the southern jaw between Collins's VII Corps on its left and Haislip's XV Corps on its right. McBride's objective was the Argentan-Sees railroad track. Shortly after jumping off, McBride's 318th Infantry Regiment became hopelessly entangled with elements of the 90th Infantry Division, which was also attacking northward. A massive traffic jam developed. Heated arguments erupted between officers of the 80th and 90th divisions.

"Get off our goddamned road!" the 90th Division officers demanded.

Leaders of the 318th Regiment of the 80th Division, convinced that they were on the assigned road, refused to budge.

Senior officers of the 90th radioed Haislip's corps CP. The 318th Regiment leaders put in a call to 80th Division headquarters. Meanwhile, the adversaries eyed each other coldly. General Haislip rushed a staff officer to the traffic tangle with a curt order to the 318th Regiment: "Get the hell off the road!"

"Like hell we will!" the 318th retorted. "We're under Twentieth Corps. We don't take orders from Haislip!"

Now the enormous traffic muddle took a turn for the worse. With a loud revving of motors and honking of horns, a long column of General Leclerc's French 2nd Armored Division charged onto the scene. In minutes its vehicles were tangled up with those of the two competing American outfits. Frenchmen left their tanks and trucks to join in the heated argument. "This is *our* road!" Leclerc's officers insisted.

The situation was just short of bedlam. Colonel Harry McHugh, commanding the 318th, dispatched a cub airplane to 80th Division headquarters for instructions, but the aircraft apparently got lost. Finally the colonel was able to reach General McBride by radio: "Fifteenth Corps has ordered me off the road. My orders are to proceed with all possible speed. What is decision?"

McBride had learned that the 318th Infantry mission had become outdated, as elements of Joe Collins's corps had already arrived on the 318th objective. "Halt in place, clear road, bivouac present position for night, await further orders," was the 80th Division commander's reply.

The men and vehicles of the 318th Regiment moved off into nearby fields. The exhausted men had barely slipped into slumber when many were awakened by loud arguments. Other elements of the 90th Infantry Division had arrived and declared that the 318th was bedded down in their assigned path of advance. Tired of arguments, the 318th colonel took the easy way out: he selected another bivouac site and let the newly arrived 90th Division elements continue onward.

At Shellburst in the Cotentin Peninsula that day, Supreme Commander Dwight Eisenhower took up his pen to issue a rare order of the day to all Allied forces. The scent of monumental victory was in his nostrils. He exhorted his fighting men to prevent a German escape from the nearly closed trap:

We can make this week a momentous one in the history of this war, a brilliant and fruitful one for us, a fateful disaster for the ambitions of the Nazi tyrants.

Few of the printed pieces trickled down to the level of the grimy, weary fighting men in the two jaws of the trap. Just as well. The foot soldier and the tanker dodging shot and shell and struggling to stay alive for another day or another hour would have been little interested in lofty exhortations to thwart the "ambitions of the Nazi tyrants."

ON AUGUST 14, General Omar Bradley fell victim to an enormous Allied intelligence blunder. He was assured that large numbers of German combat units had already fled the pocket. Based on this faulty report, Bradley arrived at a fateful decision. He decided that the five divisions holding the east-west boundary at Argentan, in the southern jaw, were excessive. Bradley did not intend to let these divisions sit idle while the German chickens flew the coop.

Without consultation with Bernard Montgomery, the Allied ground commander, Bradley ordered Patton to split Haislip's XV Corps, leaving behind to hold the southern jaw at Argentan the 80th and 90th divisions and the French 2nd Armored Division. Oliver's 5th Armored and Wyche's 79th Infantry divisions would dash eastward for the Seine River, along with Patton's two other corps, the XX and the newly arrived XII.

Bradley's plan was to snare in an even larger net the German forces fleeting through the Falaise-Argentan gap. Once Patton's spearheads reached the Seine they were to turn northward, once again cutting off von Kluge's divisions from their homeland.

General Bradley phoned Patton that afternoon and gave him verbal orders for the dash to the Seine. "Striking to the Seine means running the risk of letting the enemy escape [the pocket] more easily," Bradley exclaimed. With a mixture of anger and resignation, he added, "If Monty wants us to help him close the pocket, let him say so!"

Shortly after General Bradley issued orders for Patton's three corps to drive east and northeast for the Seine, the outspoken, pugnacious Jacques Leclerc stomped into Patton's CP. He was furious. Ever since fleeing Nazi-occupied France and joining up with General Charles de Gaulle's Fighting Free French in 1940, Leclerc had lived for and dreamed of the moment he would lead his men into Paris and evict the hated Boche. Now he learned that his 2nd Armored Division had been given the role of sitting idle at Argentan while the Americans dashed for the French capital on the Seine.

General Leclerc demanded that the French have the "honor" of reaching the Seine first. Punctuating his remarks with his customary arsenal of curse words, Patton declared he couldn't care less who reached the historic river first, "just as long as we kill Germans." Harsh words ensued. But the two leaders, mutual admirers, shook hands and parted on friendly terms.

It was nearly midnight on that August 14 when a tormented and depressed Guenther von Kluge went to bed at Sepp Dietrich's headquarters in the ornate Fontaine l'Abbé château near Bernay. Von Kluge expected the Allies to close the gap at Falaise-Argentan at any minute, trapping his Seventh and Fifth Panzer armies. He would have slept more soundly had he known of the growing discord among American and British leaders over failure to snap shut the trap, and of Bradley's decision to send most of Haislip's corps in the southern jaw racing eastward to the Seine. Unlike Bradley, von Kluge was aware of one significant factor: most of Seventh and Fifth Panzer armies were still inside the Kessel.

On the morrow, von Kluge would hold an important conference at Nécy with generals Eberhard and Dietrich. He would have to arise at dawn in order to keep the 9:30 A.M. appointment. It might require considerable time to weave through German traffic jams, and to take to roadside ditches to avoid death from the rockets and machine guns of Allied fighter-bombers.

20

A Field Marshal
Is Missing

A BRIGHT DAWN of August 15 ushered in a day that would result
in one of the great mysteries of the war in Europe. Field Marshal von
Kluge, solemn faced and clutching his baton, climbed into the back
of his Horch parked under a spreading shade tree outside the Fontaine l'Abbé. Von Kluge felt slightly refreshed after five hours of
sleep. It had been a quiet night at Bernay. No bombings or artillery
shells were heard in the vicinity.

Climbing into the backseat beside the field marshal was his son,
Lieutenant Colonel Hans von Kluge, and in the front seat with the
driver was an aide, Lieutenant Karl Tangermann. Accompanying
von Kluge to Nécy for his appointment with Eberhard and Dietrich
were a motorcycle and sidecar in the lead and a radio communications truck bringing up the rear. It was a curious ensemble. Why was
von Kluge taking a wireless communications vehicle for a meeting
with two of his generals? Would not the radio truck with its long
antennae whipping in the breeze furnish a telltale clue to marauding
Allied fighter-bombers that here was a key German commander on
the road? And why was von Kluge taking his son with him?

The weather was hot as the three vehicles drove away from the
Fontaine l'Abbé. It was not long before von Kluge's little convoy was
pounced on by Jabos. The trio of vehicles left the road and proceeded
toward Nécy by cutting across fields and through forests. But soon
there was the frightening shriek of diving fighter-bombers, followed
by explosions that shook von Kluge's camouflaged Horch. The

radio truck was hit and set ablaze, the communications operator was killed and all of his assistants were wounded.

The field marshal, his son, and aide leaped from the Horch and scrambled into a ditch as bullets stitched into the ground around them.

When the fighter-bomber flight had exhausted its ammunition and faded into the distant blue sky, von Kluge and other survivors hauled themselves out of the dust and climbed back into the Horch and the motorcycle. They pressed on toward Nécy. But other Jabos, possibly stalking the big command car, circled ominously overhead as the driver pulled under a shade tree for concealment. By now the field marshal was near exhaustion from scrambling into ditches, the intense heat, exasperation, and frustration. While he and his son waited about four and a half miles outside Nécy, Lieutenant Tangermann located a bicycle and peddled to the church in the town where generals Dietrich and Eberhard were to have been waiting. It was now past 11 A.M. and the pair had departed, believing that von Kluge was not going to keep the appointment for which he was now an hour and a half late.

Von Kluge, in the turmoil of the Kessel, now found that he was isolated, cut off from contact with his major headquarters. Staff officers at Oberbefehlshaber, West at St.-Germain, Army Group-B at La Roche-Guyon, and Fifth Panzer and Seventh armies became concerned, then deeply alarmed when no word was heard from the senior German commander in the West. It was as though General Eisenhower had suddenly disappeared on the Allied side. The greatest consternation erupted from the Führer. Earlier that morning the Gestapo had presented Adolf Hitler with evidence that von Kluge had been involved in the July 20 murder plot. Hitler was now convinced that von Kluge had compounded his treachery by deserting to the Allies and trying to surrender the German armies in the West.

Hitler threw one of his most violent tantrums, raving that he was "surrounded by traitors and cowards." News that American and French armies were landing that morning on the Riviera coast of southern France increased his purple-faced raging.

THAT SAME MORNING in the Ranes area of the southern jaw of the trap, chaos reigned in General Eberhard's panzer group, which had been ordered to continue its attack to capture Sees and "restore the situation at Alençon." Roads were jammed with vehicles, many knocked out by Allied fighter-bombers, others out of fuel. Units were intermingled. Movements had to be made at night and often under the guns of long-range American artillery. Tanks were immobilized due to lack of fuel or spare parts. The Feldgrau were hungry, exhausted, and confused. Units had lost their identity and cohesiveness. Stragglers wandered aimlessly about, not knowing where their formations were or what they were supposed to be doing. Always the feared Jabos were overhead, pouncing down to strafe and bomb and send fear into the hearts of tankers and grenadiers.

Despite this cauldron of chaos in German ranks, when Colonel Doan's Task Force X of the 3rd Armored Division jumped off southwest of Argentan on the morning of August 15 to capture Fromentel, it met savage resistance. Panzers hidden in caves caught a column out in the open and with their initial rounds set four Shermans ablaze. One of those knocked out was that of Captain Cyril Anderson, who two nights before had directed his lead tank to charge on ahead "until something heavy hits you." Captain Anderson lost a leg.

Major Paul W. Corrigan was in a jeep in one task force column when the string of tanks and vehicles ground to a halt. Corrigan raced to the front of the column. "What's holding us up?" he called to the lead tank commander.

"I think there's a Kraut 88 millimeter on a hill up there covering the road."

"Then fire a few rounds at it and keep going."

Corrigan decided to stay behind the first tank to make sure there were no unavoidable holdups. After the forward tank had passed a narrow dirt road Corrigan and his driver saw a German motorcycle with a sidecar and passenger barreling down the side road toward them. The jeep lurched to a sudden halt; Major Corrigan leaped out with his .45 Colt pistol and the driver with a carbine. They picked off both Germans, and the speeding motorcycle careened off the road, hit an embankment, and overturned.

Corrigan, a battalion commander in Chubby Doan's Task Force X, thought the cyclists might have been scouts for a trailing German column. He radioed his headquarters company commander, Captain John C. Chapman, farther back in the convoy to be on the alert when his part of the column reached the dirt side road. Corrigan then waved his force onward.

A short distance ahead a German vehicle was burning brightly in the center of the road, impeding Corrigan's advance. He ordered his column into a field to eat and take a short break. Nearby was a large house, quiet and apparently deserted.

"Put a WP [white phosphorous] round into that house," Major Corrigan ordered a tanker. The shell exploded into the structure, radiating plumes of tiny white fiery particles. Moments later a stampede erupted as 25 to 30 Germans dashed out the back door and raced into the nearby woods.

Shortly afterward Corrigan was in the center of the field as his tanks started out to the road and past the burning vehicle. Suddenly he felt a sharp pain where his leg connected to his hip, as though jabbed deeply by a white-hot poker. Corrigan grabbed his leg and drew back a hand covered with blood. He had been shot, yet no rifle crack was heard.

Major Corrigan told his tankers to keep going, and Captain Chapman was notified to hurry forward and take command. The wounded Corrigan was taken back to an aid station, but not before a lengthy delay. The rear of his column had bumped into a German force coming down the dirt side road, where the major and his driver had picked off the enemy motorcyclists several hours previously, and a furious tank fight was raging.

In this vicinity, a patrol of SS troops infiltrated positions of the 703rd Tank Destroyer Battalion and captured an officer, two TD men, and two engineers. With the exception of one engineer who escaped, all were later found huddled together, with bullet holes in each head and hands tied behind backs. Americans in that sector took no prisoners that day.

EARLY ON AUGUST 15, with Patton's spearheads racing eastward from the southern jaw of the trap toward the Seine, General Omar Bradley got a jolt: his intelligence had flip-flopped overnight and now declared that the Germans had not pulled out of the Kessel after all. Elements of five badly mauled panzer divisions inside the pocket were now heading toward Argentan and the southern jaw.

Bradley knew that these German divisions had been pounded heavily by air and artillery for days, but neither Ultra nor other intelligence gave their true situation: they were short of ammo and fuel, and they were nearly spent. Acting on the latest intelligence estimate, the 12th Army Group commander had to presume that these five or more panzer divisions presented a serious threat to the considerably weakened American force in the southern jaw. He leaped into his car, sped to George Patton's CP and ordered him to halt his three-corps drive to the Seine. Patton's troops might have to return to Argentan to help.

Patton, his eyes glued on the Seine and beyond, was harsh on Bradley in his diary: "Bradley came down to see me suffering from nerves. . . . His motto seems to be 'in case of doubt, halt.' . . . I wish I were supreme commander."

On this day General Eisenhower took steps to quash what he considered a serious situation. Newspapers in the United States and Great Britain had been depressingly pessimistic during the time the Anglo-Americans were bogged down in the *bocage* of Normandy. For three weeks now these same publications had reversed course and were rife with optimism, even predicting that the war was nearly over.

The supreme commander was holding a press conference at Shellburst. Grim-faced, Eisenhower spoke sternly. He said that those who thought the conflict would be over "in a matter of weeks" didn't know what they were talking about. "Such people are crazy," he exploded with uncharacteristic lack of tact. He declared that Hitler knew that he would hang when the war ended, so had nothing to lose by continuing to fight to the bitter end.

NEARLY EIGHTY MILES west of Argentan along the Atlantic Ocean, Colonel Rudolf Bacherer's telephone rang in his underground headquarters in beseiged St.-Malo, which had been under heavy assault by General Bob Macon's 83rd Division for twelve days. Two days before, Bacherer had told his seven hundred men who were defending a strongpoint that there was not enough food or water for the entire force. So he directed "men with women and children at home" to fall out and march into American captivity. Then Colonel Bacherer, who had led a rag-tag force in a hopeless effort to recapture Avranches from the 4th Armored Division two weeks before, continued the fight.

Now Bacherer picked up the ringing telephone and was shocked.

The American voice stated, "This is General Macon. I am inviting you to surrender. We are already inside your strongpoints." Macon carried out his conversation through an interpreter.

Reflecting momentarily, Bacherer replied, "I see no cause for surrender. But I would request you to take over my wounded who are no longer capable of fighting."

Macon agreed. There was an hour's cease-fire. Once Bacherer's wounded were inside American lines, the guns roared anew.

Elsewhere in Brittany, German forces were holding out in three other major ports: Lorient, St.-Nazaire, and Brest. They were hemmed in by troops of Middleton's VIII Corps and detachments of FFI. The Brest garrison was particularly strongly held. There 32,000 Germans, many of them resolute paratroopers, inflicted a heavy toll on the Americans.

Throughout the day a frenzied search had been in progress for the mysteriously missing Guenther von Kluge. Acting at Hitler's direction from Wolfsschanze General Jodl made repeated calls to various headquarters in France. Always the question was the same: where is von Kluge? General Blumentritt, his chief of staff, stuttered out that perhaps von Kluge had been wounded and couldn't get a signal through. Eberhard stressed that he had waited three hours in the church at Nécy and that von Kluge had failed to appear. Dietrich said he knew nothing of von Kluge's whereabouts.

General Blumentritt, as von Kluge's closest confidant, caught most of the heat from Hitler. If a treacherous von Kluge had defected and was negotiating with the Americans and British, Blumentritt would have to be involved or at least know something about von Kluge's intentions—the Führer was convinced. Late in the afternoon Jodl called again. His voice heavy with emotion, Jodl had been forced to ask Blumentritt point-blank, "Has von Kluge returned or has he gone over to the enemy?"

At 6:30 P.M., with still no word as to von Kluge's whereabouts, Jodl was on the phone again to General Blumentritt at St.-Germain. "The situation west of Argentan is worsening by the hour," Blumentritt declared. He told Jodl that Dietrich, Eberhard, and Hausser agreed that "a decision will have to be made," implying a prompt withdrawal from the pocket.

"I am duty bound to report the state of the armored units,"

Blumentritt stressed, citing immense shortages of fuel, exhaustion of the troops, and heavy losses.

Jodl replied cautiously that if there was to be an effort to break out of the partially closed trap, it would require an attack. It was more careful phraseology: he was conceding German forces might have to pull back eastward, but for the record he was proposing to attack.

Blumentritt was deeply concerned that the German armies in the pocket lacked direction, with the mysterious disappearance of von Kluge. "I must emphatically state that I am in a difficult position as chief of staff when von Kluge is not here. I have the most urgent request. Someone must be appointed by the Führer to take charge. It could only be Hausser, Dietrich, or Eberbach."

Blumentritt closed the conversation by remarking dolefully, "It is five minutes to midnight."

Hitler ordered immediate calls be made to Field Marshal Walther Model, who had been termed "the savior of the Russian front" by the Führer, and Field Marshal Albrecht Kesselring, who had fought with distinction in the Mediterranean, seeking their opinions.

One hour later General Jodl phoned Blumentritt: "The Führer has ordered that SS Obergruppenführer Hausser be placed in temporary command of Army Group-B." Hausser, who had lost an eye at Moscow, would be the "safest" choice; he was an SS officer whose personal loyalty to Adolf Hitler was not in question.

At about 9:00 P.M. a mud-caked Horch drove up to General Heinz Eberhard's battle headquarters. Slowly emerging from the camouflage-painted vehicle was Guenther von Kluge, together with his son, who also happened to be Eberhard's chief of staff. "Caught in the traffic," the haggard looking von Kluge explained.

It was a curious statement. The highest German leader in the West, who was doubling as commander of Army Group-B, had vanished for more than fourteen hours and his only explanation was a simple "caught in the traffic." At a time the encircled Seventh and Fifth Panzer armies were reeling in disarray and on the verge of being annihilated, their commander was unable to reach a single radio or telephone line to check in with his headquarters.

At about the same time von Kluge was returning from the dead, some distance to the south General George Patton, himself something of a mystery man whose presence in France had been cloaked under an Eisenhower-ordered blackout for more than six weeks, was puffing on a cigar and listening to war news over London's BBC. He was jolted by what he heard.

His private secretary was just entering his office to take dictation, and Patton looked up at the sergeant and remarked dryly, "I've just learned from the radio that I'm commanding the Third Army in France." Without notifying Patton, SHAEF had lifted the blackout.

EARLY ON THE morning of August 16, some twelve hundred miles east of the flaming Falaise pocket, Field Marshal Walther Model, a monocled, diminutive, ruthless, and capable officer with proven fidelity to the Führer, received a message from Wolfsschanze: *Leave for France immediately. You are to replace Feldmarschall von Kluge as Commander in Chief, West, and Commander in Chief Army Group-B.* Within two hours the energetic Model, the fifty-four-year-old son of a schoolteacher, was winging toward Paris. Hitler's "savior of the Russian front" would now try to work his miracles on the Western Front.

Early the next morning, von Kluge drove to Fifth Panzer Army headquarters at Fontaine l'Abbé, arriving at 11:00 A.M. General Dietrich handed him a signal from Hitler that stated: "[You] are to leave the pocket immediately and conduct operations outside this sector." Von Kluge was not told that the Führer had already dispatched Model to France to replace him.

Hitler was taking no chances that von Kluge would, in his final few hours as commander in France, surrender his battered forces to the Anglo-Americans.

A weary von Kluge climbed the circular stairs of the château to the ornate bedroom of General Dietrich and from there placed a call to Jodl in East Prussia. "There's no question now of launching a full-scale attack to improve the situation," von Kluge declared. He added prudently, "All the army commanders are of this opinion."

Jodl, parroting Hitler's desires, insisted that Panzer Group Eberhard continue its assault against the southern jaw of the Allied trap.

"An attack through Argentan to capture Sees is out of the question!" von Kluge exploded. "You can send all the orders in the world. Our men are at the end of their tether. You cannot halt the enemy!"

There was a silence on the other end of the line. Then Jodl spoke calmly. "I understand perfectly," he observed. "I will let you know the Führer's decision as soon as possible."

Both von Kluge and Jodl were careful not to mention once the forbidden word: withdrawal.

Less than a half-hour later, General Jodl was back on the line. Even Hitler now realized the catastrophe facing his armies in France. "Seventh and Fifth Panzer armies are authorized to fall back," Jodl stated matter-of-factly. The withdrawal was to begin the following day, August 17. But von Kluge did not intend to wait one minute longer. He promptly contacted Hausser, Eberhard, and Dietrich and instructed them to start moving toward the Argentan-Falaise escape valve that same night.

That morning of August 16, General Kurt Meyer, the youthful commander of the battered 12th SS Panzer Division, was entrenched on Hill 159, the final dominating height between General Guy Simonds's attacking Canadians and Falaise. Meyer's Hitlerjugend had steadily been chopped to pieces while denying the Canadians a quick breakthrough to Falaise. On the height with their leader were some five hundred youths who had taken an oath to die for the Führer, if need be. Walking among his grenadiers, Meyer was proud to note that their morale was high, even though all knew this would be their "last stand."

Simonds's Canadians for two days had been pounding the Hitler Youths on the hill with heavy artillery and mortar barrages. Fighter-bombers struck the elevation, which by now was pockmarked with craters and resembled the surface of the moon. Now the Canadians were closing in to wipe out what remained of the 12th SS Panzer. Cromwells, Stuarts, and Shermans—swarms of them—were rolling across the terrain and toward Hill 159.

Overhead Typhoons circled, then dived on the Hitler Youths desperately hugging the bottom of foxholes. There were the eerie, frightening squeals of rockets being released and seconds later enormous explosions rocked the hill. Canadian tank guns and artillery loosed a mighty barrage. Kurt Meyer felt a sudden burning sensation, as if a white-hot ice pick had been jabbed into him. Blood began running down his face. A shell fragment had struck him in the head.

Meyer crawled into a ditch and there looked on helplessly as his handful of panzers dueled with swarms of Canadian tanks. Behind the attacking armor Canadian infantrymen were advancing toward Hill 159. Weak from loss of blood, Kurt Meyer was helped out of the ditch by his aide and driven back through a gauntlet of shell explosions to an aid station. There several stitches were taken in his head, after which Meyer leapt to his feet, jumped into a vehicle and returned to his grenadiers and tankers on the crucial hill.

There was nothing more Panzer Meyer could do. The hill was soon overrun.

General Simonds now rushed more forces into the assault. On either side of the main road leading into Falaise were the Cameron Highlanders and the South Saskatchwewan regiment. They attacked abreast and later that day fought their way into the flattened little town.

Prior to the June 6 D-Day in Normandy, General Bernard Montgomery had spoken of his tanks "knocking about" at Falaise that evening. Now, on D-Day plus 71, the 21st Army Group finally had reached the birthplace of William the Conqueror. The gap between Montgomery's forces at Falaise and Bradley's troops at Argentan had been narrowed to fourteen miles.

While overwhelming Canadian formations were on the outskirts of Falaise, with only a small number of surviving Hitler Youths and stragglers burrowed into the ruins to defend the town, von Kluge received a signal from Hitler: "Falaise will be held at all costs." Von Kluge turned to his aides, stating flatly, "He's absolutely out of his mind!"

With the Canadians in Falaise, the enemy plight grew more desperate, and the Germans battled fiercely in the two jaws of the closing trap to keep the shrinking escape-corridor open. Eberhard's panzers and grenadiers struck elements of the U.S. 3rd Armored Division a heavy blow west of Argentan, and parts of the 2nd SS Panzer and 116th Panzer divisions smashed into McLain's 90th Infantry Division at the village of le-Bourg-St.-Leonard, five miles east of Argentan. The Americans were driven from the town, but counterattacked that night and recaptured le Bourg-St.-Leonard in a fierce hand-to-hand fight.

The heavy fighting that took place that day on the terrain between the jaws of the Anglo-American trap proved one thing to the Allied high command: the gap was now swarming with Germans who were fighting desperately to hold it open. Vanished was the golden

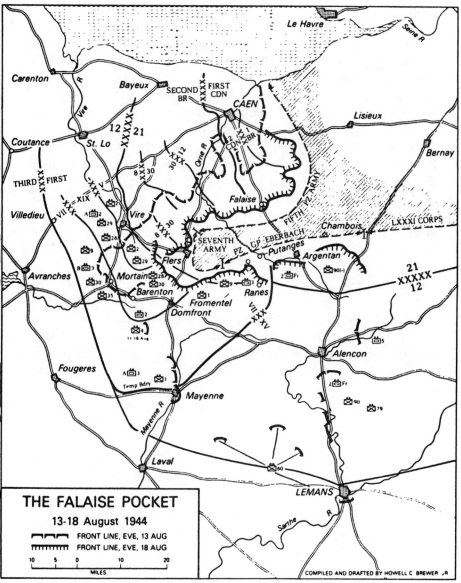

THE FALAISE POCKET

13-18 August 1944

FRONT LINE, EVE, 13 AUG
FRONT LINE, EVE, 18 AUG

10   5   0   10   20
MILES

COMPILED AND DRAFTED BY HOWELL C BREWER JR

(Courtesy of Louisiana State University Press)

opportunity of only three days previously when Wade Haislip's spearheads had, on Patton's orders, pushed on northward past Argentan and to within six miles of Falaise while encountering only sporadic resistance.

Late in the afternoon of the sixteenth, General Bradley received a call from General Montgomery who suggested that an effort be made to close the gap farther to the east at Chambois. Monty had already veered the Canadians toward the southeast with orders to fight their way through Trun to Chambois. Could Bradley assist in closing the trap by attacking toward Chambois? Bradley said that he would try.

But the American commander was racked with doubt about his ability to do it. He had learned that it was too late to recall George Patton's three corps, which were racing to the northeast and east and had already seized Orléans, Chartres, and Dreux, far from the jaws at Argentan-Falaise. Bradley was not sure his troops in the southern jaw, which included Leclerc's unpredictable French tankers and the green 80th Infantry Division of Horace McBride, could get the job done.

IN BERLIN THAT afternoon, Dr. Josef Goebbels, the Third Reich's minister of propaganda, was in a quandry over how to present the looming German debacle in France to the home front. Could the nation hold up under an announcement of another Stalingrad, this one in the West? That night over Radio Berlin, the German people were told that their armed forces had scored a great victory, having stalled the Americans at Argentan. The Americans, the announcer declared, were involved in "a desperate final throw of the dice."

21

Slaughter Grounds
in the Gap

IT WAS FIFTEEN minutes after midnight on August 17 as Major General Leonard "Gee" Gerow, Eisenhower's longtime crony, strode into First Army battle headquarters behind the southern jaw of the pocket. Gerow had been summoned from the Vire area, southeast of St.-Lô in the Cotentin Peninsula, where he had commanded V Corps, to take over leadership of the corps left behind at that jaw when Patton dashed eastward for the Seine. It had taken Gerow and a few staff officers twelve hours to make the long circuitous trek around the lower half of the pocket.

General Courtney Hodges, commander of First Army and a man of few words, was succinct in his instructions to Gerow: "You are to close the gap between Argentan and Falaise." Hodges explained that Gerow's three divisions would be the 80th and 90th Infantry divisions and the French 2nd Armored Division.

"Where are these three divisions?" Gerow asked.

"We don't know," replied Hodges's chief of staff, Brigadier General William Kean. "You'll have to find them."

"What is the enemy situation around Argentan?"

"That's been in the Third Army front. We don't know the situation there."

At 2:30 A.M. Gerow and a few of his key staff officers hopped into three jeeps and drove off through the pitch-black night. Rain was pouring in sheets. Visibility was only a few yards. A communications radio in one jeep was balky and refused to function. The tiny command group was out of contact with all headquarters. While scouring the dark and rainswept countryside in search of the three divisions, Gerow and his aides were not always certain which side of the lines they were on. There was the possibility that they could suddenly find themselves confronted with the business end of an 88-millimeter gun with an SS Tiger tank crew lining up the sights.

After numerous inquiries, the 90th Division CP was located and there Gerow got in contact with his other two divisions. He set up corps headquarters in Alençon at the Hotel de France. At dawn he met with Major General Hugh Gaffey, Patton's chief of staff, who had been sent by Patton the previous day to command the three divisions as a provisional corps. Gaffey of Third Army and Gerow of First Army were both in command of the same three divisions.

Meanwhile urgent messages were flashing between Bradley, Hodges, and Patton about the command tangle at Alencon. Bradley solved the snarl by dissolving the provisional corps, placing the Chambois-Trun sector in the First Army zone, and freeing Patton to continue his slicing drives to the Seine.

Gaffey had already issued a plan and orders for an attack to jump off at 10:00 A.M. that day to seize Argentan and drive toward a juncture with the Canadians near Chambois. But Gerow did not like the plan, canceled it, and his three divisions sat idle for twenty-four hours until a new course of action was developed. In the meantime, Germans were moving eastward out of the gap, now only 13 miles wide.

That morning the new German commander, Walther Model, burst upon the scene at Guenther von Kluge's headquarters at St.-Germain outside Paris. Model had a reputation in the German officer corps for being tough, cold, and with a will of steel. Despite his high rank, it had been his habit to be up front at the hottest spots. Energetic and lacking almost entirely in humor, Model had gained his field marshal's baton at fifty-three partly through his demonstrated ability on the battlefield and because of his utter devotion to the Führer.

Model, monocle in place, greeted von Kluge with stiff formality bordering on contempt. After all, von Kluge had failed. Model knew that to be a fact—the Führer had told him so.

Model, clutching his jewel-encrusted marshal's baton, handed a letter to von Kluge from Hitler. It stated that von Kluge was being relieved due to "ill health" and ordered him to report at once to Wolfsschanze. Von Kluge paled on reading the terse message. The Führer most certainly was not summoning von Kluge to decorate him. It could mean only one thing.

Guenther von Kluge knew that his days were numbered. He suspected that his involvement in the July 20 murder plot against Hitler had been unearthed by the Gestapo. And in the Führer's eyes von Kluge had "lost" Normandy, Brittany, and maybe all of France; the field marshal stood highly suspected by the supreme warlord of the Third Reich of trying to surrender the German armies in the West to the Anglo-Americans.

Breathing fire and brimstone, Model set off for the Fontaine l'Abbé château where he had called an urgent conference with generals Hausser, Dietrich, and Eberhard. Each was curious about what Model could do to resolve the present disastrous situation that his predecessor had not already tried. Heinz Eberhard in particular was in a foul mood. He had driven to the conference from the center of the pocket, and it had taken him eight hours to make a twenty-seven-mile trip. Traffic jams, knocked-out vehicles, and relentless Jabo attacks had slowed his progress to a crawl.

As the other generals sat in stunned silence, Eberhard related the facts of life in France to Model: The morale of the German soldier had collapsed. Each day the Feldgrau watched huge armadas of Allied bombers heading for the Reich, then return with no apparent losses and flying as though in review. Letters from home were depressing, telling only of shattered cities and civilian deaths. Deserters from the Wehrmacht were no longer conscripted Russians, Poles, Czechs, or other nationalities, but homegrown Germans. Even the SS divisions were fighting with little enthusiasm.

There were several moments of silence as General Eberhard concluded his gloomy analysis. Finally Model, placing his monocle in position, snapped, "These are opinions, not facts."

The conference droned on. Model decided to do precisely what von Kluge had been doing: retreat.

During the previous several days there had been only a trickle of Germans and vehicles seeping through the Argentan-Falaise gap. Now there was a convulsive surge to escape the bloodbath in the pocket, and a stampede erupted. As a thin veil of mist lifted on the morning of August 17, Allied reconnaissance pilots rubbed their eyes in disbelief as they circled the German escape-corridor. Down below was a massive column of two thousand enemy vehicles, bumper to bumper, often three abreast, inching ahead or stalled in the thirteen-mile-wide gap. For the first time, the Germans were risking a retreat in full light of day under clear skies favorable to Anglo-American fighter-bombers.

It was the juiciest target of the war. The entire striking power of the American and British air forces was alerted to move in for the kill. Taking off from fields in France and England, thousands of American Thunderbolts, Mustangs, and Lightnings and RAF Spitfires and Typhoons raced through unblemished skies for the strip of landscape between Argentan and Falaise where the Germans were desperately seeking to escape the trap.

There, swarms of fighter-bombers crisscrossed the sky. So many planes were waiting to pounce on the stalled German column that they often had to "get in line" to attack. The horror for the Feldgrau began as the fighter-bombers dived from out of the sun and loosed 500-pound wing bombs and poured streams of machine-gun bullets into the convoys. One flight of Thunderbolts was preparing to dive on a group of tanks and trucks when at the final moment it had to hold up—a group of Typhoons had beaten it to the target.

Up and down the stalled German column, stretching for miles, raced the fighter-bombers. When a flight had exhausted its bombs and ammunition, another group would take over and resume pounding the vehicles. The slaughter was immense. Trapped under the rain of steel and explosives, terrified Feldgrau milled about in the open, too tired or unable to dig foxholes. They were blown to pieces or cut down by spitting machine guns. Horses stampeded, hundreds of them. They knocked down the hedgerows and fences in wide-eyed panic, dragging their carriages through the apple trees and farmyards. Often the animals ran wildly even after a chunk of bomb had torn open their bodies, trailing bloody intestines.

Some of the frantic horses plunged down a steep bank and into a stream, thrashing about in their harnesses as they slowly drowned. The water soon turned red. Panicky Feldgrau who had taken refuge along the banks were trampled to death. Truck drivers, in a frenzy to escape the torrent of bombs and bullets from the sky, collided with other vehicles, often with such great impact that the occupants inside were crushed in accordian fashion. Wounded lay helpless in trucks and ambulances that caught fire and burned the shrieking occupants to a crisp. German soldiers and horses jammed together for stretches of one hundred yards—struggling, screaming masses.

Trucks and tanks blew up, sending thick black plumes of smoke into the sky. The roads, villages, woods, and fields were littered with burning, smoking wrecks. The corridor of death between Argentan and Falaise would become known to terrified Germans who had to run the lethal gauntlet as the *Jabo Rennstrecke* (fighter-bomber race course).

In the meantime, American artillery to the south and British and Canadian artillery to the north, massed hub to hub, opened an enormous barrage on the stalled German column. For hours on end thousands of shells screamed into the hapless convoy.

While the massive rain of explosives and bullets would pound the Germans in the narrow alley of death for three days and nights, the big strategic bombers—Flying Fortresses, Liberators, night-flying Lancasters and Halifaxes, any aircraft that could carry a bomb—raked the lines of retreat that reached all the way to Paris.

Airpower and shells alone could not close the trap, so while the slaughter grounds of the escape corridor remained choked with German tanks, guns, and motor transport, American, British, Canadian, and Polish foot soldiers and tankers slugged ahead against desperate Feldgrau, seeking to keep the gap open.

In the pulverized ruins of Falaise, General Henry Crerar's Canadians of the South Saskatchewan Regiment were bitterly resisted from rubble pile to rubble pile by a handful of surviving Hitlerjugend of the 12th SS Panzer Division. While the fighting was raging inside the battered town, some three hundred French men, women, and children took refuge in Trinity Church. As bomb and mortar shells crashed around the building, panic erupted and many rushed for the doors. They had to be restrained from bolting outside to certain death.

Now huge fires broke out all around the bomb- and shell-torn ancient church. Cries rang out in the jostling, terrified mob. "We'll be burned to death!" Women screamed. Most fell to their knees, praying loudly and pleading for deliverance. Flames leaped from nearby buildings and caught fire to the wooden eaves and timber in the edifice. The screaming grew louder. In the midst of the chaos, a young woman gave birth to her child.

As night fell the fierce fighting intensified. About fifty-five of Panzer Meyer's fanatic teenagers holed up for their last stand in the *École Supérieure* (high school) The South Saskatchewans grappled face to face with the stubborn Germans for three hours. Point-blank antitank gunfire set the sturdy school ablaze, but the remaining handful of Hitlerjugend fought on. Then silence fell over Falaise. Six of Meyer's men survived, four of them seriously wounded, and were taken prisoner. Sprawled about the smoking piles of rubble were the corpses of scores of Canadian and German soldiers and French civilians. The fleeing Germans had been denied the last hard-surfaced road to the east.

Nine miles southeast of embattled Falaise at noon on August 17, advance elements of Polish and Canadian forces were finding their way down the heights just north of Trun and edging into the debris-strewn town. Hardly one brick or stone remained cemented to another. Trun was found deserted. A German contingent had pulled out at 10:00 A.M.

The gap had now shrunk to a width of six miles. But the densely forested area, devoid of landmarks, had become a nightmare for Anglo-American fighter-bomber pilots. In Trun late that afternoon, the Polish commander complained to corps headquarters that his men were being steadily bombed by "friendly" aircraft.

Now the Americans on the south, and Canadians and Poles on the north, were within a brisk hour's walk of each other. Still Germans managed to seep through the ever-shrinking *Jabo Rennstrecke.*

ON THAT MORNING of August 17 in the southern jaw, Doyle Hickey's Combat Command-A of the 3rd Armored Division attacked Fromental for the second straight day. Germans resisted with artillery and *Nebelwerfer* (multibarreled rocket launcher) fire. Roads were blocked with knocked-out panzers and covered by German antitank guns. So Hickey's tanks left the roads and rumbled across fields to reach Fromental. Sergeant William Alberti, a free-spirited tanker, rode the blade of a dozer throughout the assault, firing at enemy infantry with his Tommygun while helping to guide the driver over the rough terrain.

Hickey's tanks and foot soldiers broke into Fromental and after a brief but fierce fight, seized most of the town. But a short time later they were driven out, not by the Germans but by American P-38

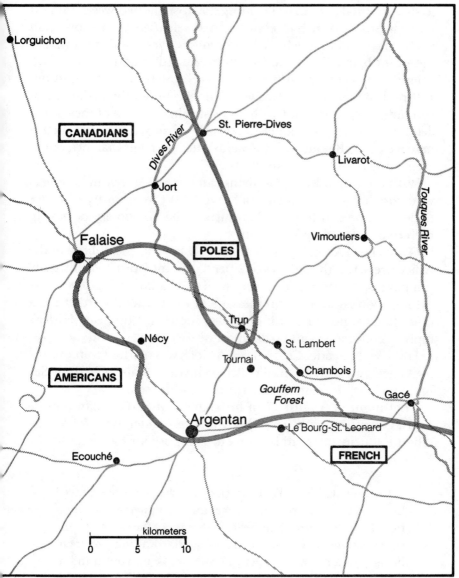

Lorguichon

CANADIANS

Dives River

St. Pierre-Dives

Livarot

Jort

Touques River

Falaise

POLES

Vimoutiers

Trun

Nécy

St. Lambert

Tournai

AMERICANS

Chambois

Gacé

Gouffern Forest

Argentan

Le Bourg-St. Leonard

FRENCH

Ecouché

kilometers

0   5   10

The Shrinking Gap (August 18

Lightnings that bombed them. Later Combat Command-A attacked Fromental again, and this time held on.

Some eighty miles west of the Argentan-Falaise gap on the seventeenth, the final curtain was coming down on the two-week drama at Fortress St.-Malo. It had been battered relentlessly for more than twelve days and nights by Allied bombers, large-caliber guns, and the point-blank fire of tanks, and assaulted steadily by the 83rd Infantry Division. Nearly out of food, water, and ammunition, stiff-necked Colonel Andreas von Aulock put out the white flag of surrender. Begrimed (but with boots shining), proud of their long, defiant stand against hopeless odds (but badly hung over after a massive farewell bout with Calvados), the Germans marched out of their tunnels with hands in the air.

With the surrendering Germans came seven American prisoners who said that they had been treated well. "We were hardly aware we under air and artillery bombardment," the GIs observed, having been four stories deep in granite.

Colonel von Aulock, the "Madman of St.-Malo," as dubbed by the Allied press, was the only hero Hitler had in the Normandy-Brittany campaigns. So he made the most of it. Radio Berlin repeatedly extolled von Aulock's final message to his Führer: "Further resistance had to end as a result of lack of food." It trumpeted Hitler's reply: "Your name will go down in history forever."

For days, long after Colonel von Aulock was residing comfortably in American captivity, Radio Berlin insisted that the hero of St.-Malo had perished among the ruins with his men.

That night of August 17 in his château at St.-Germain outside Paris, Guenther von Kluge, who would leave after dawn for Wolfsschanze, sat in the semidarkness to compose a final letter to the Führer:

> I do not know if Feldmarschall Model, who has proved himself in every respect, will be capable of mastering the situation. I hope so with all my heart. If that is not the case and if the new weapons . . . which you are so eagerly awaiting, are not to bring you success, then mein Führer, make up your mind to finish the war. The German people have endured such unspeakable sufferings that the time has come to put an end to their terrors.

Von Kluge's letter was devoid of rancor, bitterness, or condemnation of the military strategy in France that had sent thousands of the flower of German youth to their deaths and tens of thousands more into impending captivity. On the contrary, he paid homage to the warlord of the Reich:

> . . . Mein Fuehrer, I have always admired your greatness and your iron will to assert your authority and uphold National Socialism. If your destiny overcomes your will and your genius, it will be because Providence has willed it so. You have fought a good and honorable fight. History will bear witness to this. . . . I depart from you, mein Fuehrer, having stood closer to you in spirit than you perhaps dreamed.

Before dawn the next day, August 18, von Kluge, along with an aide and a motorcycle escort, drove off from the château at La Roche-Guyon where he had arrived only seven weeks before imbued with enthusiasm and confident he would drive the Anglo-American invaders back into the sea. Eastward moved the big Horch command car through the fabled battlefields of World War I. Near Metz, he ordered his driver to halt for a roadside meal.

At the conclusion, he wrote a hurried letter to his brother, gave it to an aide, Lieutenant Tangermann who had been with von Kluge three days before when the field marshal mysteriously disappeared, and told him to mail it later. He instructed Tangermann to prepare to leave in fifteen minutes, then wandered off into a nearby wooded area alone. He bit into a phial of potassium cyanide and was dead in seconds.

WEST OF ARGENTAN in the bright sunlight of midmorning on August 18. Sergeant Don J. Eckdahl, a tank commander in Rose's 3rd Armored Division, clambered down from his Sherman between Fromental and Putanges. During the past few days Eckdahl and his comrades had engaged in some of the most savage fighting of the war against SS troops battling desperately to keep open the trap's escape valve. His white teeth shone brightly in his bearded, grimy face as he shook hands with a British lieutenant.

Minutes later back at 3rd Armored headquarters, another sergeant put down his radio headset and called out, "Our guys have linked up with the Limies north of Fromental. Both outfits shot up a number of Kraut tanks before they had a chance to shake hands." The juncture that helped squeeze the Kessel even tighter culminated a 156-mile fighting march for the 3rd Armored which, along with Ted Brooks's 2nd Armored, had exploited the infantry breakthrough of First Army when Cobra was launched July 25.

In the same sector that morning, the 318th Regiment of the 80th Infantry Division jumped off to capture Argentan. Ahead of Horace McBride's raw soldiers were several hills on which were entrenched some twenty five hundred Germans supported by tanks, artillery, 88-millimeter flak guns, barbed wire, and mines. The enemy position offered a direct view of the flat ground over which the Americans would have to advance.

Almost at once the inexperienced 318th Infantry, most of its men under fire for the first time, bogged down. Colonel Harry McHugh, the regiment's commander, rushed to the point of attack and began kicking and cursing his men to get them moving. They clung to the ground. To encourage his reluctant warriors in their first big fight, McHugh calmly strolled along a road devoid of cover. He received no fire. His men scrambled to their feet and almost at once were raked by machine-gun fire. Shells began screaming in. Colonel McHugh called for tanks and tank destroyers, but could not find his armored liaison officer. A short time later five Shermans arrived and lumbered forward along a narrow dirt road. Hidden German anti-tank guns opened up and in minutes four of McHugh's tanks were blazing torches. The fifth Sherman bogged down in the mud. The attack to capture Argentan ground to a halt.

On the right of the 80th Infantry Division that morning, Colonel Robert L. Bacon's 359th Infantry Regiment of the 90th Division was perched on a hill overlooking le Bourg-St.-Leonard. Bacon's men had balcony seats to the carnage being inflicted on fleeing German columns by devastating artillery fire. Yet when Bacon's men jumped off to link up with the Canadians and Poles at Chambois two miles to the north, they were halted by savage resistance not far from the line of departure.

August 19 broke sunny and clear. Allied fighter-bombers, like swarms of angry bees, were over the battlegrounds early. The escape alley was still teeming with Germans, most of them frantic. Confusion within their ranks increased overnight as French civilians stealthily removed road signs. Inside a tiny patch of terrain barely six miles by six miles were crammed two army and four corps headquarters; remnants of one parachute, six infantry, and five panzer divisions; and assorted stragglers and service units. It was almost impossible to fire an artillery shell or drop a bomb into the pocket without hitting German troops or their vehicles.

At seven o'clock that morning, a grim-faced Paul Hausser strode into the farmhouse headquarters of the II Parachute Corps. General Eugen Meindl, the imperturbable corps commander, knew something important was in the works. "I presume the lid is on the kettle," Meindl observed matter-of-factly, meaning the pocket had been closed, "and we will have to break out."

"Actually, the kettle isn't covered yet," Hausser replied. He said that there was still a gap less than two miles wide between Chambois and St.-Lambert. Starting at ten thirty that night, Meindl's paratroopers were to move eastward cross-country toward the Mount Ormel hills seven miles away. "Your men are to advance in Indian file," Hausser explained. "They are not to fire their weapons until daylight. Fire all your artillery ammunition today, then destroy your pieces."

Later that morning Hausser was conferring in a ditch behind a farmhouse with his chief of staff, General von Gersdorf; General Kurt Meyer; and others. The group was pounced upon by fighter-bombers, and a nearby ammunition truck exploded. Von Gersdorf was painfully wounded. After he was removed for treatment, the conference resumed. Participants nearly had to shout to be heard above the crescendo of American artillery shells crashing on all sides.

Late in the afternoon of August 19, Lieutenant Jan Karcz, leading a troop of the 10th Dragoons of the Polish 1st Armored Division, and his 60 men were taking a breather on the eastern approaches to Chambois. They had been fighting all day since jumping off with their regiment after dawn from Trun. Karcz, perspiring profusely and holding his helmet, glanced around the terrain. He had never seen such carnage. Horse-drawn equipment, dead and wounded horses littered the premises. Some animals, screaming from hideous wounds, were dispatched with pistols by Karcz's men. The road into Chambois and streets in the town were jammed with knocked-out panzers, and piles of German corpses were strewn about in grotesque fashion. Scores of enemy wounded, many groaning and others begging softly for help, were scattered over the landscape. The town was a shambles, and much of it was on fire. The Allied dive-bombers and artillery had done their job.

At the same time the Poles were assaulting Chambois from the north, American Captain Laughlin E. Waters was leading his company of the 359th Infantry Regiment in an advance through the orchards and fields toward the town. Waters and his men were puzzled, and angry. They had been periodically raked by machine-gun fire from all sides, and suspected it was coming from "friendly" troops. The situation in the fast-closing gap had grown chaotic. American, Polish, and Canadian troops and tanks, converging on Chambois in an all-out effort to snap shut the trap, were intermingled with German troops and panzers desperately seeking to escape the net.

Shortly before 5:00 P.M. Lieutenant Karcz received orders to move into smoking, battered Chambois with his sixty Poles. Wending their way toward town through mounds of corpses and piles of smashed German equipment, Karcz and his men were soon hampered by 200 dazed, confused Feldgrau whom they had ambushed and captured. The prisoners were dispatched to the rear. On the outskirts of Chambois a concealed German machine gun suddenly chattered angrily, and Lieutenant Karcz was struck by a bullet. Refusing evacuation, he was patched up and led his men on into the burning town.

Suddenly a shout rang out that a large force of enemy soldiers was attacking Chambois from the south. Peering through binoculars, Lieutenant Karcz was alarmed by what he saw. Some eight hundred yards away, a long skirmish line of infantrymen was moving directly toward him. He immediately deployed his men in defensive positions on the southern outskirts, and put in an urgent call for reinforcements and artillery fire on the approaching force.

The enemy formation halted while some distance away. Karcz pondered his next move. Should he order his men to open fire? Or was this enemy force in the mood to surrender? He watched and waited.

Having ordered his G Company of the 359th Infantry to take cover outside Chambois, Captain Laughlin Waters moved forward to reconnoiter. He was concerned by the silence inside the ruined town and could see no activity. Was he leading his men into an ambush?

Suddenly he spotted a figure moving out of Chambois to his

north. The figure stood surveying the scene to the south. It appeared to Waters that the man was wearing a British officer's uniform. The figure was Lieutenant Karcz, who was clad in his Polish uniform, which was similar to that worn by the British.

Whoever this unknown figure was, Captain Waters was thinking, he does not appear to be a German. The American emerged from his concealment and began walking toward the Polish officer. As Waters drew closer, Karcz could see that what appeared to him to be the silhouettes of German helmets at a distance now took on the distinct shape of American steel headgear.

Lieutenant Karcz breathed a deep sigh of relief. On a hunch, he had called off the artillery barrage he had requested. As the American and the Pole neared each other, Captain Waters broke into a run, and while going full tilt joyously grabbed Jan Karcz and lifted him off the ground, swinging him around as though he were a rag doll.

At that precise moment—5:55 p.m., August 19—the Argentan-Falaise pocket was snapped shut. The link was tenuous, and the Americans, Poles, and Canadians in and around Chambois and St.-Lambert braced for the blow they knew would strike soon—an all-out effort by desperate remnants of the German Fifth Panzer and Seventh armies to crash out of the net. That wait would not be long.

At 10:30 p.m., precisely on schedule, small German battle groups began heading eastward toward the loosely held gap. Fires lit up the darkness, casting eerie shadows. Artillery crashed constantly. Overhead flares from British aircraft floated lazily to earth, turning night into day. In most cases, German generals personally led the columns.

Scouts of the parachute formations, faces blackened, slipped into the night with orders to avoid contact with the enemy, if possible. General Meindl divided his mauled force into two columns; he led one; his chief of staff, Colonel Herman Blauensteiner, the other. Sneaking through the blackness, Meindl and his paratroopers slithered over fields, crawled for long distances, slipped past tank-manned strongpoints, and raced ahead when brought under fire by Canadian machine-gunners. Reaching the Dives River north of Chambois at midnight, the German airborne men silently swam across. Emerging in their soaking uniforms, they spotted the dim silhouettes of Allied tanks just ahead. Silently, like thieves in the night, they crawled past.

All the while, Allied machine-gun fire was raking the area, searching out the shadowy figures. Lieutenant General Hans Schimpf, commander of the 3rd Parachute Division, was seriously wounded in the leg by a bullet, but was helped onward by aides. Colonel Blauensteiner and most of his men made it through the gap, but not before taking serious losses, including Major Eric Stephan, commander of the 9th Parachute Regiment.

General Meindl and about 20 men stumbled onto a tank column moving directly toward them in the darkness. The Germans leaped for a ditch. They held their breaths as four tanks pulled up and stopped only a few yards away. The tankers could be heard talking in Polish. Meindl and his men lay motionless and in total silence for more than an hour. Artillery shells began crashing around the huddled Germans, but they were relieved to hear the revving of motors as the Polish tanks rumbled off into the night. With catlike caution the parachute corps commander and the rest of his group scrambled to their feet and stole silently onward.

All during the night firefights broke out along the German escape routes through the narrow gap. Paul Hausser, the sixty-three-year-old SS general, no longer was in command of an army. Instead he was wearily trudging along a road as "point man" for a small column of grenadiers and panzers. Suddenly in the blackness shells crashed around the group. Hausser, who had lost an eye in Russia, went down, his face a bloody mask. At his insistence, he was propped up on the rear of a tank, clutching his Schmeisser automatic pistol, and the column pushed onward.

As dawn approached, General von Gersdorf, Hausser's chief of staff who had been painfully wounded earlier in the day, was leading a mixed force that reached the Trun-Chambois road near St.-Lambert. Two Panthers knocked out a pair of antitank guns covering the road, and German armored cars, trucks, a few self-propelled guns and other vehicles dashed ahead along the cleared road. They promptly ran into elements of the U.S. 90th Infantry Division, who were taken by total surprise and surrendered. Von Gersdorf did not know what to do with them. So he ordered the men of the Texas-Oklahoma National Guard outfit disarmed and abandoned.

Earlier, 2nd Panzer Division commander General von Lüttwitz, fifteen tanks, and a small band of grenadiers were having difficulties. They had been pounded so hard by artillery that losses were steadily mounting, and Lüttwitz could not get out of the assembly area. He expected that the road that he and his men had planned to follow to

St.-Lambert would be under enormous artillery fire as it had been all day, but for some reason the Allied bombardment suddenly ceased. So von Lüttwitz's column headed east for the breakout.

Daylight had arrived when von Lüttwitz, who had been wounded, and his force fought their way into St.-Lambert. The pudgy commander climbed to the top of a church steeple and from that vantage point directed the passage of his vehicles and grenadiers through the bomb- and shell-ravaged town. Allied artillery had focused in on a stone bridge crossing the Dives River, and there horses, men, and equipment piled up as they were killed or mutilated by the heavy barrage. Von Lüttwitz's men kept the road open for several hours while other units passed through the escape route.

General Kurt Meyer, whose Hitlerjugend division had been virtually wiped out, was among the last to leave the pocket. He had assembled a rag-tag group of two hundred men in a few farm buildings. His force was to act as the rear guard. Reaching the Dives, Meyer and his men waded in and swam across. The river was a death trap. Perched on a hillside sloping down to the Dives was a strong force of Canadians who raked Meyer's exposed grenadiers with murderous bursts of machine-gun fire. German bodies lined both banks and floated grotesquely in the water.

What remained of Meyer's little force worked its way around the strongpoint and soon ran onto another Canadian position. The young general gave the order to charge the enemy formation. Without a sound, the Feldgrau leaped from cover and raced across a pasture toward the Canadians. Meyer, a bloody bandage around his head from an earlier wound, led the assault, firing his pistol and exhorting his men onward. The Canadian line scattered. A single thought penetrated the mind of each charging German: get out of the inferno of the pocket.

Daylight found Panzer Meyer crawling up a ridge and gasping for breath. He had been marching and fighting for many hours and had not slept in several days. His heart was heavy, as day after day he had witnessed the slaughter of his elite Hitlerjugend—boys who without question had laid down their lives for their Führer. Meyer gazed down at the plain behind him at the awful carnage thinly veiled by the early morning haze. Only weeks before Adolf Hitler had trumpeted a clarion call to throw the Allied invaders back into the sea. Now that trumpet lay broken and mute.

Epilogue

THE NARROW CORRIDOR between Argentan and Falaise through which the German armies in Normandy sought desperately to flee was one of the great slaughter grounds of the war. Roads, highways, and fields were so choked with destroyed equipment and with corpses and dead animals that passage through the area after the shooting halted was extremely difficult. The stench was so overpowering, so putrid, that those who had to be in the vicinity took to wearing gas masks. Here the once-vaunted German Fifth Panzer and Seventh armies bled to death.

Forty-eight hours after the closing of the escape valve, Supreme Commander Dwight Eisenhower was conducted on foot through the area where thousands of Allied fighter-bombers and hundreds of artillery pieces had for days and nights rained death on the fleeing Germans. Eisenhower was stone-faced in awe. Later he wrote that he encountered "scenes that could be described only by Dante. It was literally possible to walk for hundreds of yards at a time, stepping on nothing but dead and decaying flesh."

How many Germans escaped due to the Allied delay in closing the trap? The figure, buried in the fog of war, will never be known. Indeed, on August 23 Adolf Hitler demanded a report from Field Marshal Walther Model on the divisions that had succeeded in fleeing the pocket. If such a report was ever submitted to the Führer, it was never located after the war. Such was the chaos in German ranks that battle commanders themselves were unsure of how many

293

men and what equipment got out of what the Germans came to call *der Kessel von Falaise,* the Falaise Pocket.

At the time, and in postwar years, various figures have been bandied about as estimates of the number of troops who escaped. Field Marshal Alan Brooke, British Chief of the Imperial General Staff, from his vantage point in London estimated the figure at fifty thousand, which to most other Anglo-American authorities appeared excessive. British officials who had listened in ceaselessly on German wireless messages through Ultra set the number who got out of the pocket at twenty to thirty thousand. General Heinz Eberhard later declared the number who had escaped the encirclement was twenty thousand. Allied intelligence and postwar historians were inclined to go along with that figure.

However many Germans got out of the pocket, one overriding conclusion emerged: Hitler's armies in France had taken a frightful beating and suffered enormous losses in men and equipment. The war diary of Model's Army Group B, which had no apparent reason to juggle figures, later recorded that elements of six or seven panzer divisions that managed to filter out of the trap, when regrouped consisted of about two thousand men, sixty-two tanks, and twenty-six artillery pieces. General Hans Speidel, who had been chief of staff first to Rommel, then von Kluge, and Model, and later commanded NATO forces in western Europe long after the war, stated independently that some 100 tanks had made it out of the pocket.

Within the Mortain-Falaise encirclement ten thousand Germans were killed and fifty thousand captured. Those snared in the final act in the Argentan-Falaise gap were a sorry lot. Pounded for days and nights from the air and by artillery, they shuffled into prisoner-of-war cages in long, undisciplined columns, dust-covered, bedraggled, past caring. Men drooped with fatigue, eyes red-rimmed, glassy, and unseeing. Blood oozed from mouths, ears, and noses.

As great a debacle as it was for the German armed forces and Hitler, the enormous Mortain-Falaise trap was comparable to Stalingrad in many, though not in all, respects. In the German disaster on the Russian front the previous year, an entire army was destroyed and its commander, Friedrich von Paulus, became the first field marshal in German history to surrender. Along with von Paulus, 25 other German generals and their staffs marched off into captivity. In France there was no formal mass surrender, and most of the German

generals escaped. Less than four months later these same commanders would confront the Allies again, in the Battle of the Bulge.

The greatest loss to the western Allies in the failure to promptly
close the Falaise-Argentan gap when the opportunity apparently
had presented itself on August 13 was a psychological one. Had *all* of
the German Fifth Panzer and Seventh armies, together with their
generals, been killed or forced to surrender, the impact on the Reich
home front, as well as on the German armed forces, would have been
devastating. Instead, Propaganda Minister Josef Goebbels bolstered
sagging spirits somewhat by lauding the "fighting breakout from
encirclement" and portraying it in the media as "one of the great
feats of German arms in the war."

Numerous scholars of the European conflict, including Lieutenant General James Gavin (Ret.), wartime leader of the U.S. 82nd
Airborne Division, have declared that failure to promptly shut off
the escape valve probably prolonged the war in the West.

Colonel Ralph Ingersoll, historian of Bradley's 12th Army Group,
summed up the view of most American generals in late August 1944:

> "The failure to close the Argentan-Falaise gap was the loss of
> the greatest single opportunity of the war. The news would
> have come hard on the heels of the attempted assassination of
> Hitler . . . and would have been accompanied by the news of the
> liberation of Paris [less than a week later]. But as long as any of
> the German army escaped, Hitler had a chance to cover up the
> extent of the disaster."

How could a tactical blunder of this magnitude, which resulted in
less than total annihilation of Hitler's armies, have occurred? The
answer lay in an Allied command structure rife with national jeal-
ousies and in which it was not clear who was responsible to whom or
for what; personality clashes and towering egos among top American and British generals; and faulty Allied intelligence, despite the
enormous advantage of Ultra.

General Eisenhower, as supreme commander, bore the ultimate
responsibility for the Anglo-American prosecution of the war
against Nazi Germany. Therefore, some critics maintain, Eisenhower should have intervened directly in battlefield decisions when
it became obvious that there was a golden opportunity to close the

gap and annihilate two German armies. Instead, the supreme commander remained aloof, possibly due to considerations of Allied harmony. British General Bernard Montgomery, although commander of all Allied ground forces in Normandy, hardly was in contact with Bradley at the crucial point in the Argentan-Falaise actions. Montgomery and Bradley had barely been able to remain civil when they did deal with each other, but rather, from their respective headquarters, cast a jaundiced eye at each other. As a result, in the critical days at Argentan-Falaise, American Bradley and Englishman Montgomery remained apart, as though conducting separate wars.

Critics have held that when George Patton, although in violation of orders, sent spearheads northward past Argentan almost to Falaise on August 13, it proved that Patton could easily have closed the gap at that time. Patton had always made this claim, saying that his patrols had even probed into Falaise itself.

There has been considerable evidence that the coolness between Omar Bradley and Bernard Montgomery precluded the American from making a simple telephone call to his British superior at this point to say in effect: "Patton is almost to Falaise. The stakes are enormous. Why don't we just dissolve the boundary line at Argentan and let Patton close the gap?" The customarily easy-going Bradley's mood at this point was acidic. He had told Patton, "If Monty wants my help, let him ask for it!"

For his part, Bernard Montgomery, never overburdened by humility, had no intention of calling on anyone for help, least of all Omar Bradley. He himself would close the gap—and soon. Meanwhile, Supreme Commander Eisenhower, with the war in Europe at stake, maintained his self-imposed role as a sort of chairman of the board, who monitored proceedings from on high, but declined to inject himself into tactical decisions.

Privately, close comrades Eisenhower and Bradley were mystified, even angered, by Montgomery's tactics during these crucial days. With the pregnant opportunity for inflicting one of history's monumental annihilations of an enemy force, why did Montgomery employ the green Canadian First Army, game as it was, to try to close the trap? And after the raw Dominion troops failed repeatedly to break through to Falaise, why did Montgomery not substitute his battle-tested British Tommies and tankers to get the job done?

Even Colonel C. P. Stacey in his official history of Canadian operations was critical of the way the gap tactics were handled. "First Canadian Army failed to take advantage of [German disarray] on its side of the gap," Stacey declared. "Bradley and Eisenhower refused to take full advantage of it on theirs. It is true that Patton might not have succeeded in closing the gap, but the stakes were so high it was well worth trying. . . . Ultimately the boundary line [at Argentan] had to be disregarded. It would have been good sense to disregard it on August 13," when Patton's spearheads had punched through to Falaise, and then were quickly recalled by Bradley.

Could George Patton's forces have snapped the trap shut and annihilated the German armies? Evidence suggested that he could have. Major General Francis de Guingand, Montgomery's loyal longtime chief of staff, observed after the war: "It is just possible that the gap might have been closed a little earlier if no restrictions had been imposed upon [Patton] as the limit of his northward movement."

Colonel Robert S. Allen, a Patton staff officer and civilian newspaperman, wrote after the war: "The real reason [for halting Patton at the Argentan boundary] was Montgomery's insistence that he [Montgomery] close the gap. He demanded—and got his way—that Patton be halted from springing the trap."

Eleven years after the war, Omar Bradley took a swipe at Montgomery in a magazine article. "I have often asked myself," Bradley wrote, "if I should not have done Monty's work, and if we should not have closed the gap ourselves. Montgomery was scared."

Major General Wade Haislip, whose XV Corps tanks raced to the boundary line at Argentan from the south, reported he had been opposed only by feeble German units. Haislip said that "there were no [German] units worth mentioning" on his right, and those "worth mentioning" were of "negligible combat strength." He pointed out that a company of German bakers had been assigned to defend the key road center of Sees.

Despite the monumental missed opportunity for total annihilation, the indisputable fact remained that the German Seventh and Fifth Panzer armies died in the Mortain-Falaise pocket. Who was the architect of this daring strategy? There was no shortage of claimants. Bernard Montgomery took full credit for the plan. But Lieutenant General Walter "Beetle" Smith, Eisenhower's chief of staff and alter ego, after the war maintained that it was a joint conception of his boss and Bradley and that Bradley put the encircling proposal up to Montgomery, who endorsed it. Colonel Robert Allen gave full credit to his own boss, Patton, and in his memoirs Patton maintained that the Cobra breakout and the encirclement had been his conceptions and that Bradley had, in effect, given them a new coat of paint and adopted them as his own.

Not unexpectedly, Commander (later Captain) Harry Butcher, the supreme commander's naval aide and confidant, credited the whole idea to Eisenhower. For his part, General Eisenhower credited Bradley for the encirclement plan. At a press conference the following month, George Patton was asked if the Mortain-Falaise trap was an improvisation or part of the original Overlord plan. Patton replied succinctly: "Improvisation by General Bradley. I thought we were going east and he told me to move north [from Le Mans]."

Patton's more generous view toward Omar Bradley in September may have evolved from the lifting of the SHAEF blackout curtain. He never had been afflicted with an unbridled passion for anonymity. George Patton, who had embarrassed fellow officers, angered the American public, whose promotion the U.S. Senate had indignantly rejected, had suddenly burst from the shadows in a dazzling display of blazing newspaper headlines. Overnight he became America's most admired general. The British press idolized him, the American press forgave him his sins, and U.S. senators fell all over each other in quickly confirming his nomination to permanent major general.

Once Patton was revealed as the dynamo who had led the Third Army in its dash to the Seine, the fiery general could do no wrong. In the sudden new acclaim for Patton, Senator Albert "Happy" Chandler, who had helped block Patton's promotion, rose hurriedly and intoned, "At this hour he [Patton] is the greatest tank soldier in the world. . . . I have changed my mind!" Cheers rocked the august chambers.

If unassuming yet capable Lieutenant General Courtney Hodges, commander of First Army, was disturbed by the lavish praise being heaped upon the flamboyant Patton, he gave no indication of it. But many of Hodges's officers and First Army combat soldiers resented Third Army gaining "credit" for the monumental victory of The Trap. To this day, more than four decades after the event, old warriors of Hodges's First Army get red-faced with anger when it is suggested that Patton and his Third Army "won" the battle of the Mortain-Falaise pocket. It was First Army, they claim, that paved the way for the destruction of Hitler's armies there, and there is considerable evidence to back up that contention.

It was First Army that had slugged its way through the bloody swamps and hedgerows of the *bocage* to reach Cobra's jump-off line, and it was First Army that blasted a hole in the German line west of St.-Lô, which permitted First Army's 2nd and 3rd Armored divisions to bolt through and race southward down the Cotentin Peninsula, throwing the Germans in Normandy into total disarray. And when Hitler hurled his mighty panzer divisions at Mortain in an all-out effort to break through to Avranches, it was Hodges's First Army that absorbed the blow and hurled back the Germans in four days of vicious fighting, while Patton's spearheads ran wild in Brittany against sporadic opposition. Finally, Hodges's former fighting men point to the casualties sustained in fashioning the steel noose around the Germans. First Army had 19,000 men killed, wounded, or missing, and Patton's Third Army suffered about half that number.

But the mammoth victory was not solely an American operation. When Bradley's forces burst out of the *bocage* when Cobra was launched, General Montgomery's troops around Caen were facing most of the panzer divisions in Normandy. And once the trap had been snapped shut, the inexperienced Canadians and Poles, as well as veteran British soldiers, fought heroically against a final, all-out German effort to escape the encirclement at St.-Lambert and Chambois.

To this day an aura of mystery continues to hover over the day-long disappearance of Field Marshal von Kluge on August 15 during one of the most critical periods in der Kessel von Falaise. Did the German commander attempt to surrender his armies in the West to the Anglo-Americans? There is evidence that he did. Almost a year later, on June 25, 1945, *Time* magazine, without naming a source for its story, reported that von Kluge drove to a spot on a lonely road near Avranches on August 15 and waited for Third Army officers with whom he had secretly arranged to discuss surrender. The American negotiators were held up by blocked roads, the report went on, and by the time they reached the scene von Kluge, fearing betrayal, had departed.

According to Anthony Cave Brown, a distinguished British journalist, and authority on Allied cloak-and-dagger operations in World War II, Dr. Udo Esch, von Kluge's son-in-law and at the time an officer in the German Army medical corps, told American intelligence agents after the war that von Kluge "after the failure [of the Hitler murder plot] considered surrendering the Western Front to the Allies on his own authority, hoping to overthrow the Nazi regime with their assistance."

Dr. Esch added, according to the report, that "he [von Kluge] went to the front lines but was unable to get in touch with the Allied commanders." It was Esch who furnished his father-in-law with the cyanide phial with which von Kluge took his own life near Metz.

There was no doubt in Hitler's mind that von Kluge tried to surrender. At an August 31 conference at Wolfsschanze, the Führer heatedly declared, "Field Marshal von Kluge planned to lead the whole of the western army into capitulation and go over himself to the enemy. . . . It seems as though the plan miscarried owing to an enemy fighter-bomber attack" that blocked the roads.

Guenther von Kluge, a field marshal in the German Wehrmacht, the soldier who nearly captured Moscow and had been praised by his Führer for his "victorious defense" in Russia, was quietly buried in his family plot with only a few close relatives in attendance. He was denied the customary full military honors by a bitter Adolf Hitler.

Field Marshal Model, who had burst onto the scene during the death throes of the Wehrmacht in France with high hopes for "restoring the situation" as ordered by the Führer, was trapped with his tattered two-hundred-thousand-man force in the German Ruhr in April 1945. Model had let Hitler down. He drew his Luger and shot himself through the head.

300

Bibliography

Allen, Robert S., *Lucky Forward*, New York: Vanguard Press, 1947.

Ambrose, Stephen E., *The Supreme Commander*, New York: Doubleday, 1970.

Bennett, Ralph, *Ultra in the West*, New York: Scribner's Sons, 1979.

Bekker, Cajus, *The Luftwaffe War Diaries*, New York: Doubleday, 1968.

Blumenson, Martin, *Breakout and Pursuit*, Washington: Chief of Military History, 1961.

Bogen, Paul L., *The Sixth Armored Division*, Aschaffenburg: Steinbech Druck, 1945.

Bradley, Omar N., *A Soldier's Story*, New York: Holt, 1951.

Brereton, Lewis H., *The Brereton Diaries*, New York: Morrow & Company, 1946.

Brown, Anthony Cave, *Bodyguard of Lies*, New York: Harper & Row, 1975.

Bryant, Arthur, *Triumph in the West*, New York: Doubleday, 1959.

Butcher, Harry C., *My Three Years With Eisenhower*, New York: Simon & Schuster, 1948.

Carrel, Paul, *Invasion—They're Coming*, New York: Dutton, 1963.

Churchill, Winston S., *The Second World War*, Boston: Houghton Mifflin, 1949.

Cline, Ray S., *Washington Command Post*, Washington: Chief of Military History, 1951.

Codman, Charles R., *Drive*, Boston: Little, Brown, 1957.

Collier, Basil, *Battle of the V-Weapons*, New York: William Morrow, 1965.

Collins, J. Lawton, *Lightning Joe*, Baton Rouge: Louisiana State University Press, 1979.

Davis, Kenneth S., *Experience of War*, New York: Doubleday, 1965.

Eisenhower, Dwight D., *Crusade in Europe*, New York: Doubleday, 1948.

Farago, Ladislas, *Patton: Ordeal and Triumph*, New York: Obolensky, 1964.

Florentin, Eddy, *Battle of the Falaise Gap*, London: Elek Books, 1965.

Galland, Adolph, *The First and the Last: Rise and Fall of the German Fighter Forces*, New York: Ballantine, 1954.

Gavin, James M., *On to Berlin*, New York: Viking, 1978.

Gilbert, Felix, *Hitler Directs His War*, New York: Oxford University Press, 1950.

Guingand, Francis de, *Operation Victory*, London: Hodder & Stoughton, 1947.

Hausser, General Paul, *Waffen SS im Einsatz*, Göttingen: Schutz, 1949.

Irving, David, *The War Between the Generals*, New York: Congdon & Lattes, 1981.

Keitel, Wilhelm, *The Memoirs of Field Marshal Keitel* (reprinted as *In the Service of the Reich*), New York: Stein and Day, 1965.

Killen, John, *A History of the Luftwaffe*, New York: Doubleday, 1968.

Kurowski, Franz, *Die Panzer Lehr Division*, Munich: Podzan Verlag, 1964.

Lewin, Ronald, *Ultra Goes to War*, New York: McGraw-Hill, 1978.

Liddell Hart, B. H., *History of the Second World War*, New York: Putnam's Sons, 1971.

Meyer, General Kurt, *Grenadier*, Munich: Schild Verlag, 1955.

Montgomery, Field Marshal Bernard, *Memoirs*, London: Collins, 1958.

Moorehead, Alan, *Eclipse*, London: Hamish Hamilton, 1945.

Morison, Samuel Elliot, *History of United States Naval Operations in World War II*, Boston: Little, Brown, 1959.

Patton, George S., Jr., *War As I Knew It*, Boston: Houghton Mifflin, 1947.

Price, Frank James, *Troy H. Middleton: A Biography*, Baton Rouge: Louisiana State University Press, 1974.

Ruge, Friedrich, *Rommel in Normandy*, San Rafael: Presidio Press, 1981.

Schramm, Percy Ernst, *Hitler: The Man and the Military Leader*, Chicago: Watts, 1971.

Schramm, Ritter von, *The Generals Against Hitler*, London: Allen & Unwin, 1956.

Simonds, Peter, *Maple Leaf Up*, New York: Inland Press, 1946.

Speidel, General Hans, *Invasion 1944*, Chicago: Henry Regnery & Co., 1945.

Stacey, C. P., *Official History of the Canadian Army in World War II*, Ottawa: The Queen's Printer, 1960.

Strong, Kenneth W. D., *Intelligence at the Top*, New York: Doubleday, 1969.

Summersby, Kay, *Eisenhower Was My Boss*, New York: Prentice-Hall, 1948.

Tedder, Arthur, *With Prejudice*, London: Cassell, 1960.

Wallace, Brenton, *Patton and His Third Army*, Harrisburg: Military Service Publishing Co., 1946.

Weigley, Russell F., *Eisenhower's Lieutenants*, Bloomington: Indiana University Press, 1981.

Wilmot, Chester, *The Struggle for Europe*, New York: Harper & Brothers, 1952.

Winterbotham, F. W., *The Ultra Secret*, New York: Harper & Row, 1974.

Woolner, Frank, *Spearhead in the West*, Frankfurt am Main: Kunst und Wehrverdruck, 1945.

Young, Desmond, *Rommel, the Desert Fox*, New York: Harper & Row, 1950.

MISCELLANEOUS

Interviews and correspondence with many participants.

Chester B. Hansen Diaries, U.S. Army Military History Institute.

Major Kenneth W. Hechler, *VII Corps in Operation Cobra*, Washington: Chief of Military History.

Hugh M. Cole, *VIII Corps Operations, Operation Cobra*, Washington: Chief of Military History.

Index

Hickey, Brig. Gen. Doyle O., 126, 168, 255, 259
Hitler, Adolf, 14, 15, 16, 25, 26, 32, 34, 38, 39, 42, 89, 90, 114, 125, 131, 132, 135, 139, 144, 145, 153, 157, 159, 166, 171, 190, 201, 204, 206, 219, 225, 226, 231, 232, 236, 244, 249, 260, 261, 266, 269, 271, 272, 273, 279, 291, 293, 299, 300
Hobbs, Maj. Gen. Leland S., 42, 52, 62, 65, 186, 202, 219
Hodges, Lt. Gen. Courtney H., 49, 52, 62, 65, 136, 137, 186, 247, 277, 298
Hogan, Lt. Col. Sam, 183
Hooper, Cmdr. Arthur M., 143
Horrocks, Lt. Gen. Brian G., 173, 174
Huebner, Maj. Gen. Clarence R., 42, 67, 157

Ingersoll, Col. Ralph, 295
Irvin, Bede, 62
Ives, Capt. Norman S., 143

Javron (France), 256
Jodl, Col. Gen. Alfred, 38, 39, 89, 90, 114, 131, 138, 231, 232, 238, 253, 270, 271, 272, 273
Juvigny (France), 155, 156, 177, 223

Karcz, Lt. Jan, 287, 288, 289
Kaupert, Sgt. Karl, 44
Kean, Brig. Gen. William, 277
Keitel, Field Marshal Wilhelm, 31, 32, 90, 136
Kerley, Lt. Ralph A., 221, 242
Kibler, Brig. Gen. A. Franklin, 251
King, Lt. Col. Rosewell, 223

Kitching, Maj. Gen. Alan, 228
Kluge, Field Marshal Hans Guenther von, 24, 26, 30, 31, 32, 38, 39, 40, 42, 53, 89, 90, 97, 123, 125, 132, 135, 136, 145, 146, 153, 157, 159, 165, 166, 171, 176, 180, 187, 188, 201, 204, 225, 226, 231, 232, 235, 238, 244, 253, 261, 264, 265, 266, 270, 271, 272, 275, 278, 279, 284, 285, 300
Kluge, Lt. Col. Klaus von, 84, 265
Koch, Col. Oscar, 159
Koukl, Master Sgt. Frank A., 33, 34
Kraiss, Lt. Gen. Helmuth, 77, 78
Kruse, Tech. Sgt. Norman, 224

La Bazog (France), 183
Laison River, 257, 258, 259
Lammerding, SS Lt. Gen. Heinz, 177, 186
Landrum, Maj. Gen. Eugene M., 74, 75, 147
La Roche-Guyon (France), 26, 30, 32, 40, 53, 249, 260, 285
La Tournerie (France), 177
Laval (France), 192, 193
le-Bourg-Saint-Leonard (France), 247, 274, 286
Leclerc, Maj. Gen. Jacques P., 229, 230, 231, 239, 240, 248, 264
Leigh-Mallory, Air Chief Marshal Trafford, 28, 43, 48, 49, 50, 56
Le Mans (France), 84, 125, 132, 170, 189, 191, 195, 213, 214, 226, 235
le-Mesnil-Adelee (France), 155, 177, 223